THE MIND
OF THE
CEO

JEFFREY E. GARTEN

BASIC
BOOKS

PERSEUS PUBLISHING

Published by Basic Books and Perseus Publishing, members of the
Perseus Books Group

ISBN: 0-465-02616-8

Library of Congress Cataloging-in-Publication Data is available.

The paper used in this publication meets the requirements of the
American National Standard for Permanence of Paper for Printed
Library Materials
Z39.48-1984.

First Paperback Edition, January 2002

01 02 03 / 10 9 8 7 6 5 4 3 2 1

CONTENTS

List of Interviewees

As background for this book I interviewed a number of business leaders. Following is a list together with the dates of our meetings.

C. Michael Armstrong, Chairman & CEO, AT&T Corporation, July 15, 1999

G. Leonard Baker, Jr., Managing Director, Sutter Hill Ventures, November 17, 1999

Susan V. Berresford, President, Ford Foundation, November 18, 1999

Michael Bloomberg, CEO & Founder, Bloomberg L.P., July 19, 1999

Michael R. Bonsignore, Chairman & CEO, Honeywell International Inc., July 14, 1999

Richard Branson, Chairman, Virgin Management Ltd., May 4, 2000

Dr. Rolf-E. Breuer, Spokesman of the Board of Managing Directors, Deutsche Bank AG, July 30, 1999

John Browne, Group Chief Executive, BP Amoco p.l.c., October 27, 1999

Stephen M. Case, Chairman & CEO, America Online, Inc., September 24, 1999

Kenneth I. Chenault, President & COO, American Express Company, September 13, 1999

Michael S. Dell, Chairman & CEO, Dell Computer Corporation, December 2, 1999

Roger A. Enrico, Chairman & CEO, PepsiCo, Inc., July 8, 1999

William Clay Ford, Jr., Chairman, Ford Motor Company, October 19, 1999

Victor Fung, Group Chairman, Li & Fung Limited, October 1, 1999

Orit Gadiesh, Chairman, Bain & Company, November 12, 1999

Christopher B. Galvin, Chairman & CEO, Motorola, Inc., July 14, 1999

Andrew S. Grove, Chairman, Intel Corporation, November 2, 1999

Minoru Makihara, Chairman, Mitsubishi Corporation, July 26, 1999

Ira M. Millstein, Esq., Senior Partner, Weil, Gotshal & Manges LLP, May 4, 1999

Yoshihiko Miyauchi, Chairman & CEO, ORIX Corporation, April 27, 2000

Mark Moody-Stuart, Chairman, Royal Dutch/Shell Group, September 17, 1999

Rupert Murdoch, Chairman & CEO, The News Corporation Limited, April 22, 1999

Hiroshi Okuda, Chairman, Toyota Motor Corporation, June 11, 1999

Jorma Ollila, Chairman & CEO, Nokia Corporation, October 28, 1999

Henry M. Paulson, Jr., Chairman & CEO, The Goldman Sachs Group, July 19, 1999

Nancy B. Peretsman, Executive V.P. & Managing Director, Allen & Company Incorporated, July 18, 1999

Franklin D. Raines, Chairman & CEO, Fannie Mae, November 19, 1999

Leonard Riggio, Chairman & CEO, Barnes & Noble, Inc., August 10, 1999

Jürgen E. Schrempp, Chairman, DaimlerChrysler AG, November 22, 1999

Stan Shih, Chairman & Co-Founder, The Acer Group, August 5, 1999

Frederick W. Smith, Chairman, President & CEO, FedEx Corporation, August 14, 1999

George Soros, Chairman, Soros Fund Management LLC, August 4, 1999

Martin S. Sorrell, Group Chief Executive, WPP Group plc, July 19, 1999

Donald Valentine, General Partner, Sequoia Capital, November 17, 1999

Lawrence A. Weinbach, Chairman, President & CEO, Unisys Corporation, April 14, 1999

John F. Welch, Jr., Chairman & CEO, General Electric Company, October 21, 1999

James D. Wolfensohn, President, The World Bank Group, October 18, 1999

Interviews were also conducted with the following executives who have since resigned their positions:

Richard L. Huber, Chairman, President & CEO, Aetna Inc., May 15, 1999

Rebecca P. Mark, Chairman & CEO, Azurix Corporation, September 23, 1999

G. Richard Thoman, President & CEO, Xerox Corporation, June 16, 1999

In addition, I talked to three historians: Ron Chernow, the biographer of J.P. Morgan and John D. Rockefeller; Richard Tedlow of the Harvard Business School; and Emma Rothschild of Kings College, Cambridge University, England.

PREFACE TO THE PAPERBACK EDITION

Since I originally wrote *The Mind of the CEO,* several important events have occurred. Dwarfing everything is the terrorist attack on the World Trade Center and the Pentagon on September 11, 2001. The full implications of this event are still not clear, but among other things, an already slowing global economy has been further undermined by massive political uncertainty. No one can know how deep the economic slump will be or how long it will last, but it certainly raises all the pressures on CEOs that I discuss in this book. The specter of a long war against terrorism could also add impetus to the political backlash against globalization that was already building, as evidenced by rising protests at the Economic Summit of major governments in Genoa, Italy, in July 2001 and the seriousness with which governments, international institutions, and companies are taking the issues that the demonstrators have been raising. Many of the CEOs whom I interviewed warned about this trend, and in this book I underlined the importance of their devoting more attention to political and social issues and asserted that these matters would become mainstream strategic concerns for business leaders. I believe this assessment is more true today than ever. Finally, a new presidential administration has settled in in Washington, one that is unabashedly pro-business and is staffed by several former CEOs. It is too early to tell how the performance of President Bush's team will influence some of the themes in the book—the relationship between CEOs and the government, for example, or the prominence of the American model of capitalism—but these remain big issues that cannot be divorced from what will be in CEOs' minds as the decade evolves.

Despite the changes in the business and political climate, not to mention the rapid turnover of CEOs, as of this writing, nearly all of the people I wrote about are still firmly in place. The three exceptions are General Electric's Jack Welch, who retired; Honeywell's Michael Bonsignore, who resigned after the failed merger with GE; and PepsiCo's Roger Enrico, who stepped down as chairman and CEO to the position of vice chairman to make way for younger talent. It was my original objective to interview leaders who were not only prominent and had something important and thoughtful to say but who also had substantial impact on the global business scene. I'm pleased to see that it worked out that way.

New Haven
October 2001

ACKNOWLEDGMENTS

I am most grateful to my former assistants Anne Herold, who so steadfastly helped me to secure and arrange the interviews on which this book is based, and Laura Pham Lewis, who helped with background research at every stage of the project.

I could never have produced this book without Mary Ann Green, who handled the production, draft after draft, late into the evenings and on too many weekends to count. There is no way I can thank her enough.

Finally, for all their superb help I am indebted to two editors, freelancer Sara Lippincott and William Frucht of Basic Books, and to my agent, Raphael Sagalyn.

For Ina

INTRODUCTION

Suppose you had a chance to travel around the world and speak to dozens of the most successful business leaders, one on one. Suppose further that they talked to you frankly about their goals and strategies and what keeps them awake at night. What would you think about these captains of industry who sell trillions of dollars worth of products and services, employ many millions of people and develop our path-breaking technologies? Would you find them impressive or ordinary? Would you judge their visions bold enough for the changing times? What kind of impact would you think they will have on shaping society in the early twenty-first century? What kind of impact would you think they *should* have?

In late 1999, I had this very experience. I interviewed forty men and women whose jobs and ideas affect just about every part of our lives. I tried to get into these people's heads. I wanted to understand the environment in which they were operating, the opportunities they saw, the obstacles they faced and what worried them most. I wanted to know what they thought about the challenges posed by the Internet, the New Economy and the management of gigantic corporations spanning many national cultures, and what role they saw for themselves in building the foundations of capitalism in our times. When I was done, I tried to come to grips with what I thought of the environment CEOs faced, how they were dealing with it, and what more, if anything, they ought to be doing.

✧ ✧ ✧

Jack Welch, chairman and CEO of General Electric, held forth before an audience of MBA students at Yale recently. I was in the audience, and that's when the idea for this book arose. Welch, of course, is one of the most successful business leaders of our times, having taken GE from a market value of $12 billion to over $500 billion in his twenty years at the company's helm, and having set the standard for other CEOs on corporate restructuring, quality control, globalization and how to take a traditional industrial and service company into the Internet age. The room was packed. Students were sitting on the floor in front of the first row of seats, in the aisles and cramming the doorway, and yet the audience seemed totally motionless in its concentration on what Welch was saying. When he finished speaking, he asked if there were any questions, and at least twenty-five hands shot up immediately. He pointed at one eager young man. "Shoot," he said.

"Lots of companies are merging these days," said the student. "If I found myself in charge of one of these big new conglomerates, what would be your advice to me?"

Welch took off his coat and threw it on the chair behind him. He walked in front of the podium, rolling up his shirt-sleeves at the same time. "You have to think about that company as being a big house," he said. "The house has several floors. Think of each floor as a layer of management. Then there are interior walls. Think of them as separating different divisions of the company." His eyes were glistening and he moved closer to the audience. "Then you get a hand grenade," he said, his arm curling upward and his fist tightening around an imaginary object. "Then you pull the pin."

He paused. It seemed as if all the students were leaning forward. "And then"—now he dropped his shoulder, stooped, and slowly swung his arm in a long arc as if he were bowling—"you roll the sucker right through the front door of the house and blow up every floor and every wall."

He straightened up, smoothed one hand against the other. "And now you are ready to do something with that company."

America's legendary CEO went on to explain that his strategy for GE was to create an organization without any boundaries, a culture in which ideas flowed freely from the division that made aircraft parts to the one that made lightbulbs, from the subsidiary in Shanghai to the one in Cincinnati. But first, he said, you had to tear down the existing barriers.

Tearing down barriers is at the heart of Welch's strategy for GE, but the idea resonates nearly everywhere. It describes what is happening within companies of every industry as hierarchies are flattened, barriers to internal communication are removed and employees become more entrepreneurial. It reflects what is going on among corporations as they join forces in all kinds of partnerships to expand their range of products and customers. It is a metaphor for what the Internet is doing around the world. It is the essence of the blurring of national borders, the phenomenon we call globalization.

Jack Welch is one of many top business executives who have come to the "Leaders Forum" at the Yale School of

Management to tell their stories. Another is Sir John
Browne, chief executive of British Petroleum, who over the
past four years has acquired two large American firms,
Amoco and Atlantic Richfield, and thus has become a pio-
neer in the creation of the new transatlantic mega-firms.
Browne also came to Yale in the fall of 1998 to talk about how
leadership entails not just focusing on the bottom line but
also on the relationship between a company and the communities in which it operates. In his talk he committed BP to
voluntarily reduce carbon emissions below levels recom-
mended by governments or targeted by other firms, a
groundbreaking announcement that was instantly reported
around the world. When he finished, a student posed a
broader question: "How do you think about the links between big multinational firms like yours and society at large?"

Browne slowly walked up the central aisle, about twenty
yards up, and stood right next to the student. He spoke so
softly that the small portable microphone hooked to his tie
barely picked up the words. "Companies are an integral part
of the societies in which they work," he said, with unmistak-
able earnestness. "We don't make our profits and then go
and live somewhere else. This is our society, too. The people
who make up our company are also citizens. They have
hopes and fears for themselves and for their families. Companies that want to keep operating successfully have to uphold their employees' values, just like their customers' values. We cannot isolate ourselves. We have to be engaged in
public policy issues. We have to be constructive."

Browne's words illuminate another vital issue. In a global
economy where Adam Smith has decisively won the day and

where governments have far less control over economic and technological forces than at any time in memory, what are the roles and responsibilities of big international companies? How should we think about the relationship between their mission to enrich their shareholders and their obligations to other groups such as customers, employees, suppliers and the communities in which they work? These questions raise others. Just how much power do leaders like Welch and Browne have at the dawn of the new century? What opportunities do they see, and what constraints? How do they define their biggest challenges, and what should we think of their perspective on them? Listening to Welch, Browne, and many others who have come to Yale, I found myself wanting to talk more intimately with some of them and with many more who had yet to make it there to find out what was on their minds.

✧ ✧ ✧

Top executives of global companies lead organizations with enormous reach. Among the people I interviewed, for example, Stephen Case, chairman and CEO of America Online, will, once the merger with Time Warner is complete, sit on top of the world's largest communications conglomerate, which has at least 22 million Internet subscribers and reaches some 65 million households via sales of books and magazines. C. Michael Armstrong, who runs AT&T, directs a company with over 60 million customers. William Clay Ford Jr.'s Ford Motor Company has sales that exceed the gross national product of most countries. Leonard Riggio's Barnes & Noble accounts for about 10 percent of all books sold in the

United States. Jorma Ollila's Nokia constitutes over half of
the stock market capitalization of Finland, its home base, as
well as 25 percent of all global sales of cellular phones. Sir
Martin Sorrell's WPP, which is acquiring Young & Rubicam,
is about to become the world's largest advertising and communications conglomerate. Rupert Murdoch's News Corporation beams news, sports and entertainment from Boston to
Beijing and is becoming the most formidable media company in the United States. Henry Paulson Jr.'s Goldman
Sachs advises some of the world's largest firms regarding
their structures and strategies and accounted for 20 percent
of all money raised for initial public offerings in the United
States in 1999. Rolf-E. Breuer's Deutsche Bank is the largest
bank in Europe and, depending on how you measure it, in
the world. George Soros, the world's best-known global investor, has moved international markets with his business decisions or his public policy suggestions. Susan Berresford's
Ford Foundation supports philanthropic causes through offices in sixteen countries.

CEOs are also major actors in the drama called globalization. Their companies move the money, information,
goods and services that are knitting the world together. They
therefore have a crucial impact on economic growth, employment, technological development, and the environment. They will influence values relating to the balance of
private and public interests—how much free market and
how much regulation, for instance. They will guide the socially explosive activities that fall at the intersection of science and technology, commerce, and values—biomedical research, genetically modified foods, privacy and personal

security. They can be a progressive force in building capitalism around the world or they can constitute a rearguard action against political and economic change. However they behave, their influence will be at least as important as that of national governments and international institutions—probably more so.

❖ ❖ ❖

I talked to leaders here and abroad from a wide range of industries: telecommunications, computers, automobiles, aviation, energy, finance, law, health care, media and entertainment, publishing, advertising, consumer products, economic development and philanthropy. I spoke not just to people who ran global companies but also to those who financed and advised them. I looked for men and women who were highly respected by their peers and recognizable to a large audience. While deliberately excluding the new breed of successful dot-com entrepreneurs, I did not ignore the enormous wave of entrepreneurship around the world. My sample included some who founded major operations and continue to run them, including Frederick Smith, Rupert Murdoch, Michael Dell, Stephen Case, Michael Bloomberg, Leonard Riggio and Richard Branson. I also selected leaders who were exceptionally innovative in large organizations, adapting technology, decentralizing decision making, stimulating new ideas throughout their organizations, and motivating their employees to be creative.

I went to prominent venture capitalists to get their views: Donald Valentine at Sequoia Capital, Leonard Baker at Sutter Hill Ventures, and Nancy Peretsman at Allen & Company. I spent time with Ira Millstein, who leads Weil, Gotshal & Manges, a prominent U.S. law firm, and has been an advisor to various presidents, governors and international institutions. To gain some historical perspective, I spoke also to three influential historians: Ron Chernow, the biographer of J. P. Morgan and John D. Rockefeller; Richard Tedlow, a business historian at the Harvard Business School; and Emma Rothschild, an economic historian from Cambridge University in England.

In making my selections I knew I was not talking to the typical CEO. The men and women in this book are at the top of the pyramid. From the resources they oversee to the pressures they face, they constitute an elite class, a distinct group worthy of observing. I am also aware that generalizing about leaders who are involved in a range of industries requires omitting a large number of important concerns that relate to specific companies. An investment bank faces different day-to-day opportunities than an automobile company. Nevertheless, there is no shortage of information on individual executives and their firms, and I want to complement what exists elsewhere by focusing on what they have in common. A media company and a high-tech manufacturer are both preoccupied with the Internet, globalization, getting closer to customers, figuring out how to tap into exceptional talent around the world. This book, therefore, does not attempt to cover all the important questions surrounding CEOs or even most of them, but rather looks at business leadership through a wide-angle lens.

As a business school dean, I know as well the extent of scholarly research that exists on all aspects of business management. I've come to respect this work enormously, and a good deal of my professional time is devoted to creating an environment where it is encouraged and promoted. But as someone who has spent most of his life on Wall Street and in Washington, I lay no claim to scholarly knowledge in this area. This is not a theoretical book, and there is no pretense that it is based on hard analytical data. To the extent that it provides insights into business strategy, it is the result of what CEOs are saying to me and the thoughts they provoke.

My objective has been to reflect the most important thoughts that run through the minds of some of the world's leaders as a group. I was looking for patterns from which to draw conclusions, patterns derived from what was said and what wasn't.

Most important, I make no pretense of being an objective observer. Although I drew from the interviews, I wanted to describe not just what the world's top corporate executives are saying but what it made *me* think about. I have been interacting with top business leaders throughout my career. When I was on Wall Street some were my clients. When I was undersecretary of commerce, I helped many of them to expand their company presence abroad. As a columnist at *Business Week,* I write about them. As a dean I now call on some of them to help educate our students. In this book I want to talk about the awesome challenges that CEOs face as seen through what they have said to me and as filtered through my own experiences and my own thoughts.

✧ ✧ ✧

Finally, let me explain how I went about writing this book and how it is organized. When I began this project, I had no preconceived view of how it would turn out. In effect, I conducted an experiment by talking to top businesspeople to see what they thought. Because the interviews—which averaged sixty to ninety minutes each—covered a wide range of topics, many ideas arose. I subsequently zeroed in on those few themes that emerged most frequently and that I felt were most fundamental to CEOs' thinking. As I sat down to write, in some cases I felt it was enough for me to be just an observer; in others, I wanted to comment; in yet others, I felt compelled to go further and offer some thoughts about what CEOs should do in the future. In some ways this is a book of essays. But there is a train of thought that ties them together, and it goes like this:

Global CEOs are in the middle of the third industrial revolution and face three kinds of challenges. First, they have their hands full with the central strategic problems of how to take advantage of the Internet and the global economy. Second, they face certain everyday dilemmas of leading and managing corporate Goliaths. And third, they have roles to play on the world political, economic and social stage.

While the strategic and everyday problems are almost overwhelming in themselves, CEOs are doing the best that can be expected, often against trends and pressures that are much more powerful than they are. That notwithstanding, where they fall down is in the third category: They have not sufficiently understood or accepted their roles as leaders in helping to create the rules and the institutions for trade, finance and communications and for defining social responsibility for global companies. I am not naïve, however, and I acknowledge that because the business pressures alone are so awesome, it simply may not be possible for global CEOs to add to what they are now doing by substantially expanding their service to society more generally. If this is true, however, we will all be worse off.

New Haven, Connecticut
November 2000

1

*Masters of the Universe
or Lost in Space?*

L eonard Riggio, chairman and CEO of Barnes & Noble, was talking fast, and his entire compact body seemed to be in a state of animation. We were discussing the business climate and how it was changing. "Put it this way," he said. "Everything is in play."

In those four words he captured the environment in which CEOs operate today—the possibilities, the vulnerabilities, the uncertainties. Riggio caught, too, the tension between the various jobs that chief executives have to perform as they scramble to lead their companies and as they come to grips with their changing positions in society.

This tension will shape this third industrial revolution that we are all living through. How *do* the requirements of running a highly competitive and profitable company interact with other pressures on CEOs to build a better global society? One answer is that they really don't; business executives worry about shareholders, customers and employees, while governments and public interest groups deal with the rest of us. But this response is too simplistic. In the real world, CEOs—particularly the kind interviewed for this book—are required to play roles beyond the narrow scope of their businesses, if for no other reason than that their companies affect the lives of so many people and communities around the world. But how far does this role extend? How far *should* it extend?

The best starting point for this discussion is something that two CEOs from different countries and industries told me. "Unless you are competitive," said Michael Armstrong, chairman and CEO of AT&T, "then all other issues are moot." Or as Jürgen Schrempp, chairman of Daimler-Chrysler, put it, "Only a profitable corporation can think about being a social enterprise, too." Without underestimating the formidable obstacles CEOs face in running successful companies, I will nevertheless argue for a broader conception of business leadership than now exists in the minds of most top executives. While they are naturally riveted on meeting quarterly earnings targets, and while unrelenting attention to shareholders is the best market discipline that anyone has yet conceived of, most top executives still construe their jobs too narrowly. Their critical task is to build value for shareholders over time, not just to please speculators and day traders who buy and sell securities according to the latest headlines. This means that CEOs will not only have to run profitable companies, but they will need to build great institutions that provide customers with superior products and services, create high-quality jobs, and in the process make life better for the population at large. They will also have to devote far more effort to helping to devise the rules under which twenty-first century trade, finance and communications systems will evolve, and to lending a hand to build the institutions that will be the global counterpart to the arrangements on which national economies rest.

There are a number of reasons for this more expansive view of corporate leadership. First, a company will have a better chance of finding and keeping loyal customers and talented employees—the essential ingredients for creating value in the new economy—if it offers brands and creates relationships that can be trusted. This, in turn, requires CEOs to chart and execute a steady course over several years, and not bend like a bough in the wind every time market sentiment shifts.

Second, while everyone might agree that only democratically elected governments have a clear mandate to represent the popular will when it comes to issues like new laws or social institutions, there are some realities that must be taken into account. Public sectors are simply not equipped to do what they ideally should in the midst of today's rapidly changing world. Below the very top levels they lack the talent. And while many national budgets are in surplus today, over time governments will not have the financial or technological resources to keep up with powerful and capricious markets. They are already overwhelmed by the enormity of capital flows across borders, the forces unleashed by the Internet, and the demands of citizens for stronger and more flexible safety nets in the face of changes wrought by globalization.

Third, because we are in a transition between the industrial age and the information age, a large vacuum exists concerning the regulatory framework for the global economy. We have very few of the international institutions that will eventually be required. There is nothing equivalent to a central monetary and banking authority, no global Securities & Exchange Commission, no global Food & Drug Administration, no common set of antitrust procedures. There is an absence of international arrangements for all the new problems that are arising, including environmental protection, labor standards, the Internet, the Human Genome Project and global fraud and corruption. Even what organizations we do have—the International Monetary Fund, the World Trade Organization, the World Bank, the International Labor Organization—are mired in political controversy over what they should be doing, and their operational effectiveness has suffered accordingly.

Fourth, the environment for global business is more fragile than it appears. A powerful political and social backlash is building against continued liberalization of global trade and finance. The protests at the meeting of the World Trade Organization in Seattle in November 1999, and subsequent demonstrations in Washington and in Prague, were just the beginning of a trend in which public interest groups and disaffected citizens around the world are joining together to form a counterweight to what they see as the unbridled power of global companies.

What I will be suggesting, therefore, is that CEOs see themselves in a new light, adopting more of a proactive stance than they have thus far. This isn't just a question of civic-mindedness, for many CEOs have been quite generous in supporting charities and important causes. Nor is it about marginal improvements in exercising "social responsibility" through corporate foundations, because that is definitely happening already. The imperative is not a stepped-up public relations campaign, and it's not a question of lobbying governments more effectively on behalf of business interests.

I am proposing something more far-reaching: CEOs ought to think more broadly about what true business leadership means today. Of course they need to run their companies well, but they ought also to realize that they should take more responsibility for shaping the environment in which they and everyone else can prosper. They should be corporate chief executives, but also business statesmen. The wider mission has as a prerequisite the need for their companies to be competitive and profitable, but it also entails more involvement in building the future regulatory framework of the global economy and working with public authorities to create it and make it work. It includes helping to define the role big corporations ought to play in solving many of our social problems before they become too severe to handle and before multinational companies become scapegoats for causing the problems in the first place. In my interviews, no one asserted that a free market alone, without effective government rules and institutions, would work to the benefit of business and society. They were much less clear about what that framework should consist of, how to establish it, and what their own roles should be.

In advocating a broader and more proactive role for business leaders, I am not equating the private interests of business with the public interest, nor saying that markets are the only mechanisms to deal with the needs of our citizens. I am suggesting that the definition of the public interest has become too complex to draw bright lines between the public and private sectors as we have tended to do in recent years.

We all know, as well, that there is a long history of business pursuing its self-interest in ways that are antithetical to the general welfare. Companies in industries such as oil, automobiles, pharmaceuticals, media, entertainment, and, of course, tobacco have all come under political attack in recent years for charges ranging from fixing prices, to environmental degradation, to marketing music and movies that celebrate violence to children. Even today, with elaborate and sophisticated government regulation in place, there is a substantial amount of fraud and deceit, stimulated in large part by the profit-at-any-cost motive. Of course businesses have been pouring money into political campaigns in an effort to buy political favors, and I am not advocating that government cease its vigilance or slow its attempts to fashion sensible regulations and enforce them vigorously. On the contrary, I believe in stronger and more effective government and in business leaders doing more to police their own activities.

The question is whether the world's most important business leaders can transcend their immediate competitive preoccupations and formidable strategic requirements to create something more for the society in which they operate and on which they depend. There are intense counter-pressures, and it is not at all clear that this can be done. But the assumption of a more substantial leadership role for top business executives is more than a worthy goal. It is essential to the continuation of economic and social progress in this new century.

❖ ❖ ❖

Let's step back and reflect on the circumstances that surround today's business leaders. CEOs are at the center of a struggle for the soul of the global company and the soul of society—both of which are closely linked. In the business world, technology and globalization have created a level of competition that will lead to new categories of winners and losers and force a transformation in how companies are organized and led. The impact of these changes will spill over into the workplace and economy. It will also spread to the political realm as citizens and governments search for new regulatory systems for both the national and global economies.

This is not the first time in modern history that the world has witnessed such a profound and complex interaction between business and society while both were reeling from all manner of new pressures. If you examine the past two industrial revolutions—England between 1750 and 1840, and America between the late 1860s and the 1920s—you can see many of the same phenomena that we are experiencing today. Then as now, new forms of business and work patterns emerged. England witnessed a large-scale move from farm to factory; in America, local firms expanded nationally for the first time. In past industrial revolutions, the spirit of innovation was unusually intense, with new technologies such as the steam engine, the railroad, the telegraph and the telephone all reinforcing one another and fostering new businesses that were soon organized and managed in new ways. Financial markets grew exponentially, even as they experienced their booms and busts. Immense fortunes were made, and legendary business tycoons such as J. P. Morgan and John D. Rockefeller wielded substantial influence in the business world and beyond. Governments were much smaller in England and America in the eighteenth and nineteenth centuries, and at first what powers they did have were no match for market and technological forces. Yet when public officials felt sufficient political pressures to deal with increased poverty, oppressive working conditions and rules for fair competition, the public sector simultaneously reformed itself and intervened in the economy with substantial effect.

Nevertheless, it is likely that the business and societal challenges of the late twentieth and early twenty-first centuries will be seen as even greater than in previous epochs. Talking to Ron Chernow, the biographer of J. P. Morgan and John D. Rockefeller, I got a clear picture of how things moved slower a century ago and how business leaders had more time to plan their strategies step by step. Chernow noted that Rockefeller often spent hours staring out his office window and just thinking. Yesterday's tycoons paid scant attention to shareholders and disclosed the barest of information to the public. The giants of the Gilded Age wielded near total control over their boards of directors, almost all of whom were insiders or partners in the enterprise.

In those days the media were typically much less investigative than they are now, and unlike current CEOs, the Rockefellers and the Morgans could lead the most private lives, without the pressures of their every move and every decision being reported around the world. Indeed, their situation was in great contrast to the "open book" nature of the lives and activities of today's CEOs and their companies, pressed as they are by shareholders and the public for reams of detailed information on a continuous basis. "Rockefeller didn't have a lot of audiences," said Chernow. "For most of his active life he was completely reclusive and mysterious, really invisible to the general public. And this was typical of a lot of businessmen of the era. Their idea of publicity was no publicity. They had no interest in burnishing their image because there was nothing, from their point of view, to be gained from it. The public was a damned nuisance to them."

Compared to today's CEOs, who are in constant motion between North America, Europe, Asia and Latin America, the titans of yesteryear didn't have to travel abroad, with all the mental and physical strain that entails. Rockefeller built the world's most powerful international oil company without venturing outside the United States until his mid-forties, and then only as a tourist. In the first two industrial revolutions, corporate competition was mostly local, not global.

Business leaders during the second industrial revolution were free of today's government constraints, as well as the pressures of modern corporate governance. "They didn't have income taxes; they kept everything they made," said Harvard Business School historian Richard Tedlow. "Aside from a few railroad companies, you would also have to look long and hard to find a nineteenth-century business leader who was thrown out of his company by a board of directors. Nor was there the pressure from big institutional investors, as there is today."

The life of CEOs was much easier even through most of the post–World War II era. Up until the 1980s, when Japanese companies and corporate raiders upset the existing business order, American companies basked in domestic prosperity, faced no threats from abroad and were under no pressure to change their fundamental business models. It was possible to build a niche and exploit it with a generic strategy. A CEO could choose to be a low-cost producer or an upscale provider. Either way, there were ways to erect barriers to competition. A great brand such as Johnson & Johnson could act as a deterrent to potential rivals. A particular production advantage such as Sony's mastery of miniaturization could keep others out. A regulated monopoly such as the old AT&T could also create a zone of protection. With less competition, the big moves, the big gambles, the dramatic organizational changes were nowhere near as necessary as now.

Indeed, the imperative for today's CEOs is not just to find the right business model but also to keep changing it to meet the pressures of unprecedented competition. It's not just that competition is so fierce but also that in many ways it is qualitatively different. For example, in the 1980s American manufacturers faced an assault by Japanese companies like Toyota and NEC—companies that had mastered quality, inventory control and so on. But at least the American CEOs could study the competition, deconstruct what made it so good and adopt the better features of their rivals' strategies. Today, however, the corporate race is less *against* some identified competitor than *for* markets that don't yet exist, for consumer needs that have not yet been identified, for young talent whose full creativity has yet to blossom. There is no rabbit to lead the dogs around the track.

In the past, the elements of corporate competition were simpler. You tried to make a better product, and you aimed for respectable growth in revenues and profits. Today, these achievements still count, but the financial markets, which ruthlessly value and revalue companies on a continuous basis, are looking at much more. It's not enough to have strong growth; hypergrowth is the yardstick. It is not enough to succeed in being within a range of earnings; a CEO must hit or exceed a precise target. It's not enough to make good products; Wall Street is looking also at your business model and asking a host of questions: Is your organization Internet savvy? How fast can you expand your business? How good is your management team? Who are your corporate partners? What kind of intellectual property do you have now and are developing for the future?

Products and services, producers and customers, executives and entrepreneurs—all are being joined in new ways. Big decisions are being made at warp speed. Nothing is static. Everything is in a state of change.

On a broader societal level, the changes may well be unprecedented, too. Whether or not the Internet is as transforming a technology as, say, the telegraph or the radio, it is spreading around the world much faster than previous pathbreaking technologies did. You don't have to argue that globalization is a new phenomenon to conclude that it encompasses more of the globe than ever before and that its roots now run much deeper than during any other time in modern history. The implications of these trends are many, but at least two are highly relevant to the world of today's CEOs. First, more opportunities and also more risks abound than ever when it comes to the future of their companies. After all, the number of new markets will be unprecedented but so will the competition, and so will the pace of technological and political change that will shape the markets themselves. Second, as the world gets smaller, CEOs will be unable to escape involvement in some of the most difficult political, economic and social problems of our times. There will be no way to avoid operating in countries with fragile economies, weak democratic structures and mega-cities with severely overburdened infrastructures. Exploding populations with growing health problems and environmental nightmares will be part of the scene too. There will be a need for more laws, standards and governing institutions in this new world; otherwise, there will be destructive chaos as different economic and cultural systems clash with no mediating or arbitrating arrangements to solve the ensuing problems. There will also be a need to accommodate billions of people who are now very poor, and who may soon be very angry at the global disparities they can now see so clearly for the first time in history because of modern communications. In September 2000, James Wolfensohn, president of the World Bank, gave a quick summary of this grim situation at his organization's annual meeting in Prague. "Something is wrong," he said, "when the average income for the richest twenty countries is thirty-seven times the average for the poorest twenty—a gap that has more than doubled in the past forty years. Something is wrong when 1.2 billion people still live on less than a dollar a day and 2.8 billion still live on less than two dollars a day." Years ago these kinds of inequalities might have been ignored or finessed. But it's probable now that in a world growing more interdependent by the hour, rich countries in general or global CEOs in particular will have to confront these problems sooner rather than later.

C. Michael Armstrong is Chairman and CEO of AT&T Corporation. After thirty-two years at IBM and four years as CEO of Hughes Electronics, he joined Ma Bell in 1997 with a mandate to bring it into the new economy. I first met him in 1994 when I was the undersecretary of commerce for international trade and he, then at Hughes, had just been appointed chairman of President Clinton's National Export Strategy, with the job of coordinating the input of top American business leaders on the making of U.S. export policy. At the Commerce Department, we had spent weeks preparing an elaborate agenda for the first meeting to help him get started. When the time came to begin, my staff and I were standing around in a government conference room waiting for Armstrong to arrive. We expected him to come with an entourage of assistants; instead he walked in alone and warmly greeted everyone, making the rounds and shaking hands. He radiated the confidence, enthusiasm and energy of a seasoned politician. Then he sat down. I was about to give an overview of the administration's policies and objectives, but I never had a chance. I never even opened the briefing book. "Here's what we're going to do," he said, in a tone that indicated he was already running and we had better catch up. He had arrived with his own agenda, knew exactly what he wanted to accomplish and from the first minute it was his show. His voice was soft and his face often broke into a smile as he talked about what the group's priorities would be, chief among them an effort to rein in the government's inclination to slap unilateral export controls on countries that ran afoul of American foreign policy goals. He came across as "Mike"—friendly, accessible. But there was enormous force and clarity in what he was asking the Clinton administration to do. You had the sense that if you were making a movie and said "Get me a CEO" to the casting director, he'd give you Michael Armstrong.

Five years later, when our interview for this book took place, Armstrong was still the picture of a major CEO. "I've seen an awful lot of history made in a relatively short time," he said. "I joined IBM when the most popular form of data processing was punch card accounting, and I saw the evolution of computers from mainframes to PCs. I went to Hughes in 1993, when space was basically a government environment and satellites were used mostly for spying, and helped usher in the era of private commercial space communications. And here at AT&T, I can see the whole world of communications exploding. Remember this: It took radio fifty years to reach fifty million people, it took television thirteen years to reach fifty million people, and it took the Internet half that time— six years or so—to reach 100 million people. We are laying enough fiber each day to go around the world twice. Internet traffic is doubling every hundred days. The borders are coming down, and it's an irreversible trend, whether they are tariff borders, monetary borders, political borders, ethnic borders—they are coming down."

Asked whether there was something different about the extent of change at the beginning of the twenty-first century compared to just a few decades ago, he replied, "Two things are radically different. The pace has been faster. And the global reach has been unprecedented. I don't care whether you are in a Communist country, a kingdom, a dictatorship, or a democracy. The Internet reaches your people and e-commerce reaches your business and your institutions. With your keyboard and your mouse, you can reach the whole world. I think it's a revolution unparalleled in history."

Henry Paulson, chairman and CEO of Goldman Sachs, talks about change from the vantage point of someone who has spent nearly his entire professional life at the same investment bank, with the exception of a few years in the early 1970s in the Pentagon and White House, his first jobs out of Harvard Business School. Paulson and I were classmates at Dartmouth College, where he was an all-Ivy League football lineman. We were also colleagues in the Nixon White House, where, at the age of twenty-six, he became the deputy director of the Domestic Council under John Ehrlichman. I had not seen him except in passing for most of the next two decades, but I had never forgotten an incident that revealed his determination to win at everything he did.

It was January 1973, and we were in the middle of a game of outdoor paddle tennis. I had been playing racket sports since the age of eight, but Paulson was new to the sport. As the game went on, I was maneuvering him from one side of the court to another, back and forth, back and forth. Although he was in great shape, he was tiring, and the cold air—it was about ten degrees Fahrenheit—made him short of breath. I was beating him badly, and he asked to stop for a second. No problem, I said, let's just call it a day and pick up the game later. No, he replied, I just need a minute. He then leaned over the side of the court and vomited. Come on, I said, let's go inside. We can continue next weekend. His body was hunched over, his face was flushed. He didn't say anything for what seemed like a long time. Then he slowly straightened up. Okay, he said, I'm ready to continue. I offered again to postpone the match, but he wouldn't hear of it. I worried that he would injure himself and wondered if I should be less aggressive on the court. The thought didn't last long. Within minutes he came on like a raging bull, and I was on the defensive—and he proceeded to demolish me.

A quarter century later, I was sitting across from him in his Wall Street office, a modest room for the chief executive of the world's premiere investment bank. His shirtsleeves were rolled up to the middle of his forearms. He was leaning forward, his words tumbling out faster and faster, his restless energy filling the room. He gave me the impression of being tough and forceful, without the slightest trace of arrogance. In fact, like many of the CEOs I met, he seemed awed by the situation he found himself in, the range of opportunities and problems, the speed with which things changed and decisions had to be made, the amount of sheer gut instinct that had to go into weighty decisions on which billions of dollars and the fate of companies rested. Seeing the way he was leaning forward, I got the sense that he subscribed to a theory, perhaps intuitively, that you had to keep moving forward always. There was no neutral gear, no resting position. "So what's changed in the time you've been at Goldman?" I asked.

"What hasn't?" he replied. "When I came to the firm in 1974, there were very few mergers being done anywhere, and today that market is something on the order of $1 trillion. There were hardly any high-yield or derivatives markets, both of which constitute so much of our business today. Investment bankers dealt with chief financial officers and didn't make presentations to boards of directors, as we routinely do today.

We didn't meet with heads of governments, didn't help to restructure whole industrial sectors around the world. When I joined the firm, Goldman had only twelve hundred employees compared to over fifteen thousand today. We had only thirty-two employees overseas and three little foreign outposts, whereas today we have twenty-five offices and at least half of our employees are overseas. Despite all that's happened in the last twenty-five years, the pace over the last five has been the fastest, driven in particular by globalization and technology. I do believe that we are at one of those crossroads in history—an inflection point, to use a cliché—in which massive changes are occurring."

Nancy Peretsman is executive vice president and managing director of Allen & Company, a small but influential corporate matchmaker and investor in large-scale business deals. The firm's crowded offices are on New York's Fifth Avenue, near the Plaza Hotel, and we met in a conference room, where coffee, fruit and bagels were available on a silver tray. Peretsman has been centrally involved in some of the highest profile media and entertainment transactions in recent years, having represented CBS in its sale to Westinghouse, advised Barry Diller in creating USA Networks, and counseled Oprah Winfrey on the expansion of her empire. She apologized in advance for the need to step out a few times to take phone calls, since she was in the middle of a deal that had, she said cheerfully, "fallen apart and been put back together twice in the last twenty-four hours." She was remarkably relaxed, given that she was shuffling between our interview and her office. I asked her how she saw the changing business scene. She zeroed in on the creation of new businesses, but she drew a distinction between today and previous eras, noting why business models can change so fast and why the scale of the deals can be so large.

"Historically, most capital formation was funding new businesses," she said. "In cases like the cable industry or the cellular industry, you had to get the business proposition ultimately accepted by the consumer. Why should you buy cable? Why should you get a cellular phone? Why should you buy a computer? Today, something different is happening. This whole Internet industry, in many parts, is not asking you to do something you didn't do before. It's just changing how you do it. Unless you believe that the number of books has changed exponentially, Amazon.com's growth has clearly come out of the hide of other [booksellers]. Ticketmaster's on-line growth came out of people who used to pick up the phone to order a ticket and now find it easier to order by computer. So you haven't changed the consumer proposition; you've just changed who it is that's making the sale. The growth [in these kinds of Internet businesses] has been meteoric, because historically to build a business required gaining consumer acceptance. But [with e-commerce] I just gave you an easier and cheaper way to buy what you already buy. We're changing not what people are doing as much as we're changing how they are doing it. I can't think of anything we've seen like this. . . . Two years ago Priceline.com didn't exist. We're going to do $500 million of revenues this year. When else in history did you go from zero to five hundred million in that period of time?"

Not all business leaders view change the same way, of course. Andrew Grove, the legendary chairman of Intel and

Time's 1997 "Man of the Year," is a case in point. A Hungarian refugee who arrived in the United States in 1956 unable to speak English, he worked his way through City College of New York, where he majored in chemical engineering, then obtained a Ph.D. from the University of California, Berkeley. He cofounded Intel in 1968, became CEO in 1987, relinquished the title in 1998, and became chairman. If any business leader personifies the realization of the American dream, it is he. We met at Intel headquarters in Santa Clara, California, amid the rabbit warren of cubicles that constitutes Grove's working environment. I reminded him of a phone conversation we had in November 1993 when I was a senior trade official at the trade negotiation in Geneva that was about to launch the new World Trade Organization. Early one morning, about 1:00 A.M. Geneva time, I began to phone a handful of American business leaders to give them an update and seek any last minute advice they had. I reached Grove and he gave me a few thoughts to pass on to Mickey Kantor, the chief U.S. negotiator. Grove said he remembered me "as the only official who would listen to what I had to say," an outrageously self-effacing comment from a business leader who drove a good deal of high-technology trade policy toward Japan in the late 1980s and early 1990s. In any event, from the minute we sat down I felt as if we were having a conversation in a Parisian café, with nothing to do but kill a few hours over coffee, so personal and thoughtful were his comments.

"Are we in a true revolution? Has technology revolutionized the way we live in the United States or the rest of the world?" he asked rhetorically. "I don't think so. I don't

think this is a revolution in the sense that it represents a
step function—a sea change—in the quality of what happens in our lives. How revolutionary was the creation of the
supermarket compared to the general store, or the down-
loading of music from the Internet compared to going to
Tower Records? Those are changes, yes, but evolutionary
ones. The steam engine was a revolution. The railroad was
a revolution. The equivalent today would be space travel."

What the Intel chairman worries about is the accelerating
pace of technological development. "One problem is that
the success of the cycle of innovation, which has created all
the improvements we see around us, is leading to good financial results and even to more funds flowing to support
new technologies," he said. "This is creating an accelerating,
dizzying dance in which you are chasing your tail in a circle,
faster and faster, until you are getting ahead of yourself. For
technological change to penetrate society, however, it has to
be invented, has to be proved, has to be deployed, and deployed widely. Then it becomes a platform on which other
developments are built, and then the cycle starts all over
again. We make a cult of how wonderful it is that the rate of
change is so fast. But . . . what happens when the rate of
change is so fast that before a technological innovation gets
deployed, or halfway through the process of its being deployed, [an] innovation sweeps in and creates a destructive
interference with the first one? If you look at the Internet
technologies, for example, there are business methods that
are being pioneered, Web-based techniques and infrastructure, and they are tumbling out so fast that Approach M is
barely beginning to be deployed when a better idea—

M+1—comes along and says, Don't bother with that. Deploy me. And these things are just tumbling on each other and the end result could be a traffic jam in which users and suppliers—and investors—are all choking on this."

✧ ✧ ✧

I found the business leaders I interviewed to be uniformly thoughtful—even philosophical—but I also found them to be pragmatic and non-ideological. They are acutely aware of the changes sweeping over our society. They believe that the lines between producers, suppliers and customers are blurring, and the borders between countries and industries are dissolving. As a group they sense that we are in the early innings of a business and societal revolution that will continue for many years to unfold in unpredictable ways.

They live in a world that includes too much unsifted information, multiple constituencies with different objectives, pressure to act with extreme speed in an environment of conflicting market signals and untested technologies. It is a world of tremendous uncertainty, where the trade-offs between one course of action and another are almost impossible to quantify and require an unusually high dose of gut instincts. Consequently they place great weight on finding simplicities that work—following basic instincts, identifying first principles clearly and remaining true to them in good times and bad.

They talk about the importance of serving customers and of finding and keeping the best talent for their organizations. They are preoccupied with absorbing new technologies and turning them to competitive advantage. They see the marketplace in global terms, although they are deeply rooted in the societies in which they grew up. They acknowledge the importance of what has come to be called "corporate social responsibility"—protecting the environment, contributing to education and training, working closely with the communities in which their firms operate—but they are concerned about being held accountable for a widening range of problems outside the orbit of their control and corporate mandate. Despite the trend to downsize government and the support for more market-oriented economies around the world, top business leaders are uncomfortable assuming responsibilities that have traditionally rested with the public sector. Count on me, they say, to provide advice to lobby government or when my direct interests are at stake. But beyond that, public leadership belongs to someone else.

In their thoughts about fundamentals, I did not find large variations among CEOs of different industries. Perhaps this is because there is so much blurring between making a product and providing a service (think, for example, about how manufacturing and service mesh in industries such as computers, automobiles, and telecommunications). Nor did I see great differences among nationalities, perhaps because all major companies are no longer national but global, or because all CEOs face similar problems.

Another background factor is at play too: The phenomenal decade-long business expansion in the United States coupled with the end of the Cold War. In the business community there is a psychology of prosperity and unlimited opportunity, without much on the horizon that will put an end to the good times. "Over time, I feel the spread of free and open markets is inevitable and irreversible," says Rupert

Murdoch, Chairman and CEO of the News Corporation. "Our opportunities," says Christopher Galvin, Chairman and CEO of Motorola, "are nothing short of spectacular." "I cannot imagine being able to have all this knowledge and all this intellect and being able to put it in people's hands and having anything negative over the long haul," says Jack Welch. Today's CEOs have no firsthand knowledge of a full-scale economic depression, and most have limited experience with operating in a serious recession. Vietnam excepted, war is not part of the personal history of any of them. We can only speculate how this positive environment has affected the CEO's mind-set. Perhaps it accounts for the luxury of looking at business leadership in relatively narrow terms, recognizing the broader societal impacts but not feeling a pressing obligation to get deeply involved. Perhaps it accounts for their optimism about the future, or the reluctance to see serious social and political problems on the horizon. But were the world to go into an economic or political tailspin, it is likely that a lot of what's in the mind of CEOs today would change substantially.

✧ ✧ ✧

There is no elegant theory of management that CEOs can use to deal with their many problems—no one-size-fits-all, no ten rules to surefire success. When you review all that arose in a wide range of interviews, you are left with an unsatisfying feeling of untidiness. The parts don't add up to any simple theory. There are too many contradictions. Guess what? That's real life for CEOs. But after you've heard what the chief executives have to say and after you've thought about what they didn't say and what their body language communicated at certain points in the discussion, you do come away with a picture of the revolution in which they find themselves.

When it comes to the Internet, for example, traditional companies need to preserve their enormous base of valuable assets while refashioning their strategies and their corporate cultures to take advantage of this fantastic new communications medium. As they do so, their biggest confrontations will not be with the dot-coms, which they will demolish, but with one another—a bloody battle that is just now unfolding.

In developing businesses in the world economy, they have to go beyond extending their company's geographical reach to figuring out how to build a truly multicultural workforce and top management team, how to create organizations that can extract maximum benefit from all their assets around the world, and how to come to grips with overseeing enterprises that are bigger than most countries. In the arena of economic and social policy, they are buffeted by potentially contradictory goals—how to continue to create value for shareholders, how to make a significant contribution to society, how not to be held accountable for what they believe governments ought to be doing.

In the meantime, they need to preserve the time-tested leadership qualities, such as maintaining consistent moral values. They need to be leaders who are trusted to be effective, to be fair and to walk through the fire with the troops, even as they change the nature of their companies through mergers, alliances, restructurings and in many cases large-scale layoffs, and even as the gap between their compensation and that of their employees widens. CEOs need to excite the markets, their customers and their employees with a powerful vision for the future, though they know they will pay dearly for unrealized dreams. They need to enrich their shareholders with an ever-rising stock price, quarter after quarter, while paying increasing attention to "stakeholders"—customers, employees and suppliers on whom the long-term value of the company depends.

Balancing all these objectives simply may not be possible. "Balancing" implies that you can have it all if you find just the right weighting for all the elements. But that assumes a point of equilibrium where all goals are pursued in the right proportion and in viable relation to one another—and that the balance is sustainable. This is not the real world of CEOs. New opportunities, new setbacks, new competitive challenges are the order of the day, and the only constant is the need to make trade-offs. "Juggling" is a better metaphor than "balancing," for it connotes many objectives that have to be kept in play all the time. The relative position of the objectives changes, and sometimes one is dropped and has to be picked up. The juggling, moreover, must be performed at ever-increasing speeds. And it takes place on stage with the entire world looking on and making judgments about how things will go tomorrow and the day after.

The juggling act has certain implications. CEOs are not looking too far into the future, so preoccupied are they with what they need to do every day. It is equally difficult to exercise peripheral vision, so pressing are the immediate demands on them. They are nowhere near as much in control of their fate as they may appear by virtue of their position and the status accorded to them by society. As a group they are certainly not using their collective influence to build the kind of foundation on which a less volatile and more sustainable variant of global capitalism could rest, nor do they give the appearance of heading in that direction. They are assuming that governments and international institutions will take care of building the architecture of the international marketplace, when in fact the powers of governments and international institutions are highly constrained. As a result, a dangerous vacuum has opened up and is growing wider.

In the end, I found myself wondering whether these CEOs are leading the third industrial revolution, being carried by it or being consumed by it. I saw evidence of all three possibilities. I concluded that the men and women who run the most powerful corporations are not masters of the universe—not by a long shot. Nor are they lost in space. The reality lies somewhere in between.

The fragility and vulnerability of their situations were poignantly described by AOL's Stephen Case. No one has a better claim to being at the forefront of developments in business and society, but listen to what he said in a talk to investors and analysts in the spring of 1998. "I sometimes feel like I'm behind the wheel of a race car. I need to keep my eyes on the horizon, but I need to keep my attention on the rearview mirror to see who is gaining on me. From the passenger seat, consumers are telling me where and when they want to be dropped off, and behind me my shareholders and business partners are engaged in backseat driving. One of the biggest challenges is that there are no road signs to help navigate. And in fact, every once in a while a close call reminds me that no one has yet determined which side of the road we're supposed to be on."

PART ONE

CHALLENGES OF THE
NEW GLOBAL ECONOMY

2

The Next Internet Wars

"**W**e've got to integrate the Internet into our basic business," Henry Paulson told *Forbes* in the spring of 2000. "It's no different than the telephone . . . it isn't rocket science, it's basic plumbing. What you are really talking about is business strategy." This deceptively matter-of-fact comment reflects a universal awareness among CEOs that the changes wrought by developments in cyberspace are deep and permanent. As the Internet pushes business and society in new directions, CEOs are obsessed with trying to understand what it means for their companies and how they can use the new technologies to be competitive. Dealing with the Internet raises every conceivable challenge. It represents the need to understand and incorporate new technologies. It requires coming to grips with globalization. It challenges traditional notions of leadership. It forces cultural and organizational change within the firm. It raises a host of new issues about the links between business and society.

Can big corporations compete with the newer companies that have been established around the Internet itself? Does the future belong to the lithe and cool companies like

Amazon.com, or are the old economy organizations poised for a resurgence? Here is what I conclude after hearing many CEOs on the subject: While top business leaders are suitably humble in the face of the Internet, they are not cowed. After overcoming some major handicaps, they will overwhelm the dot-coms by beating them at their own game or merging with them. Indeed, during the time I wrote this book, the landscape was already changing dramatically in this direction. But the survival of traditional companies won't be the big story of this decade, because from the vantage point of just a few years from now, victory over the Internet start-ups will have proved relatively easy, and the more ferocious competition will occur among the corporate Goliaths themselves.

In this war the differentiating factors will depend on how well CEOs can integrate the Internet into their overall strategies. This includes figuring out how to use the Internet to get closer to customers and suppliers, respond to changes in sales patterns in hours instead of weeks, squeeze inventories to a bare minimum, connect with other companies that have more specialized expertise than their own companies do and manage those relationships. Competition among the Internet-enabled giants will also entail finding the best talent and creating an environment that will make them productive and happy to remain with the company for a meaningful period of time. While the race will require understanding the new communication technology and its implications, even more than that it will be about basic business acumen, aided but not supplanted by telecommunications wizardry. When the history of this era is written, the CEOs who will have been most revered will not be noted for their technological wizardry but for their managerial brilliance.

The big question is whether today's CEOs have the savvy and the stamina to defeat the dot-coms, which is the first leg of the race, and then run this second, more difficult and much longer race against their peers—or whether it will take their successors to do it.

✧ ✧ ✧

Consider the contest between the traditional firms and their Internet-based rivals. Can the traditional multinationals prosper in the face of competition from more nimble upstarts that innovate more quickly, command spectacular valuations and attract some of the best talent in the world? No one should underestimate the problems of many of the older and more established companies, but it's even more dangerous to sell them short.

Of course the old economy companies have some formidable liabilities. They have to deal with the past even as they restructure their entire way of doing business for the future. One of their foremost tasks is to overcome the legacy of what venture capitalist Leonard Baker calls "bureaucratic capitalism." Baker, a twenty-five-year veteran of Silicon Valley, is a rare breed who can step outside of his own space and observe the industry in perspective. Shortly after I came to Yale in November 1995, I met Baker at a restaurant on Nob Hill in San Francisco. Wanting to bring new-economy thinking to our students, I asked him if he could deliver a major lecture. I expected war stories from Silicon Valley, but when he arrived several months later he delivered a seriously researched analysis of entrepreneurship—its general historical, economic and political context, as well as the circumstances surrounding the success of various entrepreneurs through history. You had the sense that he had thought things through, tested his ideas, which rolled out fast, many with historical allusions to the impact of the Gutenberg press, the steam engine, the railroad, the telegraph and the recent revolutions in biotechnology and computing.

I asked Baker to compare the new economy to the old. "I think it's primarily about company organization and culture," he said in an interview in his office in Silicon Valley, on a street characterized by bland 1950s-style office buildings and filled with venture capitalists. "There are really only two ways to be highly profitable. One, which I call rent seeking, is to aim for the financial returns that come from monopoly or quasimonopoly status. To do this you have to be looking to erect an entry barrier to potential competitors. And when you do that, you create a culture of defense. Rent-seeking firms usually adhere to a command and control model. In this kind of culture, careers are made and rewards are dispensed based in large part on political skills. This characterizes many of the Fortune 500 companies." The second way to be highly profitable, Baker pointed out, is through innovation. "Innovation means you are creating new value and sharing it with everybody. It is a game in which everyone wins."

Did he think the culture of the Fortune 500 could be changed? "I'm skeptical," he replied. "History would say that it is extremely hard to take existing organizations and make them highly innovative. The old model of centralized leadership doesn't work in this world. The new model is one of someone whose principal job is to create a culture that makes the people around him more productive. Unless you are making thinkers and innovators out of the rank and file, there is no longer any way that you can get enough value out of the organization to be productive."

Donald Valentine is another venture capitalist, a salty elder statesman of Silicon Valley, who helped launch Apple Computer, Oracle and Cisco Systems. While he acknowledges that more of corporate America has been paying attention to the importance of new information technology, he too faults the culture of large organizations and their historic inability to recognize change and embrace it. "If it's an evolutionary change that is involved," he says, "a big company can probably incorporate it slowly and progressively. But not if it's revolutionary. Look at Bill Gates. It was just a few years ago that he panicked and saw the Internet was happening without him. If it's looking *him* right in the eye, and if he can miss it for a minute with the quality of the people he has, how can corporate America deal with such revolutionary change until they feel that nothing less than their survival is at stake?" Valentine concludes that this inattention to change in the environment is deeply rooted in old-line companies. "I think that when you get big you get pretty complacent. You believe your own propaganda. You begin to think your company will be around forever. To me it's a constant marvel how these big corporations behave. Actually, that's why the companies we invest in get launched. Our business has been very dependent on the big companies' not paying attention to what they should have been doing."

Every major company is improving its ability to use the Internet, but just because a company engages in e-commerce doesn't mean that it is an e-business. A more profound transformation is required for that—a fundamental shift in corporate mind-set about what happens within a company and how that company relates to others. A real e-business will center all of its processes around the Internet; it will embrace the structure and the ethos of the Internet itself. For example, it will develop systems to share knowledge with all its employees, with other corporate partners, customers and suppliers. This system will connect pricing, product and design information with customers and suppliers. It will be structured to create and distribute all the financial and product information that managers could want to see so that executives are better able to run the firm with the latest and most complete data. A large proportion of middle management will have to be eliminated, and traditional hierarchy will have to give way to systems that are more self-organizing.

An e-business will focus on outsourcing to entities whose specialized expertise exceeds its own, looking for every conceivable way to eliminate the costs of unnecessary intermediaries and processes so that consumers can see the true value added in what they are getting. It will create new markets by seeking out not only new customers but new suppliers and pools of talent. It will adopt a highly fluid strategy with the understanding that product cycles are much shorter, that the premium on anticipating and reacting immediately to customer demands has increased and that risk taking is to be encouraged and rewarded. It will compete in many time frames at once, much as Intel has done in establishing product development teams working in parallel not just on the next product but on two generations to come.

✧ ✧ ✧

These are formidable challenges. But they are being dealt with as one CEO after another recognizes the centrality of the Internet to a company's survival. A number of reasons lead to the conclusion that big global companies more than "get it."

First, any complacency that might have existed is gone; the fact is, virtually all CEOs of traditional companies are running scared.

Michael Bloomberg is President and CEO of Bloomberg L.P. I met him in his company's bustling cafeteria, which is open to the organization's central reception area. With employees coming and going, and a high noise level, a visitor gets the sense of the excitement and energy in the organization. Bloomberg, once a top investment banker at Salomon Brothers, left the firm some twenty years ago to start up his own company supplying financial information to banks and brokerage firms. Now he talks about the evolution of his business, how rewarding it has been to have a team that can move fast and seize new opportunities. He worries that his company is becoming too big and too bureaucratic to keep up the pace of innovation. "In two decades," he said, "we've gone from a company that was half a dozen people to over five thousand. The bureaucracy is something that I'm constantly battling. I'm trying to keep the growth from killing us."

Across the Atlantic Ocean, Deutsche Bank chief Rolf Breuer also rests none too easy. "In the short term," he said, "I worry about a crash in the markets, but in the medium term I worry that the bank is not flexible enough to react to ongoing changes." Across the Pacific, Hiroshi Okuda, Chairman of Toyota—the world's most successful car company, known for its innovative manufacturing and its quick response to changing consumer tastes—echoes the thought. "When I became president of this company [1995], it had lost its edge, in my view," he said. "Complacency had begun to set in." When I asked him what his most important accomplishments were at Toyota, he said that it was "to instill a sense of crisis so that the company would never be complacent again."

Henry Paulson looks from another angle at the danger of not being vigilant enough. "We have made some acquisitions of small technology companies that are tops in areas like electronic trading, so that we can get that technology in-house and be able to jump-start its use throughout the firm," he told me. "We are constantly reevaluating our technology and looking for the latest ways to apply it to our strategy. What I want to avoid is the situation in which, just because we have such a strong client franchise, we sit on top of our traditional business without seeing the significant changes bubbling up elsewhere. Companies too often get locked into their own business models. They become reluctant to attack their own businesses [by installing] new technology, products, services, or distribution channels. They become so focused on providing customers what they wanted yesterday that they miss the opportunity to create the products and markets of tomorrow." He said that he and his management team are always assuming the worst case, always asking "What if ?" They are constantly examining the real value they are supplying. If the product or service is a commodity, and if Goldman is charging its clients too high a price, Paulson assumes that someone will come along and knock his company out of the competition.

Martin Sorrell, chief executive of WPP, a holding company for nearly a hundred firms in the advertising, communications and consumer and product research arena, evidences a healthy degree of paranoia about the Internet. Known as a shrewd financial engineer who nevertheless builds up companies rather than dismantles them, he has over the last two decades turned a shell of a company into the world's largest advertising and communications conglomerate by acquiring J. Walter Thompson, Ogilvy & Mather and soon Young & Rubicam. Sorrell gives the impression that he is humbled by how fast the business climate is changing, even though he has been a prominent agent of that change. Like so many other CEOs, he is at once impressed by the competitive environment he faces and confident that with enough hustle he can do quite well in it. "The new media area offers us a colossal opportunity, but if you ignore it, it could become a colossal threat," he says. "We all recognize that we have a traditional business model. Is it going to survive? How is it going to change? And we are doing two things. First we are pushing our existing businesses to use new channels such as the Internet. But the traditional channels never move fast enough. There is an inertia that you can never overcome. What you have to do is go direct and invest in the new technologies such as a direct marketing company that is Web-based. Three years ago I said to the CEOs of the companies we own, 'Look, I may have to do something at the center of WPP that destroys some brand value elsewhere. Yes, this is cannibalization. You may have to eat your own children, because if you don't, somebody else will. Either we reinvent ourselves, or someone else will do it for us.'"

❖ ❖ ❖

This healthy sense of fear calls into play the global companies' significant advantages. As Jack Welch says, "The traditional company that moves quickly should find this a better game than ever." He's right: Multinationals have well-established brand names around the world. They have years of experience with the products they make and sell, and in most cases a lot more knowledge about them than they actually use. They have long-standing relationships with huge numbers of customers and suppliers. They have a deep reservoir of talent in many countries, and they ought to have major advantages in harnessing intellectual capital and gleaning valuable market information from every corner of the globe. They have an extensive history of moving goods, services and information across borders. They have unrivaled experience in the capital markets, as well as historic ties to a broad range of players in the financial system: banks, bondholders, shareholders around the world. They have important relationships with governments, built up over many years. It will take new dot-coms a generation at least to replicate these advantages.

The international reach, knowledge and experience of the giant multinationals have given them unmatched capabilities to develop products and services and sell them around the world. It ought to give them the advantages of finding talent where others cannot. Their global research, the costs of which could be spread across an enormous base of operations, should position them in the forefront of innovation. Big companies also have the assets to take significant risks and fail. Because they are on the ground in so many areas of the world, they can swoop in when economic conditions make timely and advantageous deals available. They will be in a much better position than their purely Internet-based competitors to offer consumers various channels of distribution—phone, fax and Internet, along with physical stores—a variety that is surely the future of retailing. The fact that they operate all over the world can be a hedge against normal business cycles, too.

In contrast to most Internet start-ups, moreover, established companies have already overcome many crises—recessions, currency and stock market debacles, political turmoil in various countries—and they have figured out a way to navigate storms that most of the new-economy companies have not yet experienced.

Big global companies also have enormous potential to increase their productivity and profitability. When Ford Motor Company says it wants to reinvent the way an automobile business works, it has the laboratory of an $83 billion annual budget for purchasing supplies and a test bed of thirty thousand suppliers. In just a few years, the company aims to save as much as $8 billion from lower-cost supplies and boost supplier productivity by 10 percent. GE plans to use the Internet to reduce overall administrative costs by 20 percent, to cut the time of building turbines by 20 to 30 percent, and to otherwise increase efficiencies throughout the far-flung empire by orders of magnitude. Royal Dutch/Shell has used its new international network to locate some 30 million barrels of oil reserves in Africa. Cisco Systems says it can save $500 million per year with on-line management. Boeing believes end-to-end digital systems will save between 30 and 40 percent of the cost of building a commercial aircraft.

Most traditional multinationals will not be wiped out by the new economy insurgents; rather they are likely to be spurred on by them. As Bill Gates writes, "The digital world is forcing companies to react to change and giving them the tools by which to stay ahead of it." The companies that supply the new economy with its essential infrastructure—Cisco, Oracle, Microsoft, Intel—are selling primarily not to the dot-coms but to the traditional blue chips. Many of these companies will look much different a few years from now—some bigger, some more specialized, all increasingly centered on the Internet. Many will have linked up with purer Internet companies, either by merger, investment or some other kind of alliance.

No matter what happens in the Internet arena, moreover, the physical world won't go away. Someone is going to have to drill for oil and transport it. Someone will have to grow food and distribute it. Our roads, our ports, our automobiles, our airplanes, our hospitals, our clothing, our food, our household appliances, our energy—the "physical" companies will surely be made more efficient by embracing the Internet, but the new communications medium alone cannot perform these and many other vital functions.

"Most popular guesses about the Internet's commercial future have concentrated on fashionable new companies run by geek billionaires. . . . Dizzyingly rated firms such as Amazon, Yahoo!, and eBay that have hogged the limelight," editorialized *The Economist*. "Yet far more significant is the effect the Internet will have on established companies. 'The storm that's arriving,' said IBM's Louis Gerstner, 'is when the thousands and thousands of institutions that exist today seize the power of this global computing and communications infrastructure and use it to transform themselves. That's the real revolution.' "

✧ ✧ ✧

And that is what has been happening. "Our industry and the tools that it creates are really at the center of a whole series of changes that are occurring in the way companies work, and we might be somewhere between 5 percent and 20 percent of the way through the conversion," says Michael Dell, chairman and CEO of Dell Computer Corporation. "So in large part I think the next five years are going to be a lot about taking some of the things that a few companies like ours are experimenting with and really proliferating that across a huge variety of companies. And that's going to have a pretty profound effect on the way the economy works, the way businesses interact, where companies find real value, and how and to where capital flows."

Old-line companies are establishing e-commerce marketing links to their customers, allowing more frequent and fluid two-way relationships—an arrangement that provides opportunities for customers to design products, for firms to minimize inventories and for product service to become much more efficient. They are investing in new-economy companies, buying them or merging with them. Most important, they are thinking about all the possibilities of the Internet.

Kenneth Chenault, President and Chief Operating Officer of American Express, thinks of the Internet simply as yet another historic transformation of his company. A graduate of Harvard Law School, former consultant with Bain & Co. and a twenty-year veteran of American Express, he has been designated to succeed his boss as chairman and CEO in April 2001. Chenault sat across from me in a conference room adjoining his office high up in the World Financial Center in New York, with much of the city spread out before us. He described how the company has transformed itself many times in its hundred and fifty years of existence, moving from its original mission of being a freight-forwarding company into traveler's checks, credit cards, and ultimately a wide range of travel-related and investment services. Now the company is in e-business, too, allowing its customers to do a variety of transactions on-line: to check their accounts, pay their bills, make travel arrangements.

"One thing that's very clear now is that the on-line world is going to change everything," he said. "There will be increasing focus on and need for an understanding of different distribution channels and the matching of products and services to those channels. In the past, particularly for a consumer-based company, we could afford to focus on one or two distribution channels. Now, we will be using a wide variety of channels—some regulated, some are highways available to anyone, some are through third parties, very few are proprietary. Our customers are going to want us to create value out of information we have about them, and to personalize our offer to them. . . . To do all this we are making major bets on the fusion of the Internet business with what we are already doing. We are committing a very high level of financial resources, human resources, and we are prepared to again cannibalize our business. Some people are asking whether we know how we will make money out of all this, and when. We don't have absolute certainty, but we believe this is a bet we are going to win."

Barnes & Noble's Leonard Riggio had the idea for e-commerce well before most retailers. We met in his plain conference room on lower Fifth Avenue at a time when he was under a media spotlight because Amazon.com was emerging as the clear winner for selling books over the Internet. Riggio, who began his career in 1958 as a bookstore clerk while he studied engineering in the evenings at New York University, is rightly credited with having revolutionized the concept of the bookstore, turning it from a fairly elitist enterprise to a form of popular entertainment by establishing mega-stores where customers could meet and hang out. Despite the lead Amazon.com had gained, Riggio did not appear dismayed when we spoke, and he presented a clear idea how the game will be played out.

"What I think you have here is an ebb and flow, revolution followed by counterrevolution," he told me. "Ultimately what will happen is what some people are calling the revenge of the brick-and-mortar people. You will see the merger of the revolution and counterrevolution, and you are going to see the big e-commerce practitioners and the traditional retailers merging. Maybe one will have to break the other, but we are going to come together. . . . Retail business will change, of course. The Internet will add incrementally to sales but [it will] not replace traditional sales. Suppose you sold $10 billion worth of books. Then the Internet comes along. Then you'll probably have $12 billion sold, $5 billion on the Internet, $7 billion from the stores. So there are going to be fewer stores, plain and simple. And they will be spaced much farther apart. And the ownership of both stores and on-line business will be the same. And then the stores can be more [flexible]. Fewer stores, some big, some small, and big distribution centers across the tracks, where the rent is cheap. And we put portals in the stores, so that whatever you want to buy off the shelf you can, but if you want to tap-tap-tap on the keyboard and order the rest and ship it home, you can do that, too."

In late 2000 Riggio was still trying to find the right formula to link his 550 stores and brand name to e-commerce. Barnes andnoble.com, owned 40 percent by Barnes & Noble, announced an agreement with Yahoo!, replacing Amazon.com on that popular Web site. Barnesandnoble.com said it intends to sell books, music and videos through the Yahoo! network.

James Wolfensohn, President of the World Bank, has embraced the Internet with a vengeance. Formerly the founder and chief executive of a prestigious investment bank that bore his name, he has also been the chairman of both Carnegie Hall and the John F. Kennedy Center for the Performing Arts. The hallway leading to his spacious office in downtown Washington, where we met, is lined with his own art collection.

Wolfensohn took me to what he called the World Bank's "systems learning facility," a conference room with multiple screens. He described how the World Bank has used the Internet. "We have just run a course for seven African countries, five participants each, on the subject of corruption in government." He described how the Internet allows this kind of instruction to take place in cyberspace, not just between Washington and officials in one country but among the World Bank and several countries at the same time. "If you do that for investigative journalists, which we've done, or help parliamentarians around the world to better understand the democratic process, or give farmers extension courses, or highway builders information they need, or people in villages help to construct sewage facilities, think of what you can achieve," he said. Wolfensohn talked about transforming his organization into what he calls a knowledge bank that would house the experience that the World Bank has had in mounting projects all over the world. Anyone wishing to find out how an urban planning project was handled in Bombay, for example, could find out with a click of a mouse. Wolfensohn was also using the Internet to link up experts around the world in areas such as civil engineering or education so that they could share experiences. "You get a sense that the revolution in knowledge and the ability to store it and access it and then distribute it in multiple languages changes the pace at which you can transmit it but also gather it, because it's two-way. You have the possibility of enormous gains. This is not pie in the sky. This is today."

The integration of the virtual and physical worlds is happening in industry after industry. In the late 1990s, for example, firms like Merrill Lynch and Morgan Stanley Dean Witter were seen as dinosaurs, easy prey for upstarts like Ameritrade or E* Trade, who invented trading on-line. But by mid-2000, projections showed that the six full-line service brokers, including Merrill and Morgan Stanley, would have more on-line accounts by the end of the year than all of the hundred-plus e-brokers combined. While more customers are using the Internet to trade, they want to combine ease of execution with advice from a seasoned broker. Most of these new customers aren't day traders but conservative investors. The e-brokers, in response, are adding investment advice to their portfolio of services, but this transition is proving more difficult for them than going the other way was for Merrill Lynch, et al. Put another way, e-business is becoming mainstream for the brokerage business.

Automobiles are another example of the marriage of bricks and clicks. In mid-2000, DaimlerChrysler was considered an e-business laggard. Then it initiated what could be considered a counterattack against Internet sites like Autobytel.com, or CarsDirect.com by establishing Web sites that would allow customers to configure cars on-line and search dealer inventories for cars they might want to buy. Meanwhile, the Internet would link auto dealers with one another to better control overall inventory, match customer needs more efficiently and lower the cost of office supplies by aggregating purchases to get discounts. This move was a huge leap for the company, but only the beginning of many more Internet innovations.

In the retailing industry the virtual and physical worlds are coming together, too. An interesting example occurred last August when Toys 'R' Us and Amazon.com, once fierce rivals, announced plans to merge their on-line toy sales and concentrate separately on what they do best. The traditional toy company will coordinate the selection, purchasing and inventory management, while Amazon will handle distribution and customer service.

By the summer of 2000, moreover, the overall impact of pure "e-tailers" on the business environment had failed to live up to expectations of a number of celebrated forecasters. According to the *Financial Times,* just three companies—Amazon.com, eBay and Priceline.com, accounted for ninety percent of the market value of the entire U.S. e-commerce retail sector. Total on-line sales were projected to amount to just 2 percent of the retail market, a third of the sales made by traditional catalogue companies, by the end of 2000. None of this should be interpreted as portending the demise or even the slowing down of on-line retailing. Far from it. The implication is that more and more e-commerce will be done by traditional firms with the infrastructure for customer service, fulfilling orders, handling exchanges of unwanted products and so on—and using the Internet as one of several channels of distribution.

Beyond the way companies are using the Internet to serve consumers, progress is also being made as virtual marketplaces allow more efficient transactions between producers and suppliers—the business to business, or B2B, market. In 1998 there were virtually no B2B electronic businesses. In 2003, however, the volume is expected to approach $2.5 to 4.0 *trillion.* Thus Ford, General Motors and DaimlerChrysler are experimenting with pooling resources to create a dot-com start-up to streamline the process of procurement on some $250 billion of purchases each year. The exchange will not only cut the costs of supplies but handle currency conversions and keep track of export regulations. The cascading impact on suppliers and *their* suppliers is not possible to estimate, but a radically new and more efficient purchasing system is being born. Ultimately, the benefits will accrue not only to the auto companies' bottom line, but also to consumers who will be able to order specific models with their own selections of options—on-line or off—much more quickly.

Other industries and firms are trying to follow similar paths. Sears, Roebuck & Company and French retailer Carrefour S.A. are joining forces to create the largest e-commerce supply exchange for their industry. Procter & Gamble, Nestlé, H. J. Heinz and other consumer products companies, some fifty altogether, are creating an Internet marketplace, too. The same phenomenon can be seen in industries such as steel, energy, aerospace, chemicals, banking and health care. Even the U.S. farm sector is deep into e-commerce as companies like Cargill and Du Pont join forces to create an electronic marketplace. Many of these new marketplaces will fail either for technological reasons or, possibly, because of antitrust violations. Many are sure to move ahead in one form or another, and these efforts ought to be seen as merely a small part of what established multinational companies are doing to use technology to revolutionize their businesses.

Big companies are rapidly ramping up their efforts to embrace the Internet in other ways: investing in start-ups, establishing dot-com subsidiaries, creating in-house venture funds to finance e-business proposals from their workers. Even quintessentially new economy companies like Dell Computer are investing in other companies to maximize their involvement in innovative ventures; in Dell's case, there are over eighty such ventures. In addition, big companies are turning to newly formed groups for help in integrating the Internet into their businesses, or creating innovative business structures to maximize the effectiveness and the value of their Internet operations. Accel Partners, a U.S. venture capital firm, has teamed up with McKinsey & Company and the leveraged-buyout-firm of Kohlberg Kravis Roberts to provide such services. Goldman Sachs, the Boston Consulting Group and the venture capital firm General Atlantic Partners have formed iFormation to do the same for clients.

There are lots of inflated projections concerning the change that the Internet will bring, but you need not rely on them to get a good sense of what is happening throughout the economy. In the first half of 2000, investment in high-tech industries in the United States soared at an annualized pace of three times the rate of total business investment. This happened at a time when the bubble burst for pure Internet companies, deflating the value of many of them to small percentages of their original market values and creating financing problems for most of them. It's a good bet that the Internet-driven phase of American growth, in which the new communications technologies are spreading rapidly throughout the old economy, has just started.

By the spring of 2000 it was becoming clear that investors were applying more traditional criteria for evaluating the dot-coms than had been the case. Investors were concluding that on-line companies would need to be judged by the same standards as their off-line rivals, by profits and cash flow and not just by growth at any cost. All this coincided with the realization on Wall Street and among Internet company executives that as companies grow, traditional management questions arise relating to organization, human resources, financial planning and real estate acquisition. Internet companies were searching desperately for managers who had traditional business experience to plan strategies and to manage growth. By the fall of 2000, many of the New Economy icons were badly tarnished. Microsoft and Intel had lost huge percentages of their market capitalization, and the business models of Amazon, Priceline, Yahoo! and eBay were increasingly questioned by financial analysts and investors for their long-term viability. Popular commentary focused on the folly of Wall Street and the media for having overhyped the new Internet companies. A new line of thinking was evident: traditional firms would absorb the better ideas which the dot-coms spawned. "Virtually every smart idea a dot-com entrepreneur has ever dreamed up has been duplicated by established concerns with deep pockets and staying power," said *Business Week.*

Having exalted the New Economy for years, however, the media was now going too far in the other direction in implying that the dot-coms were history, or that the old-line firms had the Internet in their DNA. True, the revolution was spreading to the traditional companies. But it was nowhere complete in terms of technological development and certainly not in terms of the ability of corporate management and the workforce to fully incorporate everything the Internet offered. In fact, as Leonard Riggio said, revolution and evolution were coexisting, and a new kind of mega-firm was just beginning to emerge.

❖ ❖ ❖

And so the big question for multinational companies is not whether they will be thrown off course by the newer Internet companies but how they—every one of them Internet-enabled—will compete with one another. Because of the Internet, all prices will be transparent and subject to comparison, a far-reaching change in the business climate, where real comparison shopping on a global scale was never possible before, either for consumers or businesses themselves. Companies will be using the Internet to communicate better with their customers and suppliers, knit their far-flung workers closer together, mine the considerable knowledge scattered throughout their empires, reduce costs with more efficient inventory management and otherwise streamline operations. In doing all this, they will *all* become more productive, and they will create an environment so hypercompetitive that it will be almost impossible to raise prices. In fact, they may well be competing in an increasingly deflationary environment that they themselves will have helped to create. A lot of us will benefit in our capacity as consumers who are getting more value for our purchases, but not as shareholders of the companies whose profitability is under extreme pressure. The cutthroat environment will make it nearly impossible to hold any kind of lead, by virtue of innovation or product differentiation, for long. Overall, the Internet-spawned challenge that CEOs will face in the next several years will be different in kind and far greater in degree than that of the late 1990s.

What then will separate the winners from the losers? Success will depend not on technology but on leadership, management and strategy. The point is made by Orit Gadiesh, the flamboyant chairman of the global consulting firm Bain & Company and a former soldier in the Israeli Army. Just back from a six-week trip to visit clients throughout Europe and Asia, she talked excitedly about the importance of fitting an e-business strategy into a company's approach to serving its customers, not as something apart. "There is a tendency to obsess about having an e-commerce strategy, but this is the wrong way to think about it," she said. "You need an overall strategy [of] which e-commerce is an important part." She referred to recent decisions at Levi Strauss. The firm had a brilliant Web site but had recently shut it down because the price of sales over the Internet was out of line with retail sales in stores. According to Gadiesh, the company needed to think through its overall sales strategy first and then figure out how the various sales channels fit together.

Jack Welch embodies the philosophy that the Internet must be an enabler of basic business strategies. You use the Internet to do what you want to do faster and more efficiently, but your fundamental objectives don't change. "We are already using the Internet to become quicker, to squeeze more costs out of the system, to take the intermediaries out of the transactions," he says. "We have a strategy and the Internet makes it more effective."

Welch searched for a piece of paper to illustrate his point. He walked to his desk, picked up a document, brought it back to where we were sitting, and started scribbling on the back of it. On one side of the page he wrote "GE." On the other he wrote "Customer." He drew a two-headed arrow between them. His concept was a simple one: GE is about finding and keeping customers. Use the Internet any way you can and experiment with as many different approaches as you can to enhance your company's relationship with the customer. "But never allow anyone, a dot-com or any other company, to get in the middle of this relationship," he said. "Anyone." He paused after the second "anyone," his eyes flashing, the nonverbal equivalent of an exclamation mark. GE had never allowed any interlopers before the Internet, he said, and nothing had changed except that GE now had to provide its customers with whatever a dot-com intermediary could deliver. If the customer needed more information, he said, his people would see how the Internet could be used to provide it to dispense more or better information. If prices were not competitive, GE would figure out how the Internet could be used to reduce cost of supplies or inventories. In other words, the business fundamentals don't change; only the tools do. Welch leaves little doubt that there is no room in his empire for employees who don't learn how to use those tools.

A crucial differentiator will also be employees—their energy levels, their adaptability, their willingness to experiment and to take risks. "I think if there is anything to worry about, it's whether or not you've got the energy in the organization to truly understand the rapidity with which the impact of the Internet is going to happen," said Welch. "My people understand it, but we don't yet have the entire organization engaged. The Internet is not yet all-consuming. So I guess the biggest challenge is can we get enough energy, enough excitement, enough momentum into people's bodies to be sure they're reacting and leading this revolution—because it is, truly, a revolution."

A third factor in winning the Internet wars will come down to the business model, that is, how CEOs make the most of all of their assets—customers, employees, suppliers, relationships with communities and governments—and, particularly how can they get value from each, and how can they tie them together so that the total value is more than the sum of the parts. In this regard, the Internet is the key tool, because it can enhance communication as no other medium has been able to do. It can integrate the constituencies of a company by allowing them to share information and act almost simultaneously on it, such as when a customer's order in Kansas City must be filled in Kuala Lumpur, or when the blueprints of a new project are being designed by teams of architects and engineers living in different parts of the world.

No one can tell what the best business models will be, and in any event they are likely to be constantly changing. In this uncertain environment, we can expect a series of landmark business deals, each of which creates a potentially new trend. When AOL announced its merger with Time Warner, most observers were stunned, but soon afterward the logic of linking old and new media seemed inevitable. If tomorrow Wal-Mart bought Amazon.com, or Merrill Lynch linked up with Priceline.com, new precedents would be set. The point is that the market will be experimenting with combinations that few thought of initially. Some of these dramatic experiments will be colossal failures, whereas others will constitute a new direction that other companies will emulate.

We are also on the cusp of all kinds of new markets in finance and business, not just markets where you buy and sell a product on the basis of price, but where you simultaneously have access to enormous amounts of information about the people and institutions you are dealing with. To take one example, an auto company won't just buy a steering wheel online; it will also know whether the makers of that part are environmentally conscious. Just a few years from now, billions of people—that's not hyperbole—will carry cell phones with access to the Internet, a situation whose impact on business (let alone on politics and economics) defies imagination.

In 1996 the late Jerry Junkins, then chairman and CEO of Texas Instruments, gave me some advice about designing courses at Yale that take account of the Internet. "Assume that all information everywhere will be available to everyone at no cost," he said. "That's about where we'll be in the early part of the next century." It seems as though we're getting there, but it would be wrong to think of that as the end point. It is just the beginning of the beginning.

This much is for sure: Company structure will have to be redesigned over and over; experiments in strategies, projects and people will be continual. Those organizations that are uncomfortable living on the edge are unlikely to win the brutally competitive contest in which they find themselves with old and new players from around the corner to around the world. You can count on this as well: The most successful CEOs will be able to accommodate whatever trends emerge and whatever curve balls are thrown, in large part because they will never lose sight of their fundamental strategies: to win over consumers, surround themselves with the most talented people, enhance the reputation of their brands and incessantly communicate their strategies to investors, customers and employees.

The winning business model will include not just concepts but execution. How closely can you link a company to its customers? How skilled are you in creating an efficient worldwide supply system that, among its other virtues, eliminates the need for costly inventories on-site? How good are you at managing your outsourcing and your strategic alliances with other companies? Can you provide new product offerings on a fluid and continuous basis, rather than at intervals of one or more years? Can you put together special teams to accomplish specific projects, disband them and establish different ones quickly and effectively? Can you make decisions quickly? Can you kill a project early if it appears that the initial decision was wrong? Can you create an environment that promotes collaboration and can you reward people who make this happen? In the brutal wars among Internet-enabled companies, these are some of the attributes that winning CEOs will need.

✧ ✧ ✧

No one can confidently predict where the Internet will take us any more than someone could have known how swiftly the steam engine would lead to industrialization, or how radically the telegraph would revolutionize financial markets, or that the railroad would lead to the formation of national and global companies and that the automobile would create the suburbs. All we can be certain of is that the Internet will have a pivotal influence on how we produce and distribute goods, how we receive and disseminate information and how we communicate on every level. It will empower consumers in ways still only dimly imaginable and it will change the structure of heavy industry, telecommunications, energy, finance, media, health care, leisure, and recreation. It will create what management expert Peter Drucker calls a "new mental geography," in which distance is eliminated and there is only one economy and one market—global in both cases. As the Internet becomes a contest not between the traditional companies and the dot-coms but among the big boys themselves, it will become a battle among corporations with enormous resources and geographical reach, fought on terrain where price increases are almost impossible and achieving monopoly positions is increasingly difficult under the intense glare of antitrust government watchdogs. The financial markets will be passing judgments on winners and losers every day, taking account of plans, execution and quarterly profits. The wars to come are sure to be bloody.

3

Being Global

The merger that created DaimlerChrysler, says Honeywell chairman and CEO Michael Bonsignore, "was really one of the pivotal events in my thinking. Boeing–McDonnell Douglas, Exxon–Mobile—you saw these combinations and you thought 'My goodness, all bets are off.' There is no more conventional wisdom on what is possible. I began to think of the stewardship of a 114-year-old company and asking myself, 'Is a $10 billion company going to survive in the next decade?'" Bonsignore's anxieties led to a major change for his company: In late 1999 Honeywell merged with AlliedSignal to form a new firm, Honeywell International, with three times the sales of the "old" Honeywell. Bonsignore then faced the challenge of putting together two distinct cultures—his company, with its anti-conglomerate stick-to-your-knitting philosophy, and AlliedSignal, which was a multimarket, multi-product corporation prone to go after markets even if they were relatively unassociated with one another. As it turned out, the new entity struggled to deliver on its promise from the beginning. During 2000, shareholders drove down the market value by over 30 percent. In October 2000, Bosignore

helped engineer another mega-deal, this time putting the
company in the arms of GE. Now size and uniform culture
would be better assured, but at the cost of Honeywell's existence altogether.

Bonsignore's thinking and the headaches he took on because of the original transaction are hardly unusual. Nevertheless, I found that many top business leaders have been involved in international business for so long that they may be
overconfident that they understand the game. Some have
lived and worked abroad. Some have managed large projects
and operations or engineered financial deals that encompass
several countries. Important as the world economy is to them,
and as aware as they were of the intensifying competition for
world markets, I did not detect the same enthusiasm, urgency
or imagination in their discussions of global strategies as I did
when talking about the Internet.

I did not sense the same awareness that, just as it was critical for the Internet to become part of a company's DNA, so
was it essential for a company to have global mentality that
was deeply imbedded in all it did. Among other things, that
would mean having a global vision, a global strategy, a global
hiring system, a global training program, a global procurement and supply system and global R&D operation. It would
mean coming to grips with the tensions between having one
corporate culture and one which also included people and
markets of many different national cultures. It would imply
creating a global system of financial and psychological incentives that aligned the activities and interests of every part
of the company with its central vision and strategy.

To be sure, none of these issues is new to CEOs of multinational companies, and many chief executives are seized

with them. But in the New Economy, they often appear as yesterday's problems because they have been around for a long time and are not as sexy as the Internet. But the fact is that no one has yet found the right formulas to deal with them satisfactorily, and so the relative complacency I felt is likely to be a major liability for many CEOs.

After all, when it comes to global strategy, here, too, the ground is shifting. Not long ago, the essence of a successful corporate foray into the international arena was to expand into as many countries as possible, but today any dot-com can hawk its products from Baltimore to Brisbane without moving from its founder's spare bedroom. Multinational corporations once scoured the earth for low-cost labor and production facilities, while today the premium for most companies is finding highly skilled talent around the world, no matter the price. There was a time when the big global companies were really pure reflections of their national cultures and policies, but the successful corporation will soon have to be multinational in the literal sense. There was a time when companies with powerful brands—Coca-Cola, Procter & Gamble, IBM—could sweep into third-world markets and blow away the existing companies, but today tough local competition is emerging in industries such as soft drinks in India and computers in China.

While international companies were never simple to run, the size and complexity of the firms that are now arising out of mega-mergers raise fundamental questions about how much is too much for a CEO to effectively manage. As more companies set up the full range of their businesses abroad, including advanced research and development, and as more of their subsidiaries become deeply entwined with local strategic alliances, the job of maintaining an intra-company culture will become overwhelming. In addition, CEOs will need to be prepared for a global economy in which so many countries of varying states of sophistication are important markets, and for a highly volatile global financial system that is sure to be characterized by recurrent crises.

One assumption that will have to be discarded is that being big and multinational is in itself a competitive advantage. An increasing number of such firms are moving into all corners of the earth, growing by acquisition after acquisition. The decisive difference between success and mediocrity—which is to say, between success and failure—will be the ability to transform global reach into real value for customers that competitors cannot provide. This task requires more brains than brawn. It involves creating a truly multicultural organization to take advantage of the enormous diversity around the world. It requires imagination going well beyond the kinds of recent corporate reorganizations that have focused on the relationship between product lines and geographical regions. Getting the strategy right will be a never-ending preoccupation for the CEOs who succeed in the wired world market.

✧ ✧ ✧

Not long ago, for most companies being "international" meant conducting an import-export business. If an American corporation had some outposts overseas, they were designed to facilitate the movement of goods to and from the United States. Except among mining and oil companies, little or no production occurred abroad. The next stage in the evolution of global firms came when companies set up overseas branches and subsidiaries to serve specific geographical markets. For example, the Ford Motor Company simply owned a company within, say, England, and Ford would produce cars there for British citizens, but its British operations were usually tightly directed by, and heavily dependent on, the Detroit home office. The same national focus and reporting lines to the United States applied to Ford's subsidiaries in France and Japan.

Then, in the 1980s, came the multinational company in which production of foreign subsidiaries was integrated, and the end products themselves became internationalized. Toyota could produce transmissions in Japan, axles in Malaysia, car frames in Indonesia and assemble the complete auto in Thailand, from which it proceeded to export. This type of integrated production is becoming the norm not only in manufacturing but also in finance, law and consulting businesses, where specialists from all over the world deliver an integrated service. Thus Goldman Sachs can provide advice to China's telecom industries by bringing together its specialists from New York, London, Tokyo and Hong Kong, with expertise on communications technology as well as listing requirements and underwriting techniques in the U.S., Europe, and Asian markets.

The latest evolution of international business has been the growing number of mergers of companies of different nationalities. Some of these have been in the same industry, such as the melding of British Petroleum and Amoco, Daimler-Benz and Chrysler, Deutsche Bank and Bankers Trust, Bertelsmann and Random House, WPP and Young & Rubicam. Others have brought together disparate businesses that the information age is linking together, such as Vivendi, with its communications capabilities, and Seagram's, which owned Universal Studios. In these cases, it's not just production that is being internationalized but a corporation's culture and its people.

The pace of change will only accelerate. In Europe and Japan rigid economic models are being jettisoned in favor of less overbearing government regulation, more attention to shareholders, and labor policies that allow wages to rise and fall with the market and workers to more easily move from job to job. This restructuring of economies has only just begun. Big emerging markets like India, Indonesia, and Brazil are still in the early stages of their full participation in the world economy, and their impact on global finance and trade has also only begun to be felt. China, in particular, is a work in progress. For all the publicity about its turn toward market-oriented policies, for all the attention given to the pragmatism of some of its top government officials, no one knows what the future will hold for internal developments in this nation of over a billion people just beginning to experience economic freedom.

McKinsey & Company predicts a phenomenal expansion of world trade. While 20 percent of the goods and services produced now enters international trade, McKinsey says the proportion could increase to 80 percent within thirty years. In this environment, we can count on increased competition as trade and regulatory barriers keep dropping and a new spirit of innovation and entrepreneurship catches on in both advanced and emerging markets. New firms will be popping up everywhere, adding to the supply of products and services, increasing consumer choice, and driving down prices. A wave of large mergers and a growing number of strategic alliances among corporations of different nationalities will create new classes of rivals. CEOs will surely be exposed to new and higher levels of risk arising in a highly competitive environment where so many changes are occurring at once, but at a pace that varies from country to country and region to region—changes in the number and nature of players, in the mind-set of those who set the rules and in the rules themselves.

It's also certain that the new business-to-business markets will open up opportunities for new suppliers that were never on the radar screen. They will come from China, Indonesia, India, Brazil, Mexico, South Africa, Turkey, to be sure, but also from entrepreneurs in developed countries. The Internet will allow companies to scan for opportunities around the world as never before. A steel plant in South Korea that has excess capacity will be able to find the customer in Argentina who needs an immediate special delivery. An agricultural business in Poland, needing an added supply of tractors on short notice, can spot an opportunity to buy surplus equipment from Komatsu in Japan. All this Internet-aided business will put enormous pressure on global supply-and-demand management by big companies and compel a level of flexibility and adaptability that will test all CEOs. As the system of production and consumption becomes more rationalized, the substantial overcapacity that exists in the production facilities of industries like autos, petrochemicals and semiconductors will have to be eliminated. Many companies, and countries, and millions of workers will experience the impact of these future dislocations.

✧ ✧ ✧

One factor in the rethinking of global strategy is a growing need to tap into regions of the world where considerable pools of expertise exist that have so far been unexploited. This is a preoccupation of leaders like Frederick Smith of FedEx. Smith conceived of the business of express mail while a student at Yale in the mid-1960s. After a stint in the Marines with two combat tours in Vietnam, he started the company and in the process revolutionized not just how mail is sent but how inventories around the world are managed. He has taken more direct charge of his international operations than most CEOs. I first met him in 1995 on a trade mission to China led by the late Ron Brown, then secretary of commerce. Smith impressed me as being exceptionally knowledgeable about China. I recall his drawing Brown aside before a meeting with a Chinese minister and suggesting, in his slight Southern drawl, what was likely to be on the minister's mind. In those five minutes, Smith imparted more insight for the meeting than our entire briefing book, which had been prepared over many weeks and with the help of the U.S. Embassy and intelligence services. Now, four years later, in our interview in a New York hotel, Smith was talking about contracts he had signed with aircraft manufacturers in the Czech Republic. He is among the first major western aircraft users to do so, and he feels that he's found a new reservoir of expertise. "There's a huge factory over there and nobody else would give these guys an order," he said. "But I was very comfortable with the fact that they could make wonderful airplanes. They did a hell of a good job for the Germans during World War II, just for starters."

American Express's Kenneth Chenault is also preoccupied with finding people who are as yet undiscovered and underutilized. "There are no longer any boundaries to where talent is, and where and how it can be deployed," he said. "The battle at home and around the world is going to be for ideas and nontraditional thinking, and we have to look at the entire global marketplace as the playing field."

The search raises the issue of how best to manage people from vastly different cultures within one multinational organization. Jack Welch told me, "You have to lead a global organization by engaging everybody. You have to globalize your intellectual capital. You have to get every mind into the game." But are CEOs willing to find minds that are truly different from what they are accustomed to, or simply foreign minds that think more or less like the people in their own company do? The question is posed by Susan Berresford, who has spent nearly her entire professional life at the Ford Foundation. We met in her office not far from the United Nations. On the bookcases was a set of exotic wooden artifacts from Africa. Draped over some of the chairs were colorful textiles from Indonesia and India. Amid all this we sat at a modern glass conference table. Berresford put the issue this way: "Are we looking for people like us, but with different nationality? Sort of like us? Or are we looking for people who are considerably different by virtue of history, culture, experience, and language? How far are we really willing to go?"

For most companies, whatever they would say publicly, the likely real answer is "not very far." American multinationals are on the lookout for, say, Chinese students who speak excellent English and hold an MBA from a recognized U.S. university. But this isn't diving into a diverse global gene pool. How many companies are looking for future executives from Fudan University in Shanghai? In many ways you can't blame them, for the process of finding, evaluating and integrating people who are truly different is enormously difficult and time-consuming. Just achieving ethnic and racial diversity within national firms, where people come from similar backgrounds, is a long way off in virtually every country, as recent racial-diversity problems in prominent U.S. firms like Texaco and Coca-Cola indicate. When BP acquired Amoco, it reached out to experts (including some in universities like Yale) to better understand the history, culture and legal dimensions of workforce diversity as it had evolved in the United States. Clearly, Britain and the United States are more aware of and concerned with achieving diversity than most other countries. Companies in continental Europe, and certainly in Japan, are far less progressive.

As important as creating a multicultural management team is, no one should underestimate the difficulty. I had a taste of the complications in the mid 1980s when I was in charge of Lehman Brothers' investment banking activities in Asia and living in Tokyo. For eighteen months, I oversaw the restructuring of a gigantic near-bankrupt shipping company headquartered in Hong Kong. Our restructuring team was composed of Americans, Japanese and Hong Kong Chinese. It was easy enough for us to discuss strategy. However, in the heat of the crisis, when we were moving fast to negotiate with individual creditors of many different nationalities, many misunderstandings and increasing tensions arose within our own team.

For example, Japan had no tradition of debt restructuring as we in the United States knew it. Generally, if bankers wanted to save a bankrupt company they just lent it more money. So our Japanese team members had a very difficult time grasping that you can write down the size of the debt, or transform one kind of debt into another, and demand certain performance changes from the indebted company in return. In Hong Kong, on the other hand, there was no such thing as Chapter 11, a provision in U.S. bankruptcy law that allows a debtor some breathing room by protecting assets from being seized while devising a reorganization plan. Instead, as soon as a Hong Kong company couldn't pay its debts it was liquidated, and all its properties were auctioned off. In this case, however, we had agreement from all the creditors to adhere to a de facto Chapter 11 arrangement. But our Chinese colleagues did not fully understand that the hangman wasn't just outside the door, and they were itching to make small side deals with creditors to keep them from forcing a liquidation.

Transparency was also a problem. The Americans on the team felt compelled to make sure everything that was happening was as public as possible. Our experience told us the worst thing that could happen in a big corporate restructuring was that some lender felt another was getting favored treatment. The only way to instill confidence that every aspect of the restructuring deal was fair was to let everyone know exactly what was happening and what was being offered to every creditor. Accordingly, we felt that open communication was essential not just with the creditors but also with the press. But Japan and Hong Kong had a tradition of backroom dealing, with favoritism to the powerful institutions and close friends. The notion of spending time cultivating and educating reporters so that they could present the story in an accurate and timely way was totally alien to the Asian members of our team.

The most difficult thing for me was basic communication within the team when we were under pressure. We were moving fast and a lot had to be left unsaid. I had a knot in my stomach all the time, because I was sure that some of my Asian colleagues were hearing the words but not really understanding them. This wasn't anyone's fault; the American, Japanese and Chinese experiences were just very different. I confess that I wished many times that the team was composed only of Americans like me.

✧ ✧ ✧

Another task for CEOs will be to incorporate an increasing number of highly educated and skilled people into their organizations. Unlike low-cost laborers, whose expectations center mainly on basic needs, these so-called knowledge workers will be more difficult to accommodate. Their aspirations for advancement will be greater. The best of them are likely to be heavily courted and wooed not just with high remuneration but with visas and geographical and organizational mobility. Finding them and keeping them will require multinationals to build new sets of relationships with those foreign institutions where skilled workers have links, such as universities and research centers. Given the rapid advancement of knowledge today, multinational companies will have to learn to spot and cultivate talent in earlier stages of development, much as athletic scouts look for future stars among the very young. For global corporations, most of whom are still struggling to internationalize their top management staffs, this kind of recruiting breaks substantial new ground.

The ability to use a diverse workforce to upgrade the knowledge base of a company will be an invaluable asset to CEOs. Consider the importance of sharing information across borders. "You have so many different cultures in the world, and it's incredible from the standpoint of idea generation," DaimlerChrysler's Jürgen Schrempp told me in our interview in Stuttgart. In the same way John Browne changed the structure of the petroleum industry with his European-American mega-merger, Schrempp shook up the auto industry by linking Daimler-Benz with Chrysler. After that colossal transaction, people began to invoke "the age of Daimler-Chrysler" as a synonym for the new era of globalization.

Schrempp is as intense as any CEO I have met. A serious mountain climber in his free time, on more than one occasion in our session he punctuated his thoughts with a flourish of his clenched fist as if he were going to pound the table. He exuded passion throughout the interview—on his strategies, on threats to business from too much regulation, on his personal interest in economic development in South Africa, at one point leaning forward with such energy that he seemed to come unconnected from his chair. "At Daimler-Chrysler, we are able to tap into our great talent in the area of research and development, but we must now do the same with the entire value stream of the company, whether it's accounting or purchasing or anything else," he said. "The challenge, quite simply, is to share knowledge wherever we possibly can. But there are cultural barriers to sharing, and breaking down the walls is difficult. The traditional thing was

'I'll always have something in my drawer which is private for me—my knowledge because I want to be superior.' The Internet makes it easier to break down the barriers, of course, but we still have a way to go to maximize what will be possible and essential."

If DaimlerChrysler is struggling, you can be sure that other large multinationals are too. After all, it is a global corporation composed of employees of two companies that had long done business in one another's home territory and sprang from two advanced societies that had shared culture for many generations. The world is much bigger and more diverse than the United States and Western Europe, and the global company of tomorrow will need to put deep roots in less familiar ground—Asia, Latin America and ultimately in Islamic countries.

The course of DaimlerChrysler tells a good deal of the globalization story: the need for geographical reach and the problems of achieving it, the importance of cross-cultural diversity and the difficulty of making it work, the promise of leveraging assets around the world and the obstacles to making it happen. A year and a half after the company went public, the shares were trading at barely half their original value, with financial troubles plaguing Chrysler in particular. Despite Schrempp's efforts to create a multinational culture, several of Chrysler's most highly regarded top executives left. While some synergies from the combination of the two companies were evident, the integration of businesses, which were supposed to lead growth, took a backseat to more cost cutting and layoffs. An overwhelming proportion of management time went into the post-merger integration, with significant costs for the operations itself. While it's still too early to say how the merger will fare over time, the transaction shows from a CEO's standpoint that running a major global company is fraught with hazards.

Despite all the travails, Schrempp isn't finished. In mid-2000 DaimlerChrysler took control of Mitsubishi Motors in Japan. This transaction will add new complications to the management of cross-cultural differences, to say the least. In addition, the heavily indebted Japanese automaker requires a financial turnaround. Say this for Schrempp: He is determined to make DaimlerChrysler a truly global firm, no matter what the hurdles. In our interview, which preceded so many of his late 2000 headaches, he described his vision of serving all major markets by having production capacity in each. "Thirty-percent in North America, thirty in Europe, and thirty in Asia," he said. He seems to be undeterred from getting there.

Diversity may be essential to building the intellectual capacity of a company to develop and exploit markets, but a tension exists between diversity and a unified corporate culture that enables a company to efficiently execute strategies, communicate among its component parts, differentiate itself from other companies in the same business, and not run afoul of its core ethical standards. Unless carefully managed, extensive diversity could lead to corporate chaos. Striking the right balance represents a new frontier in management.

Hiroshi Okuda, former president and now chairman of Toyota, came to Yale in 1997. His visit illustrated that the search for diversity is further complicated by the fact that most

CEOs are deeply rooted in their own national cultures. I first met him in 1991, when I was an investment banker and he was in charge of all of Toyota's finances. It was a moment I'll never forget. A colleague and I flew from New York to Toyota City, near Nagoya, for a one-hour meeting with him. The plane arrived on time, but we were snarled in traffic and arrived thirty minutes late, leaving us just a half hour to make the presentation. My colleague took the lead in explaining our proposal: Toyota should invest some of its money in highly complex investments known as "financial derivatives," which at the time was a novel idea in Japan. It took twenty minutes to make the pitch. Okuda listened intently. When it came time to respond, he demonstrated that he was not a traditional Japanese executive. He did not nod politely, did not ask a few basic questions to make us feel he was interested in what we had to say. Instead he burst into a smile, which was immediately contagious. "You're kidding, right?" is a rough translation of his opening remarks. "I didn't understand a word of what you said," he continued, but in a way that made us laugh, too.

When I became the dean at Yale some five years later, I had it on my mind to introduce this iconoclastic Japanese leader to our students. He had never spoken in an American university and his staff were nervous. "What if he gets a nasty question?" they asked. "Well, he'll just have to handle it," I replied. Knowing that Okuda would be a big hit under any circumstances, I suggested that he sit on a stool on a slightly raised platform and have a give-and-take with the students, some two hundred of them. Very reluctantly the Toyota staff agreed.

Okuda gave a short talk from behind the podium and then moved to the stool, in what might have been unprecedented informality for a Japanese CEO. A student asked him if it was true that Japanese universities don't encourage independent thinking.

"Yes, that is the case," said Okuda.

"Well," replied the student, "How do you, as a major employer, feel about that? Doesn't it undermine the potential for new ideas, creativity, and entrepreneurship?"

"I admire your system in the United States," Okuda said, "but you have to recognize that Japan is very different. I'm not saying one system is better than the other. They are just very different. We at Toyota would have a lot of problems with entry-level people who are too unstructured in their thinking. We'd rather train them our way. In terms of our overall performance as a car company, Toyota can always do better, of course. But all in all, our educational system hasn't worked too badly for us."

The audience was impressed with Okuda's directness and sincerity. But when I interviewed him a year later in Tokyo, he lamented Japanese insularity. In fact, both he and Minoru Makihara, the stately, Harvard-educated chairman of Mitsubishi Corporation, emphasized their concern that the cultural conformity in Japanese companies was a debilitating disadvantage that would increasingly handicap the global positioning of their companies. In their minds, overcoming the problem would be at best a long-term affair.

An increasing diversity of talent will be the overwhelming competitive advantage of the future. Companies that put in place the policies and structures to make this happen will be the winners, for as the world continues to open up, so will markets that no one can today foresee. These will range from global businesses for niche products to local markets in the interior of China, India, Indonesia, Brazil, Russia, and many other countries. Big companies need antennae that they have only begun to develop, such as management that understand how to gauge what local people in new markets want, how to market the product or service, how to tailor financing and delivery precisely to local needs. No computer will provide this information; only people can, and the more diverse the opportunities, the more diverse the talent a CEO needs. If a company is to live up to its worldwide potential, the diversity of an organization should reflect the diversity of the international environment.

The ability to relate to individual communities in the global economy—whether they are defined by geographical boundaries, income or ethnic relationships—is becoming increasingly crucial because of the Internet too. Never before have consumers been able to shop the world for precisely what they want, and never before have sellers been under more pressure to customize their products and services. So here's the irony: The same technology that is making the world economy more integrated and more navigable is also enhancing its segmentation and diversity.

Diversity is relevant to all layers of a company—the workforce, the top management, the board of directors. National preferences, language barriers and prejudices being what they are, we may not see the emergence of truly diverse companies for many years, if ever. This won't mean the end of globalization, of course, but companies that remain insular in their mind-set and their capabilities will be at a severe disadvantage.

❖ ❖ ❖

A great multinational company ought to be a "knowledge factory" gathering information and insights from all corners of the world, applying them in various combinations in other locations. John Browne, CEO of BP, understands this well. A petroleum engineer whose entire career has been spent in the same company, Browne may be the chief executive who is the most articulate about the nature of global business, the opportunities and limitations of corporate power, the role of companies in society at large, not to mention global corporate strategies themselves. "On the other hand we understand that everything is local," he said to me. "Customs are local, customers are local and communications are local. But the purpose of a great company is that every local action should create learning that we can use elsewhere. As a company operating in so many countries, that is the great advantage that we have to leverage. A global firm ought to be able to gain advantage over others by taking what it learns in one part of the world and do something elsewhere it could never have done."

The question for CEOs is "How do you enhance learning throughout the organization?" Having the right people—a corps of employees reflecting true global diversity—is one vital element. So is using the Internet to access and distribute the enormous amount of information that exists within a firm. Companies such as Merrill Lynch have intranets, which document their thousands of deals done around the world and allow their investment bankers to learn from their colleagues' successes and failures. But this is just the beginning. A great multinational company will examine every one of its assets around the world—its factories, research labs, distribution outlets, marketing teams, partners big and small—and it will treat them not only as overseas subsidiaries, branches and facilities but also as global learning centers. These centers will view the world through local eyes, reporting to top management on how to find new ways to penetrate world markets from the vantage point of what was once considered the periphery—be it Charlotte, São Paulo or Warsaw—but which is now just another global center. CEOs and their teams will also have to be supreme trend spotters. A new fashion craze in Spain could quickly end up influencing retailing in, say, the United States or Japan. A new manufacturing technique in Scandinavia could be transferred to the United States or to Japan. Those leaders who can see these kinds of developments in one part of the globe early and experiment with them elsewhere will create the value for customers. However, the right communications systems have to be in place, the culture of cooperation must exist throughout the company, and financial incentives must encourage managers to share information and to work together on the execution of deals.

Leveraging global reach can include experimenting in countries that provide environments that are different from one's home base. Even before U.S. banks were able to be investment banks and deposit-takers at the same time—when Depression-era laws mandated separation of the two activities in the United States—they experimented with investment banking products in London, where there were no such legal restrictions. Today General Motors is using a state-of-the-art stamping press and ultra-lean workforce in Gravataí, Brazil, to experiment with a kind of modular assembly method that would be a radical departure from the way cars have been built. The process involves suppliers from all over the country. It would have been difficult, probably impossible, to break new ground this way in a traditional, rigidly unionized environment like that of the United States or Germany.

All this is easier to describe than do. Top management has to be strewn around the world, and yet they have to be a closely knit team. Otherwise, good ideas from Bangkok or Caracas, especially those very valuable ones that break the mold, will never reach the CEO's office.

✧ ✧ ✧

How to organize a company for global operations? Even the most internationally experienced business leaders continue to experiment, for no one has the right formula. CEOs may in fact be underestimating the extent of the organizational transformation that will need to take place in the best firms. They talk about the tension between organizing a company along product and geographical lines. They are worried about missing opportunities for growth by merger or acquisition. These are important concerns, but they are just the tip of the iceberg.

Three examples of what CEOs are doing today illustrate some of the current thinking about organization, and how much farther there is to go. Michael Bonsignore is a Naval Academy graduate and an engineer who speaks four languages. He has lived in five countries, and ran Honeywell's European operations before becoming its chairman and CEO. While he considers the globalization of Honeywell one of his major accomplishments, he admits that getting the organizational structure right is a never-ending effort. We met in his Minneapolis office shortly before he moved to Morristown, New Jersey to take control of the enlarged company that included AlliedSignal. He told me, "When I first became CEO, the big issue was one of mind-set. We had to get the words 'domestic' and 'international' out of our jargon. I can remember all these internal debates about how much of our sales come from outside the U.S. And I tried to convert that line of thinking so that we looked at the *world* as a place to do our business. I worked to convince everyone that we should make our investments wherever in the world they would be optimized. We put worldwide teams together. We brought the various representatives of all the regions of the world together to plan our engineering and manufacturing. We would no longer build a factory in France at the same time we were building a factory in Singapore, both of which would have done overlapping things." But for Bonsignore even the right way of thinking about being global didn't solve the organizational questions of how to do it. "We have tried a lot of organizational structures—tight, loose, central, decentralized. We're still working at it. I've always likened this to a job that is never done. If you take comfort that you have the right structure in place, you are probably in trouble."

Mark Moody-Stuart runs Royal Dutch/Shell, one of the oldest multinational enterprises anywhere. A Ph.D. in geology from Cambridge University in 1966, he has spent his entire professional life at Shell, with assignments in Oman, Brunei, Nigeria, Australia, Spain, Turkey, Malaysia and the U.K. In the late 1990s, he presided over a reorganization of the corporation designed to align its focus with at least two global trends. One was the rise of global firms to which Royal Dutch/Shell wished to sell its products, airlines and auto manufacturers, for example. These companies want to deal with one or just a few suppliers, not one in each region in which they operate. (The same goes for their advertising and financing requirements.) The second trend is the rise of the global consumer, an international middle class with broadly similar tastes. To appeal to both international companies and consumers, Royal Dutch/Shell decided to break down its national fiefdoms and create global groups that could see the entire world through the lens of products and not geography. Rather than organizing to sell petrochemicals to one customer in France and one in Japan, the Anglo/Dutch company structured itself to serve the needs of, say, Airbus Industrie on a global scale. With this structure, Royal Dutch/Shell had a more streamlined view of the world and could move more quickly too.

"We used to have a kind of federal system—and a fantastically successful machine it was—to match the time in which it operated," Moody-Stuart told me in his London office. "It was an era of strong national boundaries, reinforced by all kinds of trade barriers. We set up what you might call a family of national companies—Shell Singapore, Shell Brazil, Shell Oil in the U.S. And we built the company on the basis of countries aggregated into regions. But the world doesn't work like that anymore. You want to keep the autonomy and freedom of action of a smaller unit, but the basis on which those units are built changes from being a national unit to being a customer or a business-based unit. So [now] we have a global chemicals group, or a global aviation group—better to serve our global customers. And these same customers are served around the world by the same unit. We deliver better because we have global scale in the product and the right global alignment of people."

One of the more interesting works in progress that I heard about when it comes to organizing for international business involves Stan Shih, chairman and co-founder of Acer, a manufacturer of computer equipment and one of Taiwan's largest and best-known companies. Shih founded the company in 1976 and took it public in 1988. His aim was to go beyond the typical pattern of manufacturing in Taiwan—copying what western companies do—and instead make original products under the Acer name. His big markets have been developing countries, especially China and India, although Acer also sells in Europe, and, to a lesser extent, the United States. From the beginning, Shih touted his ambition to create a new model for multinational management.

To expand internationally Shih built a network of companies around the world that cooperated with one another but were virtually independent. They shared the Acer brand, and Acer's central management in Taiwan took small stakes in each independent Acer firm. The theory was that each unit could be publicly listed in the country in which it operated and remain especially close to customers in the local markets. The hurdle was to create one culture and set of standards throughout the many companies. This required a strong sense of common mission and a powerful but collegial management team throughout the empire. Shih bolstered the sense of teamwork by spreading stock ownership and incentives throughout his twenty-three thousand workers, becoming the first major CEO in Taiwan to do so.

Shih began this experiment in 1995 based on a combination of old and new ideas. On the one hand it resembled the informal web of business empires built and controlled by Chinese families whose members live throughout East Asia. On the other it anticipated the Internet model of a decentralized network. However, Shih's plan seems to have worked with mixed success. How much of the problem was due to management deficiencies and how much reflected the cutthroat computer industry itself is not clear. By 1999, Acer was changing its product mix to include software and multimedia products. It was building an incubator for new ideas in Taiwan in the form of a special industrial park for venues that would produce creative ideas in the Silicon Valley mode. Shih was still trying to find the right mix of organization and products, and a global niche for a non-Japanese Asian-based company. "We are seeking a structure that gives us extreme flexibility to move quickly and respond to local conditions in a creative way," he told me, clearly determined to keep trying to find the right formula.

Since my interviews took place, two of the world's largest international companies found themselves in circumstances that further illustrate how even the biggest and most experienced multinationals can flounder in their efforts to get the organizational structure right.

Let's look at Coca-Cola. Ever since the death in 1997 of Coke's legendary leader, Roberto Goizueta, the company has had problems. Recession in Asia, financial turmoil in Russia and Latin America, health and safety issues in Europe, diversity problems at home—crisis after crisis has overtaken the company. It all proved too much for Goizueta's immediate successor, Douglas Ivester, who was forced to resign in early 2000. He was succeeded by Douglas Daft.

Part of Daft's calculation was that Coca-Cola had become much too centralized and had lost its ability to understand local markets. "For a couple of years the world was moving in one direction, and we were moving in the other," he wrote in the *Financial Times* in March 2000. "The world was demanding greater flexibility, responsiveness and local sensitivity, while we were further centralizing decision-making and standardizing our practices. . . . We must [now] lead a Coca-Cola business system that not only has the professional expertise, management systems and capital structures required for success in a globalized economy, but which is also able to act nimbly and with great sensitivity in every local community where our brands are sold . . . the next big evolutionary step of 'going global' now has to be 'going local.' " Daft says Coke's operations will now be guided by three principles. First, "Think local, act local." Second, focus on marketing and outsource everything else. Third, be a model citizen in every country. "We must remember," he wrote, "we do not do business in markets; we do business in societies."

Procter & Gamble is another example of a company still trying to find its way. In 1999 it launched a large-scale global reorganization. The six-year plan was to transform the company from one based on country-specific organizations, as Royal Dutch/Shell had been, to one organized along product lines, what were called "global business units," each devoted to a different set of products, such as beauty care or food and beverages. In the event, the execution of so radical a change proved the undoing of Durk Jaeger, the chairman and CEO, who was forced to resign after only seventeen months in office. Too much change happened in too short a time: Reporting chains were disrupted, key employees left, overlapping management jurisdictions created too much organizational complexity, and amid the turmoil P & G neglected the marketing of its core products. The new CEO, A. G. Lafley, is being forced to rethink P & G's entire approach to global business.

❖ ❖ ❖

In the future, great companies will recognize that whereas once the big challenge was getting access to new geography, today—with ever-lower trade barriers and the Internet—access is increasingly cheap. The premium is now on figuring out how operating around the world allows you to deliver more real value to customers than otherwise would be the case. This requires ever more depth in all segments of the business, and then the ability to link the various specializations of those segments, which include finance, human resources, product knowledge. Global companies will therefore need to be organized by centers of core capabilities and excellence. Of course, the precise formulas will vary by industry, but the best companies will develop great depth in certain products and services in parts of the world where the talent and infrastructure are most conducive to it. From that base they will then deploy those capabilities where and when they may be needed around the world. There will no doubt be more than one center for a set of products and services, but not too many of them. For example, a company like Philips Electronics has its headquarters for digital set-top boxes in California, where the industry is most advanced, but it has headquartered its audio business in Hong Kong, the center for innovative consumer electronics. Sony has its consumer electronics headquarters in Japan, its music business is run from New York, and its motion picture operations from California. Extreme specialization located in the center of wherever that expertise is best cultivated, but linked to other parts of the company, will be a big competitive advantage.

The trends are clear, but not yet as strong as they will have to be. The vanguard may be represented by American computer companies that have discovered research capabilities in Scotland, taking advantage of a strong education system and network of universities interested in research. They've also discovered excellent software engineering talents in Bangalore, India. As the future unfolds, we should expect more such efforts. Companies interested in developing product and service expertise relating to aging populations, for instance, will be investing heavily in Japan where the population is aging rapidly; these companies will be able to use what they learn there in other countries with similar demographics. Companies wanting to build and market products to quickly expanding middle classes in emerging markets will do their research in Asia and Latin America and get deep into the fabric of a few countries in those regions. Henry Paulson makes the point with respect to Goldman Sachs: "We don't measure ourselves with pins on a map. We need to be where we can be big and real. To do something well you need critical mass, and you must put your very best people there."

Like so much of what CEOs need to do, establishing centers of in-depth specialization is more complicated than it sounds because it runs into another imperative: control and coordination. I once interviewed Nobuyuki Idei, president of Sony, for my *Business Week* column. The subject was the tension between centralized management and the imperatives of decentralized specialization. I asked him whether a lifestyle company like Sony, which originated so much of its creative content in the United States, shouldn't really be headquartered in New York or Los Angeles so that management could be closer to the heart of the company. There was a long pause. "I deal with this by being in the United States at least once a month," he said. "But we are rooted in Japan." From the tone of his voice, the careful selection of his words, his body language, I sensed he wished it were otherwise.

John Browne once raised a similar issue with me at a restaurant in Davos a year before I interviewed him for this book. "Why do we need a headquarters at all?" he asked, only half facetiously. Then the discussion turned to the difficult issues of so radical an option. The paradox is that at a time when geography seems less relevant than ever, the importance of being located in the right place for the right activity or product has only increased.

✧ ✧ ✧

Another preoccupation of CEOs derives from the trend toward growth by acquisition and merger. This kind of growth carries with it enormous problems of cultural compatibility, not to mention integration of systems and management philosophies. The simple but key question is this: How big is too big for a CEO to manage? How do you think about the limits of the span of control? Is the merger wave akin to the fad for gigantic conglomerates, which ended with almost all of them being broken up?

The march toward corporate concentration on an international level has been greater than at any time in the last century, with global mergers having reached some $3.4 trillion in 1999 compared with less than $1 trillion in 1995, and with nineteen of the twenty biggest mergers ever happening in the last two years of the 1990s. Consolidation is rampant in most of the big industries: energy, automobiles, finance, telecommunications, entertainment, publishing, media, food, consumer products. You can see it coming in transportation, law and other areas. Not all linkups are global, but the bulking up of national entities, such as the merger of Citibank and Travelers, or of AOL and Time Warner, is impetus for other firms to achieve greater size, and going abroad to do that is frequently a good counterstrategy.

Big cross-border deals happen for many reasons. When John Browne's BP bought Amoco and Atlantic Richfield, Rolf Breuer's Deutsche Bank bought Bankers Trust and Jürgen Schrempp's Daimler-Benz bought Chrysler, these men felt that their industries were consolidating and that you had to be enormous to survive. In each industry, however, size offered different advantages. The oil companies had to cut costs in the face of declining prices and the need to free up more funds for exploration, and economies of scale helped. In banking, a handful of companies was going to dominate certain global businesses, and Deutsche Bank, already the largest in Europe, wanted to be one of them. In autos, Daimler-Benz wanted to expand not only its geographical reach deep into the United States, but also the range of models it could sell.

But each of these mergers was about acquiring talent and knowledge too. As a British citizen, John Browne wanted to get inside the U.S. culture to fully understand a multicultural society. Rolf Breuer needed the financial engineering and trading expertise that only a Wall Street firm like Bankers Trust could provide. Jürgen Schrempp had his eye on Chrysler's superb marketing skills.

The merger wave has its substantial complications, to which even CEOs who led it will admit. John Browne frankly discussed the obstacles inherent in the strategy. One is to make the deals work for shareholders in the face of evidence that a large number of mergers simply don't benefit them over time. "Statistically, studies show that most mergers have failed," he says. "So far things are going very well for us, but we are very rigorous about how we follow through with our strategy. There is always risk in the implementation technique itself. We make many choices—about what we keep, what we buy, where we invest. Every day we do this."

A second complication is the enormous time, effort, and range of managerial problems involved in bringing organizations of different nationalities together. "I have sat in management meetings when there was lots of complaining about the balance between the number of Germans and Americans," Jürgen Schrempp recalled. "I said, 'I don't understand you guys. Can't we get beyond nationality? What difference does it make?' If you put ten people of different cultures around a table and they try to find an answer to a problem, at the end of the day you get a better one [than by] putting ten Germans, or ten Americans, or ten Italians around a table. In this respect I don't think we can call ourselves a global company yet. We are not yet global thinkers when it comes to top management or below. That is the job that I and my top team will have to accomplish in the next decade. The future of the truly global company is [one in which] nationality or color play no role."

It's impossible to tell whether the mega-merger trend will continue. As trade barriers fall away and financial markets become even more seamless around the world, we may well see many more huge cross-border combinations, particularly in Europe, where the game has just begun, and in Asia, where it's hardly started. But there is a high probability that these deals will fall apart. CEOs will find these corporate behemoths too complicated to manage effectively and to squeeze out the profitability that investors will be demanding. This will be especially true as two trends converge: The slowing of the phenomenal U.S. business expansion and the deflationary pressures caused by increasing competition among Internet-enabled companies. In addition, antitrust officials in the United States and Europe are already taking an increased interest in some industries where dominating positions can quickly emerge. Regulators' proposals to break up Microsoft, and their veto of the WorldCom acquisition of

Sprint, illustrate what we will see more of in the future. Whatever happens, though, business leaders will need discipline to center their attention on a few critical issues, even in the face of the enormous scale of their operations. For example, Jorma Ollila, chairman and CEO of Nokia, talked to me about the critical reorganization of his company. Today Nokia is among Europe's—indeed, the world's— most impressive business successes, but it arose from a collapsing conglomerate only in the last decade. In 1992 Ollila, a former Citibank executive with degrees from the University of Helsinki and the London School of Economics, took the reins of a Finnish conglomerate in deep crisis. Together with a young management team, he foresaw the opening of the European telecommunications markets and the establishment of a common technical standard for wireless communications. He then proceeded to fill a global niche by narrowing Nokia's product lines from twenty-eight businesses to four, all of them related to mobile communications. In effect, he bet the entire company on this new and much narrower strategy. First he looked at Europe, then Asia and the United States. "You really have to have the best people in certain focused areas in order to get the very best products to consumers," he said. "If you are in a broad sweep of business, you tend to fall into a mediocre way of running things. Suddenly top management doesn't understand all the businesses you are in."

Narrowing the range of businesses was also on the mind of Jürgen Schrempp, who forced Daimler-Benz to change from diversifying into a variety of high-technology industries, including aerospace, to diversifying within the automotive sector. Schrempp slimmed down the company from thirty-five business units to a small handful. "We found that the [high-tech] diversification strategy wasn't the best," he said. "It had to do with the world changing, and it had to do—and this is my credo these days—[with the fact] that if you have an executive board, that board should understand something about the business. That sounds simple, but boards have the tendency to be a bit far away from the business—not understanding the customers, the market. Before, only one person on the board understood aerospace and the rest were automotive people."

Given the difficulty of managing mega-mergers, the alternative of concluding strategic alliances among companies of different nationalities is bound to receive more consideration than it has to date. Because alliances do not require one company's owning another or even making an equity investment in another—it can be just an agreement to cooperate on certain projects—they can be easier to negotiate, more flexible, less constrained by antitrust considerations. More important, they can be dissolved or altered to fit the rhythm of a dynamic market.

Stephen Case, chairman and CEO of America Online, sees alliances as the essence of the global Internet culture. His starting point is that the boundaries of many industries—such as communications, technology, media and financial services—disappearing. "It's all blurring together," he told me. "The communications world is blurring together with the technology world . . . and that's blurring with the world of financial services . . . and that with the world of media. So I think you are going to see a blurring within industries and across industries . . . and alliances [among companies in different industries] are going to be essential as never before. [These days] you need to reorganize the need for interdependence. . . . No company, no matter how successful, can go it alone in this new world." AOL has teamed up with a huge range of companies around the world from Bertelsmann in Germany to China Internet Corporation. In an interview with *Business Week,* Robert Pittman, president of AOL, explained, "We do it [AOL's international operations] all with local partners, because we can get the advantage of their local knowledge, local relationships, local culture, with the advantage of our infrastructure. Long-term, that's an unbeatable combination."

Kenneth Chenault also emphasized that alliances are at the core of American Express's strategy. By August 1999 the company had concluded nearly fifty link-ups with banks overseas. Other kinds of partnerships included Delta Airlines, Hilton Hotels, Disney and IBM. He recounts how important partnering has become in the company's turnaround from its sagging performance in the early 1990s. "One of the critical decisions [we made] was . . . that we needed to partner with other companies, companies that historically we might have considered to be competitors. Hence the initiation of an incredibly transforming strategy, and that's our network card strategy where we are working with banks to issue American Express–branded cards. [This] is allowing us to build substantial scale. We are in fact getting a lot of scale advantage that one would get from a mega-merger opportunity."

Alliances on the scale now occurring are a relatively recent phenomena, and their strength and effectiveness have yet to be fully tested. As is true of mega-mergers, there will likely be some reduction in the exuberance with which these partnerships are being touted. It's not clear, for example, how CEOs will oversee these octopuslike entities and, even more important, who will be responsible and accountable in the event of serious problems relating to performance and reputation. In September 2000 a textbook example of such a crisis emerged as Ford Motor Company and Bridgestone/Firestone were forced to recall defective tires in North and South America, the Persian Gulf and Asia. As the crisis flared, each company accused the other of being responsible. "We had a one-hundred-year history with Firestone," William Ford told a news conference on September 14, 2000, after emerging from a board meeting to discuss the tire-recall crisis. "And though that history has been a very good one, the trust has been terribly shaken." A number of questions were raised: How could these two companies have communicated with one another so poorly? If you have an alliance and the product which it produces is defective, how are blame and liability apportioned? Who *should* take responsibility? How do alliance partners hedge against the possibility that one may damage the other's brand? And all this was between two companies whose alliance was built on foundations much stronger than many of those being formed so quickly today.

There is a third model for going global: It involves neither mega-mergers nor expansion primarily by alliance but relies instead on organic growth. This doesn't mean the absence of mergers or alliances, just that neither is on a scale that dominates all else. GE has made hundreds of acquisitions abroad, but they have been small enough so that there are very few problems in post-merger consolidation and in maintaining the GE culture—at least, that is, until its $45 billion acquisition of Honeywell International in October 2000. Another example is Merrill Lynch, which has not followed a mega-merger strategy but has grown steadily by small acquisitions and by setting up its own operations. Toyota hasn't made any foreign acquisitions of note at all.

In some ways, firms that can do this have an advantage, because their strategy and their culture are less encumbered than are the just "merged" or the alliance-dominated firms. An example is Nokia. "We grew the business by internal growth, not by acquisitions," Jorma Ollila explained to me. "The reason was that corporate culture is the key. In the high-technology arena, there really aren't many examples of successful acquisitions or mergers because you fall into a situation where the cultures clash and it's very, very difficult to weld them together. So we did it on our own. We want to be an informal, unbureaucratic, flat organization—an entrepreneurial company, where people feel that they can find an expression for their willingness to perform. It's a family atmosphere with a fierce hunger for achievement, a meritocracy with a fair way of compensating for achievement. We wanted people to look at this company and say 'This is an exciting place. Here is a management style that feels good to me. I want to give some of the best years of my life to this company.' "

But there is a price to pay for expansion by small increments. Growth can be slower, cultural diversity far less than optimal. There is no ideal balance.

✧ ✧ ✧

The most basic problem facing a CEO is to reconcile multiple layers of complexity—cultural and organizational—with all the other requirements of leadership and strategy. Running a multinational magnifies all the challenges that a purely national company once had, and adds some new ones. Several issues arise, including how to be big enough to be a credible global player but at the same time flexible and adaptable enough to move with the rapidly changing currents that the pace of trade liberalization and deregulation, the rise of big emerging markets and the Internet will bring. How do you expand your diversity of talent and still maintain a coherent corporate culture? How do you leverage your assets around the world so that you are far more than the sum of the individual parts of a global company? And how do you lead and manage a complicated multinational firm where effective control by any chief executive may simply be out of reach?

It's not that CEOs don't recognize these problems; they live with them every day. But they will have to become smarter and faster, even as they dig increasingly deeper into what it means not just to be an international company but to make the most out of globalization itself.

PART TWO

EVERYDAY CONCERNS

4

True North and Other Virtues

Jack Welch, who has been the epitome of a successful command-and-control leader, doesn't hesitate to predict the end of his own era. "Leadership of companies is going to have to become much less CEO-driven," he says. "People within the company are going to have so much data in their hands that they will be able to challenge [a CEO's] decisions all the time. The pace of events is going to be so fast that people aren't going to wait for the next layer of approvals. There's going to have to be far more delegation. There's going to have to be far more participation. The leader must become an ever more engaging coach, an ever more engaging person. You're going to have to create an environment where excitement reigns, where the challenges are everywhere, and where the rewards are both in the wallet, yes, but also in the soul."

But how?

Every CEO knows that the rigidities of the old command-and-control models of management won't work in the new world economy. They all understand the need to flatten hierarchies, streamline reporting lines, and create an entrepreneurial environment within their companies. All are obsessed

111

with speeding up decision making. It's fair to say, as well, that most top executives embrace time-tested leadership qualities. Mitsubishi Corporation's Chairman, Minoru Makihara, is one such traditionalist. "Ultimately it comes down to the ability to convey one's ideas convincingly down the line. And whether it's today or ten years ago, that hasn't changed," he said. John Browne of BP agreed: "A leader's job is to decide on what direction an organization will take. There has to be a decision. And our shareholders have to see that clarity."

The New Economy prompts major questions about the ability of CEOs to hold on to the traditional qualities of leadership in an era of blinding change. A central issue that arose from my interviews is the importance of a leader's having a strong compass in the storm we call the third industrial revolution and the sheer difficulty of staying on course. Another is the need for CEOs to be trusted by their employees, and the need for trust between a company and its constituents— and this, too, has become much tougher to achieve. I heard a ringing endorsement of the need for a CEO to be centered and trusted, but after thinking about what I was told against the backdrop of the New Economy, I felt that these qualities are becoming increasingly elusive even as they grow more important.

✧ ✧ ✧

Many theories address leadership in the New Economy. Leaders should be coaches, they should be nannies, they should be servants, leadership should flow from the bottom to the top. Most CEOs do not pay much attention to these sound-bite philosophies. In fact, most are much more preoccupied with a few basics, which themselves are hard enough to maintain these days.

Bain & Company's Orit Gadiesh acknowledged that "many of the traditional constituencies are coming unglued: people are changing jobs much faster; customers are shopping around much more than they used to. Shareholders who were once loyal are churning their portfolios at amazing rates." But she believes that despite the pace of change—or perhaps because of it—a leader who can provide a steady anchor is more critical than ever to the survival and success of a big organization. She calls this anchoring "true north," a combination of character and principle that makes it crystal clear what the leader—and by extension his organization—stands for.

Using her company as an example, she says it has always stood for results that produce action, which is a way of thinking that is at odds with most people's image of high-powered consulting firms. "You have to think about an organization in a special way if your objective is to generate bottom-line results," she told me. "It's not about writing reports. That could easily lead to nothing. People make things happen, not reports. This issue is, how do you facilitate a decision in your client? You need to focus all your work on making sure that once answers have been found, they will actually be implemented. This requires working . . . with people who will ultimately be responsible for implementation. You need to work *with* your clients, not just *for* them. That's why we don't write reports. And oftentimes we don't present [conclusions], either. We prefer that the clients, who have been working with us all along, present to the board or to the CEO. The purpose of our work is to solve a problem. It's not to arrive on the scene and demonstrate how smart we are. The work shouldn't be about the consultants but about the client."

In its pursuit of real solutions, moreover, Bain & Company will not take an assignment just to ratify what a company has already decided to do. "We won't tell a CEO what he wants to hear simply to get a contract," said Gadiesh. "Sometimes we lose business this way, but at least people know what we stand for."

True north is easier to spot than to define. It is more than such values as putting the client first or treating employees with integrity; it also differentiates leaders and their firms from competitors. True north reflects a certain consistency over a long period of time, even as the business environment or a company's strategy changes. It is the philosophy that holds an organization together and gives its people collective pride in their work. It has to begin with the CEO, but top management must infuse it throughout the organization. "You only know whether you have a true north when there are painful trade-offs and the organization is tested by adversity and emerges from it still holding on to its basic character," says Gadiesh.

A contemporary example of an executive with true north is Richard Branson, Chairman of Virgin Management. Headquartered in London, the $5 billion Virgin business empire encompasses airlines, trains, records, soft drinks, financial services, telecommunications, wedding stores and soon, perhaps, the management of England's national lottery.

We met one morning in the trendy Royalton Hotel in New York, I in coat and tie, he in black denim jeans and short-sleeved shirt, and we sank into two comfortable chairs in the lobby for a long discussion. Branson, who dropped out of school at fifteen, formed his business philosophy in the anti-establishment counterculture of the 1960s and never abandoned that cause, even as he rose to fame as one of England's great business entrepreneurs, established a world-class brand, and was knighted by Queen Elizabeth. I was surprised at his apparent shyness.

Branson doesn't use the term "true north"—in fact, I had to explain what I meant by it. But he *has* it. "The core thing is absolutely and utterly the people who work for [a] company and if those people are proud of the company they work for, if they respect it and are listened to, the company will thrive," he said. "And so I think the number one, most important role for anybody running a company is finding the time for the people who are out on the front line making things work."

Branson explained to me some of the ways he stays close to his employees. "Last night, when I came to New York, I was very tired," he said. "But I made absolutely sure that I took one hundred and fifty [of my employees] out—not to a formal dinner but to Mr. Chow's [so that we could] let our hair down, get drunk and have a good time. But I also sat down and listened and talked to them and made notes which I dealt with the next day. And it's often . . . the little things that can turn a positive work force against a company. Last night I learned that as we'd given free beers to all the [airline] crews when they arrived in their hotels, suddenly someone decided to dock their monies by $2 a beer—you know, something crass and stupid. But if I hadn't been out drinking with them I may never have learned that. And that sort of damage can be done very quickly."

Branson also makes it a point to stay in touch with employees he doesn't see. "I write to all our staff every month and tell them everything that's going on. And I find that in any one day I'll get twenty to twenty-five letters from people who work for various Virgin companies. And those letters are critical to me to be able to get feedback to make sure management is making the right decisions. . . . I suppose I've almost become—you know, we don't have a union at Virgin— and I've sort of become the head of the union, making sure that employees are well looked after and happy and enjoying the job. . . . It's not necessarily salaries that are key; I really think that would come quite low on the list. It's are they being listened to? If they come out with an idea, is that going to get through or just going to be buried? All the little things matter. Getting back to the airlines, is the uniform that the [crew] is wearing something they feel good in? Are the hotels they are staying in pleasant or are they just being put in an airport hotel?"

Branson wants his employees to have fun, and he himself sets the example. He once appeared at a London event in drag to launch a new line of wedding gowns. He posed with nude models to announce his new cellular telephone business. He drove a tank down New York's Fifth Avenue to introduce Virgin Cola to the United States. His risky hot-air balloon excursions have been publicity stunts as well as sport. "I think that too many chief executives sit in their ivory towers and plan things and forget that even the most stuffy-looking businessperson actually wants to enjoy him-

self, wants to let his hair down, wants to have a good time. . . .
If as chairman of the company I'm not having fun, I'm not
going to want to take the trouble to get up in the morning
and work really hard. So the chairman has got to have
fun. . . . So you've got to be the first into the swimming pool
with your clothes on or whatever, the first to let your hair
down, first to make a fool out of yourself on the stage
singing karaoke, to break the ice so that everybody else
knows how far they can actually go to have fun."

Many of the CEOs I met have true north. For Michael
Dell, for example, it is a relentless focus on the consumer
combined with missionary zeal. For Frederick Smith, true
north is a preoccupation with just-in-time delivery to eliminate his customers' inventory buildup. For Jorma Ollila,
it's the family-oriented culture at Nokia. For William Ford,
it's a passion for building a company that is socially conscious. For *all* of these CEOs, and for others, true north
also entails careful attention to the needs of their employees. It also encompasses an obsession with exquisite execution of plans—from speed of delivery to cost and quality
control. In these and other cases, CEOs make the point
over and over that the company must stand for something
beyond mere profitability, although that is a precondition
for success. Their companies must radiate these values
over a long period of time, through swings in the business
cycle and other shifting factors. They must communicate
their values in a clear and understandable way to all their
constituencies.

✧ ✧ ✧

True north is an intuitively attractive concept. Who, after all, would not applaud an executive with character and one so firmly grounded? Nevertheless, it's harder than ever for a CEO to exhibit true north today. In the current environment, the strategic directions for any firm need to be reassessed so often that the very idea of strategy often threatens to devolve into little more than day-to-day tactics. Organizational cultures are also changing, as one company merges with another or links up to others through corporate alliances. So many firms seem to be in a constant state of restructuring that the basics that once defined them are in danger of vanishing. Consider the rocky ride at Motorola. Christopher Galvin, grandson of the company's founder and son of a previous chairman and CEO, has worked at Motorola since holding a summer job there in 1967. Like so many of the executives I met, Galvin is instantly likeable for his openness, modesty and unrestrained optimism. I arrived in his office in Schaumburg, Illinois, the morning that the *New York Times* ran a long, flattering article about how he and his team had engineered Motorola's turnaround. I congratulated him on the achievement. "We're pleased, but there's a long way to go," he responded. He then went on to describe the past few years at the company and his experience of revamping its fundamental culture.

In the late 1990s, Motorola was in deep trouble, in part because it missed important trends in the market for cellular phones. The company had once thrived on a system that fostered the iconoclastic entrepreneur, "the person way out on the edge," he said. "The culture encouraged inventions and spin-offs and celebrated the inventor. As a result there was an almost unending proliferation of products. There were not ten versions of cellular phones but a hundred and twenty versions," Galvin recalled. "Every radio was 90-percent unique, and therefore there was no commonality. We ended up having to build an enormous number of factory lines, and the costs went higher and higher." It was a successful strategy for many decades, accounting for a number of technological breakthroughs, but Motorola could not survive in an era where customers wanted solutions to complicated problems, not just fancy technology. By the late 1990s this company, which had invented the cellular industry, was losing customers because it was trying to dictate what kinds of mobile phones they should buy. It was being accused of selling shoddy products and was plagued by product delays. It also appeared incapable of producing digital telephones.

In 1998 Galvin and his colleagues turned Motorola on its head. Costs were slashed by $750 million, and twenty thousand of the firm's hundred and fifty thousand jobs were eliminated. The company was reorganized primarily around two businesses. Most important, the so-called warring tribes—the small innovative fiefdoms that had grown up and competed with one another—gave way to a restructured company with emphasis on teamwork and a common technology. The compensation system was changed to reward employees for collaboration. Whereas the emphasis had been on innovation for its own sake, now employees were evaluated on how well they could find out what the customer wanted and deliver the products and services that were in demand. "The most fundamental thing we had to do from a senior leadership standpoint was to reassess the orthodoxies and dogmas of the company," Galvin told me. "[We discovered that] the more incredibly complex the technology is, the more people want it simplified. We changed everything but our principles."

Motorola made a 180-degree change. It moved from an incubator for individual entrepreneurs—what Galvin calls "a personality-based organization" that fostered complex technologies and gave short shrift to consumer preference—to exactly the opposite: A collaborative and simplified internal culture that keyed on customers. It was surely the right move, but how does a leader maintain true north amid such radical change, and how will all the company's constituencies see it?

Another case is Goldman Sachs. Henry Paulson said he is open to any kind of change at his firm so long as the core values remain in place. For him this included the traditions of teamwork and the goal of serving only premiere clients in well-defined areas. But consider some of the changes that have swept over this investment bank in just the last two years. Goldman Sachs went from being a privately held partnership to a publicly listed company with thousands of shareholders. In the process, it became subject to the scrutiny of the markets and the media as never before. Overnight its top executives, generally known only in the industry, became public figures. Their net worth and financial independence soared. Responding to stock market pressures and shareholder expectations, the firm began a major expansion. In 1999 alone, it announced plans to add three thousand staff, roughly a 20-percent increase in personnel. An effort to find new talent from universities in foreign countries like China was announced, too. Once a company that promoted almost entirely from within, eschewing the normal Wall Street practice of lateral hires, it began to bring in investment banking stars from rival firms like Lazard Frères, Merrill Lynch, Salomon Smith Barney and Morgan Stanley Dean Witter. In late August 2000, there were even rumors on Wall Street that the firm, in contrast to its traditional focus on institutions and extremely wealthy individuals, was moving into brokering and trading for smaller retail clients, capitalizing on the growing importance of individual investors in the U.S. economy. Many more changes can be expected as the financial services industry continues to see bigger mergers and more activities around the world; witness the combinations of Citibank and Travelers Insurance, Credit Suisse First Boston and Donaldson, Lufkin & Jenrette or J. P. Morgan and Chase Manhattan, all quite recently. In early September 2000, Goldman Sachs was hot on the path of further expansion too, announcing its plan to acquire Spear, Leeds & Kellogg, the biggest matcher of buyers and sellers on the floor of the American stock exchanges. No doubt Goldman Sachs will try to maintain its culture, for its leadership is obsessed with doing so. But to the extent that culture is dependent on who owns a firm, who controls it, who works in it, who its customers are, and how big it is, Paulson and his team face a Herculean challenge in maintaining the values they cherish.

As traditional companies embrace the Internet economy, more and more structural and cultural change will be involved beyond mergers, restructurings and alliances. Investment banker Nancy Peretsman of Allen & Company talks about the need for CEOs "to break some glass" when it comes to their traditional constituent relationships. She is referring to the changes that are occurring as producers of information and products deal directly with their customers, rather than through layers of middlemen. When music can be downloaded directly from the Internet, what happens to outlets like Tower Records and at what point do CEOs of entertainment companies disrupt long-standing ties with such retail distributors? Auto companies like General Motors have flirted with selling cars directly to consumers; what happens to the historic relationships between Detroit and the dealerships? Goldman Sachs, Morgan Stanley and others have been customers of the New York Stock Exchange, but they are also helping to set up competing electronic stock exchanges in which they have substantial business interests. Peretsman says that those CEOs who are not thinking about how to position themselves vis-à-vis some of their traditional business relationships are going to have big problems down the road.

True north is both an invaluable concept and a difficult one to implement. Founder-CEOs—men like Richard Branson, Michael Dell, Frederick Smith, Michael Bloomberg, Rupert Murdoch and Stan Shih—have an easier time demonstrating it in their organizations. After all, it comes directly from them. And because founders remain at the helms of their companies much longer than the typical chief executive, they have more time to impart their values and philosophy throughout the corporation. What happens when they depart is another story. For them as well as other top executives, the requirement remains the same: To identify what they stand for in more than platitudes, communicate it and stick by it, all the while exhibiting extreme adaptability to rapidly changing circumstances. How many people can rise to this standard?

❖ ❖ ❖

Part of true north is being seen as trustworthy. CEOs talk frequently about the importance of trust, but in the middle of this new industrial revolution, with all the uncertainties, surprises, and market pressures, what does being "trusted" really mean?

Michael Armstrong emphasizes that employees have to believe that their company's top management has the interests of the rank and file at heart, that what the company is doing and how it's changing is good for them. "If people are going to follow your vision and take the risk of changing their habits and their practice, they must know that they can trust that the institution will not only reward them for success but that they will not be punished unduly for taking risks that don't pan out," he told me. Armstrong's ability to make good on what he knows is essential and will now be sorely tested as he tries to manage the breakup of AT&T. Rolf Breuer of Deutsche Bank agrees. "A leader must get people aligned to follow him," he said. "Employees have to be convinced that what you are doing is leading to the right kind of development for the firm. They have to feel in safe hands—that the firm's leader is really caring for the prospects of the institution, and, by extension, for each of them." Like Armstrong,

Breuer faces his own challenges in enacting his theories as his bank undergoes radical transformation from a stodgy European Commercial bank to a top global investment bank.

While trust has always been an important anchor to any CEO, its value is heightened today. In the old economy, rigid bureaucracies prescribed what people did and how they did it, leaving little room for creative judgment. Most companies operated in self-contained units and within their home countries. The pace of change was slow, and large-scale restructurings were not commonplace. All this is different now: Employees work in flexible teams with fewer guidelines than they once had; companies are more dependent on outsourcing and partnerships, and virtual organizations are becoming increasingly the norm; executing deals requires a high level of cooperation among employees resident in different countries; and every great company is in a continuous state of organizational change. The ethos of trust—between leaders and their colleagues and employees and among workers themselves—is the glue that holds everything together in the new economy. Without a CEO who is trusted, and who imparts the quality of trust, a company is in great jeopardy.

Trust is not a simple concept. It involves qualities that might be called "hard" and "soft." A leader gains trust by getting results: By setting corporate targets and achieving them, by creating value for shareholders, by running a company profitable enough to create good jobs at good wages, and by having the resources and the willingness to contribute to the communities in which the company operates.

Trust also entails creating an organizational structure that makes decisions openly and fairly. The development of a company's strategy must be seen as deliberate and thoughtful, with promotions and compensation based on objective criteria that everyone understands. Some of these goals ought to be achieved easily, but some require more nuanced approaches that marry a leader's need to be decisive with the importance of being as fair as possible under high pressure. "The environment surrounding the Internet would give you the feeling that everybody is equal in the company," Lawrence Weinbach, Unisys' Chairman and CEO, says, "but we have nearly 40,000 people here and not everyone is equal. Sometimes you have to be an autocrat. When something is very crucial to the company and you feel very, very strongly about it, you cannot allow it to be put up to consensus. There are many other times—most of the time, in fact—when you as a group have to hash out an issue and come to a decision. But you better be clear that if you do put an issue before a group and ask them to come up with an answer, you will be willing to accept it. A leader has to pick which issues go where, and he has to be up front about it."

One quality necessary to engender trust is a leader's willingness to be transparent, to explain to all of a company's constituents what is happening and why. John Browne says that when people are getting real information—as opposed to being informed by rumor or simply executive assertion—they are more apt to think that their leaders are being straight with them. "I do think that information is ubiquitous. It goes everywhere," he said. "And I think the meaning of that is, actually, that there are very few secrets. And therefore you may as well be transparent. But it's a good thing to do, as well, because transparency creates trust."

Trust also requires integrity. CEOs who say one thing and do another, those who blame others for their own faulty decisions, or leaders who ask the troops to tighten their belts while they purchase more elaborate corporate jets obviously arouse suspicion among employees. Alternatively, an executive's integrity is enhanced when he or she takes responsibility for a mistake or a strong position on ethical issues.

Important as trust is, there are several reasons why many employees feel insecure or even betrayed today. In order to achieve their financial goals—and meet Wall Street's expectations—many CEOs have had to preside over a variety of corporate restructurings that have resulted in tens of thousands of people losing their jobs. When Michael Armstrong took the reins of AT&T in 1997, he set a reduction target of eighteen thousand employees. Jürgen Schrempp of DaimlerChrysler, Richard Thoman of Xerox, and Christopher Galvin of Motorola all made comparable cutbacks in their workforces. Such actions not only affect those with pink slips but create anxieties among their colleagues who remain employed.

Another wedge between top business leaders and their employees is the impact of globalization on job security. The liberalization of trade has already resulted in the transfer of substantial manufacturing activity from the industrialized to the developing world. The pressure on jobs in the United States, Europe and Japan has already expanded beyond manufacturing to the service sector, and now even to technology and engineering, as evident in the growth of high-technology regions in India, Singapore and Taiwan. If there hasn't been a loud outcry, it's because unemployment is low. But more job transfers are in store, and, come the next recession, it will bite much harder.

Also, how can employees bank on the commitments of their leaders when those same executives may not be around for long? CEOs are in increasingly tenuous positions, their survival dependent on stock market performance, which itself is highly volatile. In addition, the job market for top corporate leaders has rarely been more active—particularly with the lure of stock options from technology companies—and many top executives are often tempted and likely to move to more lucrative positions. Here, the question of outsized CEO compensation packages is relevant. CEOs who perform extremely well are worth the fortune they take home to all of a company's constituencies. But if top executives arrive with guarantees of enormous severance packages even if they do not succeed in creating value for the company, they are not sharing the risk with employees who have no such floor underneath them. In recent years the rewards even for failure have become almost legend: Jill Barrad presided over a disaster at Mattel and took home $50 million; Doug Ivester lasted less than two tumultuous years at Coca-Cola and won a severance package of $25.5 million; Durk Jaeger was ousted at Procter & Gamble after seventeen months as CEO and took home close to $10 million. This doesn't make for much trust.

PepsiCo's Roger Enrico was the only American CEO who broached the compensation subject. We were talking about income inequalities on a global basis, and Enrico made a point about the importance of the middle class to business and the dangers of extreme income disparities. He was more confident about the problem than the solution, but he was seized by the issue nevertheless. In the past, he said, "business was not a very good steward of the broader marketplace. But what do you do about that?" I asked him how he saw things in the future. "I don't know", he answered, "but I don't think the signs are very good. And I don't have a pre-scription, so maybe there aren't any good answers. But I would say to you that just one example would suggest to me that not many people are thinking about this, and that's the disparity between CEO compensation and [the companies' employees]. Now maybe a lot of that is driven by the stock market and stock options. But I don't see a lot of discipline in that."

He then related a story. "When Don Kendall was CEO of this company he took great pride in a chart in *Fortune* maga-zine which measured performance and pay. And they put the faces of the CEOs in this chart. And Kendall was proud be-cause he was in the high percentage performance group and also in the low pay category. I mean, that really made him feel good. And he had more than enough money to live on. It wasn't like he was starving to death."

I had read that Enrico himself donated his entire salary to scholarships for employees, retaining only bonuses for performance, and asked him to explain this. "I'm not mak-ing a statement to the outside world; the outside world can do what it wants to," he said. "I'm not trying to impress peo-ple. I just felt I needed to do something."

❖ ❖ ❖

Trust goes well beyond the relationships between leaders and the people they work with. In today's business climate, trust between a company and its customers is equally crucial. This, of course, is why brand reputation is so important and valuable; a company may be constantly restructuring; it may be experimenting with new products and new ways to get closer to its customers; but if the brand denotes reliability throughout all the changes, in good times and bad, that will be an overwhelming competitive advantage over time. The same considerations apply to the links between a company and its suppliers, too.

Among the most interesting thoughts I heard from CEOs on these subjects came from Jack Welch and John Browne, who took slightly different angles on the topic of trust. Welch talked to me about how the Internet will transform relationships. "It's going to change the relationship with every constituent. Your customer is going to have a different relationship [with you], your supplier is going to have a different relationship," he said. "They are going to be much more permanent because you're both going to be more dependent on one another." He went on to say that the enthusiasm for creating new markets for producers to buy supplies in an Internet auction would work only if a company was looking to buy undifferentiated commodities. "But it will not work for sophisticated supply chain stuff, because if the supplier is really doing a good job for us, we'd better be smart enough to stay with that supplier. He'll grow, he'll become more productive. We'll pass on the productivity gains and better prices to our customer. And that's altogether different."

I asked him whether he was advocating a way of doing business based more on trust between a company and its suppliers. He agreed, but he qualified what the trust was based on. "It's not about trusting a person," he said, "but the whole operation, the integrity of the process." Because of the Internet, "You have the data. You can see through to what you want. You know where things are in their shops."

John Browne told me a story that embodies one of the ways he looks at trust, although he never used the word. It illustrates his thinking about how a global company should behave. "One of the most important changes in the business world as I've experienced it is in the way big companies exercise power," he said. "I always remember my predecessor, David Simon, who always used to talk in sporting metaphors. He used to say that when he took over in 1992, BP was a light middleweight in a ring with heavyweights. And he had to learn to understand how to conserve BP's punches and to use its speed to come around and at least gain some advantage from time to time with the heavyweights. We now punch with the strength of a heavyweight. And if you inadvertently punch with the strength of a heavyweight, you may knock someone out you don't want to knock out."

Browne then zeroed in on his notion of trust. "So this is all about power . . . and all power must be proscribed. You have to use your power to solve problems . . . like produce energy and clean up the environment. But we will not use it to do one-off transactions with people to take advantage of them, recognizing that we can't come back and do business again—in other words, create a relationship which isn't a relationship. Relationships have to be mutual. We are in business to generate wealth, but we have to do it today, tomorrow, the next day and the day after."

❖ ❖ ❖

True north, trust, and the like: Are they mission impossible? Not totally, of course. In their seminal book *Built to Last: Successful Habits of Visionary Companies,* James Collins and

Jerry Porras point out that great CEOs are less concerned with strategies, business models, particular products, or immediate financial payoffs than with building great institutions that serve all their constituencies over long periods of time. They cite CEOs like George Merck II, who in 1950 defined "true north" for the company that bore his name when he said, "We try to remember that medicine is for the patient. . . . It is not for the profits. The profits follow, and if we have remembered that, they have never failed to appear. The better we have remembered it, the larger they have been." Another of their examples is David Packard, co-founder of Hewlett-Packard, whom they quote as saying, "I think many people assume, wrongly, that a company exists simply to make money. While this is an important result of a company's existence, we have to go deeper and find the real reasons for our being. . . . Our main task is to design, develop, and manufacture the finest electronic [equipment] for the advancement of science and the welfare of humanity." The authors make it clear, however, that Packard believed in profits, too, for they were what allowed the company to pursue its broader goals. ". . . Anyone who cannot accept [profit] as one of the most important objectives of this company has no place either now or in the future on the management team of this company," Packard is quoted as saying.

In the context of the new economy, roller coaster that it is, these leaders are hard acts for today's CEOs to follow.

5

A Vision Without Execution Is an Hallucination

In the midst of an industrial revolution, all of a company's constituencies crave a simple but compelling picture of where the company is going. Such demands force business leaders to create a powerful vision and set of attainable goals. But executing that vision is more important than ever too, and the same factors that cloud a clear view of the next several years make implementing plans increasingly difficult. Not only does the underlying terrain (the technology, the people, the competition) keep shifting, but the penalty for missing targets—the price exacted by Wall Street in terms of lost market value, and the damage to a company's reputation from newspaper stories about failed goals—is getting higher. In the recent past, there have been times when either vision or execution, but not both, were of extreme importance. In the 1950s and 1960s, for example, business leaders in the United States could promote a social vision of mass consumption—two cars for every American family, say—without too much concern for quality. In the next two decades, due in large part to competition from Japan, execution was at a premium and many Americans deserted Detroit. Today, consumers want to see the aspiration *and* the reality. The vision needs to be powerful and credible. The execution needs to be nearly flawless.

What exactly is vision? It is not a mission statement describing a company's objectives, and it is not the kind of slick, cliché-ridden corporate letter that often appears in annual reports. A vision needs to be an imaginative picture of where a company will be and why that positioning will be a transforming event not just for the company but for its customers and its other constituencies. A vision needs to be sufficiently broad and deep to ride above specific transactions, such as plans for a merger or a sale of a division. When I hear CEOs explain where they want to take their companies, there is an element of personal passion, almost as if the leader and the vision were one, and the vision existed in the form it did because of the personality and character of that particular CEO. Chief executives will also give you a brutally frank assessment of the obstacles to the effective implementation of their vision. They talk passionately about the strategy that needs to be put in place, the speed of decision making that is required, the awesome challenges of communicating with all their constituencies, and the gambles that have to be taken—in short, the complexity and risks of putting all the pieces together in a fast-moving situation. What emerges from the vision-execution conundrum is a classic Catch–22. In an era of heightened competition, the vision had better be spectacular, but the more spectacular the vision, the more difficult it is to execute.

✧ ✧ ✧

I caught Stephen Case, Chairman and CEO of AOL, in his Dulles, Virginia, headquarters a few months before he announced his intention to merge with Time Warner. He walked into the conference room wearing a Hawaiian shirt and khakis, a small backpack over his shoulder and a can of Coca-Cola in hand. In our talk he painted a strikingly clear and highly ambitious view of where he wanted his company to go and what he wanted it to be. Throughout his career, he said, he had held one idea out front: "To build a global medium as central to people's lives as the telephone or television—and even more valuable." In its simplicity and grandeur, this is reminiscent of Henry Ford's goal to build a great car that "no man making a good salary will be unable to own and enjoy with his family the blessing of hours of pleasure in God's open spaces." Case described three phases in the evolution of his company. First was to build an on-line service. Then, starting in the mid-1990s, he worked on developing a structure for the business so that it could grow in an organized way. "Now," he said, "our attention is on creating a great medium and making sure that it has a positive impact on the economy and on society."

Case discussed several elements of his game plan: He wanted to double the number of subscribers by 2005, with a heavy emphasis not just on the United States but also abroad; develop services that will encourage users to triple their time on-line with AOL companies, keeping them for about three hours per day; and deliver services not just via computers but also via televisions, cell phones, and other devices that might be embedded in cars or kitchens. In the process, he wanted AOL to overtake most of the twenty-four companies rated above it in market value on the *Wall Street Journal's* list of the country's largest firms.

Case wants to use sophisticated technology, combined with simple delivery and ease of use. "I think one of the things that served this company well over these past fifteen years was that we weren't wedded to any prior culture," he said. "If we had grown up in Silicon Valley, we probably would have looked at the world through the prism of technology. If we had been born in Hollywood, the prism would have been entertainment. If we started in Basking Ridge, New Jersey [where AT&T is headquartered], we would have seen ourselves as a communications company. It's not possible for most companies to put aside decades or sometimes a century of traditions and lessons learned and not apply it to the future. Sometimes that's helpful, because you avoid making the same mistakes over again. But most of the time it's harmful, because you end up assuming that the future is going to look like the past—which in the case of our industry, it usually isn't. AOL grew up in northern Virginia, where there was really no culture, just a sleepy government town with lots of government contractors. We started from scratch. No obvious talent pool, no venture capitalists. But in retrospect it was very helpful in those formative years, because we looked at this medium through the prism of consumers as opposed to bringing any other baggage to it."

One of Case's most important goals is to establish a brand that consumers trust. "We will continue to innovate, of course," he said, "but we'll do it in stages so that every time you sign on, we don't force you to download a new browser, for example. We know people want innovation. We also know they don't want the screens to look different every day." He returns to the same concepts many times in the interview: choice, convenience, flexibility, immediacy, interactivity, personalization.

Case believes strongly in a broader relationship between AOL and the population at large. He is among the most vocal and articulate CEOs pointing out the need for careful responses to issues like privacy and the taxation of e-commerce. He has argued for stepped-up industry self-regulation and an overhaul of outmoded government regulation, which he said fails to take account of the blurring of communications technologies. Taken together, Case's vision is unambiguous: Enhancing consumers lives wherever the Internet is, setting enormously ambitious quantitative business goals and leading society into the Internet world.

Several months after I met with Case, he announced the proposed merger between AOL and Time Warner. There was no end to the speculation and commentary in the press and on Wall Street as to the motivations behind the deal. Was Case after "content" to enhance AOL's penetration in the lives of consumers? Did he anticipate the end of the boom for pure Internet companies and want to grab on to an old economy organization with tangible assets? There were other questions, too: Did Case err badly by taking AOL out of the pure Internet world? Would it be possible to combine the cultures of AOL and Time Warner, or would this mega-merger fail as so many others had? Only time will tell, but it

did strike me that Case's strategy was consistent with everything he told me. The burning desire to build the greatest
communications medium ever devised required a big step,
and access to enormous content that would compel consumers to use it. Time Warner brought not just news but also
movies and TV programs. AOL was looking for ways to link
to people's homes, and Time Warner brought broadband cable connections. The combined operation catered also to another of Case's visions—to use his company to shape the new
world of communications—and for that he needed even
more scale than he had before the merger, because the playing field was brutally competitive but also global.

And consider what Case did *not* do with this deal. He did
not make AOL fancier from a technological standpoint, at
least as far as customers are concerned. He did not change
the qualities he saw as essential to success, particularly easy
accessibility. He just gave us more reasons to log on and tune
in, and he opened up a range of possibilities that even now
no one can as yet fully foresee.

Vision isn't limited to companies associated with the new
economy. Take Ford Motor Company, one of the world's oldest manufacturing companies, the most profitable carmaker
in 1999 and the one poised to overtake General Motors as
the automotive corporation with the largest global sales.
William Clay Ford, Jr.—the great-grandson of founder Henry
Ford—has been a Ford employee since 1979 and the company's chairman since 1998. Like Stephen Case, Ford wants
to create a revolution. An enthusiastic environmentalist (and
a prospective blackbelt in tae kwon do), he bears the responsibility, just as Christopher Galvin does, of shepherding

a family dynasty through the new era. It is hard not to sense the sweep of American industrial history when you take the elevator to the executive suites, hard also not to be impressed by the optimism, sincerity and openness of the forty-one-year-old chairman in whose hands this corporate giant now largely rests.

Ford described where he wants his company to be. "We are standing on the thresholds of two revolutions in an industry that hasn't had one in almost a hundred years," he said. "One is driven by the Internet and will transform the way we deal with our customers with information and product. The other relates to how we power our vehicles. We're redefining what it means to be an industrial company."

He discussed two changes that will characterize the company in the future. "Most of our business will be touched by the Internet, and indeed already is. Our president, Jacques Nassar, says that if you go back to even a very short while ago, our whole idea of a customer was that we would wholesale a car to a dealer, the dealer would then sell the car to the customer, and we hoped we never heard from the customer— because if we did, it meant something was wrong. Today we want to establish a dialogue with the customer throughout the entire ownership experience." That is why Ford is getting into all aspects of the auto-owning experience, from financing, to parts and service, and ultimately to recycling of old cars into reusable metal. "We want to talk to and touch our customers at every step of the way," he says. "We want to be a consumer products and services company that just happens to be in the automotive business. The Internet is key to all of this."

The second part of the transformation of one of the country's oldest global companies revolves around clean fuel and the environment. "When it comes to fuel sources, we hope to lead a clean revolution," Ford told me. "The company has certified all its plants around the world under the toughest environmental standards, something I do not believe anyone else in the industry has done," he said. "We are aiming for a dramatic shift in the role of the internal combustion engine, and we have committed to have cars on the road for sale in 2004 running on fuel cells. It means that the only thing that comes out the tailpipe is water vapor."

William Ford is making a big bet that putting his company on the right side of environmental issues will pay off. "At the end of the century, many of the great ideological issues are off the table," he explained. "It's now a question of what consumers are going to be demanding, rather than what business leaders are envisioning. Consumers want a safer, cleaner, more equitable world, and they'll buy from companies that display those characteristics. I believe that companies that are responsive to these needs—assuming they have great products and services, of course—will have a commanding market position."

"I've staked much of my personal reputation on the environment," William Ford told me. "I wake up sometimes wondering whether I'm the only one who feels this way and whether I am taking the company on a diversionary course that, in the end, won't pay off. But on other nights I wake up thinking that we're not doing enough. Fact is, I see the company that gets this issue right has a chance to really put some distance between themselves—reputationally—and all the rest of the pack."

Ford is trying to position his company to embrace several powerful trends in society: high technology, webcentric manufacturing, intense consumer focus, and social responsibility as reflected in environmental consciousness. Together they constitute a new brand for an old-line manufacturing company. "We are trying to build up a lot of trust," he said, "trust that our product is good, trust that we will treat customers very well, and trust that we will stand for something that our customers and employees can be proud of."

In the months since my interview, the Ford Motor Company has faced serious problems that have threatened the credibility of William Ford's ambitious goals. The first of these came in May 2000 when the company released its first *Corporate Citizenship Report,* an unsparing public assessment of the dilemmas it faced. "Ford's activities have a significant impact on society," it said. "However ... SUVs [sport utility vehicles] ... raise issues relative to Ford's corporate citizenship commitment." The report went on to explain that these vehicles can cause serious safety and environmental problems. Yet the company said it would keep building SUVs, which according to one analysis generated $18,000 profit per vehicle. Ford's president and CEO, Jacques Nassar, said that although customers wanted environmentally friendly vehicles, they were unwilling to pay more for them or do without many of the current features of the SUVs. The *Citizenship Report* promised that Ford would continue to improve the fuel economy of all its vehicles as well as find ways to reduce the damage that SUVs caused in accidents to lower-riding vehicles. At a press conference, Ford admitted that Wall Street does not reward progressive and environmentally friendly companies, but that he continues to have environmental payoffs as an objective "five, ten, twenty, fifty years down the line."

Two months later, Jacques Nassar committed the company to increasing the average fuel efficiency of its sport utility vehicle by 25 percent over the next five years by adjusting engines and making auto parts lighter. The increase was the first fundamental change in fuel economy in any major passenger car category in almost two decades. According to press reports, Ford officials were hoping that their new proenvironmental policies would give all their brands an image of responsibility. The *New York Times* editorialized, "Environmentalists on the whole were delighted. They noted that if Ford can build S.U.V.s that yield much better mileage per gallon, other companies are sure to follow. If they do, William Ford will further solidify his reputation as the most adventurous executive in an industry not previously known for environmental stewardship."

Three months later the company was hit by a much bigger thunderbolt: The forced recall of over six million Firestone tires that had been mounted on Ford Explorers and linked, as of mid-September, to at least eighty-eight deaths. In Congressional hearings that month, everything William Ford was trying to do was challenged. At what point did Ford Motor Company know that the tires were defective? To what degree were these deaths attributable to defects in the vehicles as opposed to the tires? The crisis was in its early stages when this book was put to bed, but at a bare minimum it constituted a body blow to William Ford's vision of a new and more trusting relationship between the Ford Motor Company and its customers. Still, this was not the first large-scale crisis that unfolded for people around the world to see and in which great business leaders helped their companies to regain their reputation. In 1982 Johnson & Johnson recovered from the Tylenol scare in large part because of the skillful actions of CEO James E. Burke. In 1997 Texaco was able to handle serious problems of racial prejudice with the help of chairman and CEO Peter I. Bijur, who left no stone unturned in an effort to rectify the situation. The big question therefore is whether William Ford's vision is strong enough, and he and his team good enough, to guide the company back to where Ford wants it to be.

✧ ✧ ✧

The struggle to turn dreams into reality takes place on many levels. "Even if you have a sense of what's around the corner, if you don't have a team in place to execute your plan there's a big problem," said Stephen Case. "In the end, a vision without the ability to execute it is probably an hallucination."

One aspect of execution is the setting of fundamental principles for decision making. In large decentralized organizations, no matter how strong the leadership at the top is, the effective execution of a plan requires purposeful action in many parts of the company. Broad guidelines—operating principles—are needed for all the levels of management to use in making decisions in a rapidly shifting environment. Said Orit Gadiesh, "You can't have a long-term strategy anymore, because with it you're going to be confined and you won't be able to move fast enough. What 'strategy' is now is how you allocate your resources—which also means how you decide what *not* to do. And when I say 'resources' I don't mean just capital. I mean your time as an executive, where you put your most talented people, and what you put your brand name against. And so if you do not have infinite resources you need some strategic principles."

Gadiesh cited Jack Welch as someone who has established effective strategic guidelines. When Welch took over GE in 1981, he decreed that all of GE's companies would have to be either number one or number two in their respective global markets. He didn't tell the heads of these companies how to get there, but he made it clear that he wouldn't support businesses that failed to achieve this goal.

Lawrence Weinbach of Unisys also illustrates the way strategic principles can be used. Weinbach came to Unisys in 1997 from an eight-year stint as chief executive of the combined accounting and consulting firm of Anderson Worldwide. His job at Unisys, where he holds the titles of chairman, president and CEO, was to turn around a flagging performance. He is determined to make the most out of globalization by subjecting his entire product development and marketing operations to a standard: Will a Unisys product sell in most of the hundred or so countries in which the company does business? "I understand full well that different countries are going to change at different speeds, but because of globalization the time it takes for country X to catch up to country Y has been vastly reduced. And so I want to concentrate only on products and services that can be used in many countries over a reasonable period of time. To be a global company we can't think of one-off products, things that sell in just the U.S. or just in Malaysia, for example. We have to be convinced that we can replicate the product in at least fifty countries, sooner or later—or else you wonder whether the investment is worth it."

American Express's Kenneth Chenault is another business leader who uses strategic principles to give guidance to his ubiquitous organization. "The idea around here is that there should be clear criteria for making big decisions," he told me. "We call this 'principle-based decision making.' To deal with the changes that are occurring at such a rapid pace, the rule books don't work anymore. When things have gone wrong, what I find is that we have not established the appropriate criteria." He described three principles that he has established for all of Amex's employees. First, they have to meet the test of providing superior value to their customers. They have to ask themselves questions such as "Do we really understand what our customers want, and do we really understand the competition?" Second, they have to satisfy themselves that they are the best in the relevant category when it comes to a combination of costs, revenues and margins. And third, they must be sure they can add to the American Express brand. Amex executives have to measure their decisions against all three criteria. "What I have found is that getting people to apply criteria and thinking them through is not an easy task," he said, "but once you do it, the power it gives an organization is incredible."

❖ ❖ ❖

In late 1999 Steve Ballmer (then president of Microsoft, and now CEO) was asked by a *New York Times* reporter how his firm planned to make money from selling software over the Internet. "Don't know yet," he said, "but if you wait to have a business model in place, you'll be the last guy in the marketplace." When it comes to execution, CEOs are clearly preoccupied with the importance of having to make up their minds very quickly and with only a fraction of the relevant information. "If we want to be leaders," Lawrence Weinbach told me, "we're going to have to make decisions with maybe 75 percent of the facts [we'd like to have]. If you wait for 95 percent you are going to be a follower." But you can't will speed, he explained. Your entire production system has to be geared to it. He described Unisys's technology platforms, how they were built nearly complete, but in such a way that they could be customized very quickly.

Michael Armstrong put it another way: "In the end you have to have the guts to make a decision," he once told executive recruiters Thomas Neff and James Citrin. "You'll never have all the data you need. You'll never be able to sort through all the alternatives and risks that are in front of you. You get the right information and couple it with the right instincts to enable you to make a decision. Then you energize your organization to make that decision work in the marketplace." Armstrong further explained that in the old AT&T there was a drive to minimize uncertainty with unlimited analysis. "Yet the effort to create a 100 percent solution insured that the decision was always too late, because the market had changed," he said. "You have to accept that you'll be wrong sometimes, but in the long run you'll suffer more from consistently delayed decisions."

It is a proposition with which Kenneth Chenault agrees. "I think the premium needs to be placed on speed. We talk about the conflict between speed and perfection and one of the things that I have said to the organization is that the focus has to be on speed. That does not mean that we want to come out with shoddy products or inferior products. But the reality is, if we take too long to get it perfect, it won't matter."

The obsession with speed is widespread. Michael Bonsignore: "I think a lot of companies can get hung up on the analytical. I don't think there is time for this because things are moving all the time and you have to decide what you think the world will look like [without all the information you'd like to have]." Martin Sorrell: "I have a bad quote which I nevertheless agree with. 'A bad decision on Monday is better than a good one on Friday.' What bedevils our business is lack of speedy response." PepsiCo's Roger Enrico: "When you are faced with a decision, the best thing is to do the right thing, the next best is to do the wrong thing, and the worst thing is to do nothing."

✧ ✧ ✧

Strategic principles may be necessary and speed of decision making may be more important than ever, but they both assume an exquisite level of teamwork, which itself presupposes common understandings about corporate goals. Virtually every CEO emphasized to me that execution requires extraordinary communication efforts. Today there is so much information traveling so fast that getting a message out and heard among the clatter is a tremendous undertaking in itself. Multiple constituencies have to get the message. The information has to be clear and consistent, for with today's technology everyone gets the word at the same time. It has to penetrate the barriers of different nationalities and cultures. Discrepancies in what is delivered to different audiences will be quickly noted, and confusion can arise and spread quickly, compounding itself in a way from which it is almost impossible to recover.

Being a great communicator entails many traits. You need to connect with people on a number of levels, each of which summons a different skill. You have to present a dignified and authoritative persona, yet you have to be highly personal, and often informal, for even in the era of easy mass communication, any message is received only one person at a time. You have to understand complicated technical issues yet simplify the concepts for the general public. You need to be receptive to a wide range of questions yet maintain control of the message you want to deliver. You need to be a champ with audiences from your own industry, but your base of knowledge must be much broader, for global executives are constantly being asked in public about their views on trade, finance and the course of the economy. Today's top business leaders need to be effective in getting their points across in multiple national cultures. How John Browne, Jürgen Schrempp, Martin Sorrell and Hiroshi Okuda "play" in the United States is as important as how they come across in their home countries. The same could be said of Stephen Case, Michael Dell and Frederick Smith and their effectiveness in communicating in places such as France, China or South Africa.

CEOs need to reach their employees, often in the way that Jack Welch does with his incessant handwritten notes, phone calls and e-mails, all of which give the sense that he is everywhere at once. It's a technique that Rolf Breuer has begun to use too. "My ability to reach all ninety thousand of our employees is limited, of course," he told me. "So what can I do personally? A lot of things. For example, what I have is a personal e-mail by the name of Employer Line. Every employee can reach me directly. I guarantee that he remains anonymous. And he gets an answer within a week." For years, Roger Enrico, chairman and CEO of PepsiCo, has invited teams of up-and-coming managers to his western ranch to bond, brainstorm and think about their goals. "There are two things I try to get across," he told me. "You know this question about whether you're born with leadership skills or you learn them? I want them to believe that however you got it, if you practice and work on it, you can become better at it. And the second thing I want them to walk away with is that there's no mystery about how this corporation is run. No one is on a pedestal. If there is such a thing as a club, then they are in it. During the week I spend two one-on-one sessions with each of the participants where we can talk about anything they want including their career, their life."

Then there is the crucial issue of being direct and specific, but also being able to provide the all-important context. John Browne talked to me about the dual functions of communicating en masse and communicating with individuals. "It's a big challenge, because the agenda is always shifting for large groups and for their members," he said. "The most important thing a leader can do to communicate is to keep the bigger picture in focus, to set the context . . . to explain or reconcile the complexities that cloud the overall picture of what's important and why." He emphasized that both the public and the employees need to know what the company is trying to do, how it is doing it, how important any one event or activity is in the larger scheme of things. He used as an example the extensive press coverage in 1999 of BP's investments in Siberia, which at the time were doing poorly because of disputes with BP's Russian partners. A major event in the company's fortunes? "Yes," he said, "it's important. However, we are carrying just under $300 million of investment there, and in the scale of our operations it's tiny! We have a strategic interest in the region, but if we have to write off the investment, no one should think we have diverted any significant resources. That's the context which I wanted everyone to understand."

Another good example of providing context is a five-page letter that Harvey Golub, chairman and CEO of American Express, sent to all his employees in September 1999. The financial markets were being rocked by the combination of the Asian economic crisis, Russia's default on its debts and the collapse of Long Term Credit Management, one of America's largest hedge funds. President Clinton was calling this the worst economic crisis in half a century. American Express employees, stationed around the world, were understandably nervous about the position of their company—which was highly invested in global markets—as well as their own personal futures.

"Given the extraordinary volatility in worldwide equity markets in recent weeks," the letter said, "we wanted to share with you our perspective on the performance of American Express stock and on the current state of our business." Golub went on to discuss the volatile performance of the stock market, the impact on other companies like American Express, the actual performance of Amex's businesses, and some of its plans to deal with the situation. The letter provided a broad perspective. It gave Amex employees—and, by extension, all Amex's other constituencies—a measured way to assess the overall position of the firm. In providing a context for the crisis, it did something else: It showed that the company's leaders were doing everything they could, looking at the short-term and the long.

✧ ✧ ✧

When technology is changing so rapidly and the boundaries of markets are expanding, when competition from old and new rivals is white-hot, when your customer base and pool of talent are both restless, when you have to move at lightning speed—when all this is the case, then executing strategy often leaves leaders no choice but to take some big risks. CEOs console themselves by making the most educated judgments they can. But the fact is, they need to move in bold directions with only a fraction of the information that's vital to them and a lot of instinct. It's the only way to win in the middle of an industrial revolution. It's also inevitable that some of the big decisions will turn out to be wrong. Many kinds of huge bets are taken today: bets on technology, bets on markets, bets on the optimum size of the company.

Many bets of CEOs concern the Internet. Jorma Ollila's Nokia is already thriving, thanks to the ability of its cell phones to connect to the Internet. But Ollila is sure this is not the end of the game for the world's largest producer of cell phones, and his calm demeanor belies his intense examination of what is coming down the road as wireless handsets and the Internet link up. "In the next five years, it's hard to know how our industry will be evolving," he said. "Is it going to be one where the value chain will be dominated by software and applications and services, and if so will we, a company which is primarily a hardware manufacturer, have to be a major player? Or is this an industry where we can continue to thrive as a supplier of handsets, constantly improving our performance in that arena? The point is, we really don't know how the industry will develop, and who the key players in software and applications for wireless handsets will be. The AOLs, the Microsofts, the Yahoo!s, the Motorolas—there are lots of candidates for that space. Do we jump in to that? We have to decide on the issue of where the real value will be added in the future. It's a big decision for us."

And indeed it is. By the fall of 2000, the mobile communications industry was in the throes of great uncertainty. What kind of data and other services would be available and who would supply that information was a question that CEOs of many industries and investors of all kinds were nervously wondering. As Ollila predicted, new competitors with different skills were entering Nokia's space—Dell, Palm, Sony and others. Ollila had no more time to ruminate; he had to roll the dice soon.

Michael Armstrong has made some huge bets. Since becoming chairman and CEO of AT&T in 1997, he has been endeavoring to create a totally new company. In 1998, Armstrong set out to transform the old Ma Bell, which had failed to innovate and had become a laggard in the Internet age. Amid many acquisitions, Armstrong's biggest moves were to buy the cable companies TCI and Media One for $110 billion to become the country's largest cable provider so that he could handle all the local and long-distance phone service, Internet, and TV for any given customer, rendering just one bill. By any measure the transformation was a highly ambitious goal, because it assumed the success of unproven technology, and a complicated alliance strategy with other cable companies. It also relied on near flawless execution of a wholesale upgrading of existing systems. "If he [succeeds] he'll be the hero to AT&T that Lou Gerstner is to IBM," wrote Janet Guyon in *Fortune.* "If he doesn't, he'll be remembered not as the guy who saved AT&T, but as the one who finally ran it into the ground."

By the middle of 2000, the bet was looking even bigger. While Armstrong had been staking the future on the growth of wireless and cable communications, he had also been assuming that the traditional long-distance business, a cash cow, would provide time for the change. The latter was losing steam, however, which raised questions about whether the long-distance operation ought to be sold off. There was even speculation in the press about whether AT&T itself could be for sale. The pressure on Armstrong was mounting. "For the first time since he took over as chairman in the fall of 1997," wrote Seth Schiesel of the *New York Times,* "Mr. Armstrong himself is on the defensive. His bet-the-company vision to transform AT&T by delivering a package of interactive digital television, high-speed cyberspace access, and local telephone service over cable television lines is still largely just that, a vision."

At the end of October AT&T's stock was sinking fast, and the company had lost $70 billion of its value since the beginning of the year. The pressure was too great for Armstrong, who was forced to announce that he was splitting the company into four separate parts in order to unlock value that he felt the market wasn't recognizing. He told a group of analysts that the breakup was the "next logical step" in his strategy. He considered the press accounts that he was in retreat "not only wrong but offensive." But the *Wall Street Journal*, echoing virtually every other commentary from the media and Wall Street analysts, said on the day after the split up was announced, "The sweeping restructuring . . . is an admission that [AT&T's] recent strategy . . . had failed." Only time will tell who is right.

Deutsche Bank's Rolf Breuer is betting on the Internet, but notes the inherent gamble in how far he can go. I met Breuer, who has worked at the bank since 1956, in New York not long after the acquisition he engineered of Bankers Trust. Chairman and CEO since 1997, he had been the force behind Deutsche Bank's transformation from a plodding commercial bank to a top investment bank. He represents the group of European executives who, contrary to the traditions on the continent, are leading proponents of a business culture that gives increasing priority to shareholders. When I came into his office, he greeted me with the same personal grace as if I were entering his home. He didn't strike me as a European titan astride one of the world's oldest and largest global financial institutions. As in my meetings with many of the CEOs I interviewed, I was taken aback by the lack of pomp—or, for that matter, staff. There was a low-key solitariness to the moment that belied my expectations.

Breuer's acquisition of Bankers Trust was itself a big bet. In 1989 Deutsche Bank tried to move into the fast lane of investment banking by buying the British firm of Morgan Grenfell, but the experiment foundered on cultural differences, relating not just to nationality but also to business style. It was a huge gamble for Breuer to try again with Bankers Trust, a bigger, brasher American bank known for its appetite for risk. Breuer told me Deutsche Bank had learned its lessons from the debacle with the British, the trick being to swallow the new firm quickly and completely. "There is no longer a Bankers Trust," he said. "Only Deutsche Bank."

The post-merger integration was going well, he said, and the cultural risks that so many experts had warned him against had proved vastly overrated. "But how we approach e-commerce, that's a big challenge," he admitted. "The real question is the behavior of our customers. In five or ten years' time, will they still want to have an opportunity to visit their banker person-to-person, or will that be a thing of the past? If it's all going to be on-line, then the bank has far too many people on board, far too much real estate all over the place, and we have to get rid of that as soon as possible. On the other hand, if we go too far with e-commerce then we could lose our customers and market position." Breuer said that the decision of where the balance would be weighs heavily on him all the time.

Not long after our meeting, Breuer announced a proposed merger with Germany's Dresdner Bank. A major objective of the deal was to rationalize the bricks-and-mortar retail banking industry in Germany, which had become far too large and inefficient. Breuer made it clear to the public that one of his priorities was to enhance Deutsche Bank's global investment banking presence by merging Dresdner's and his operations into one major powerhouse. It was a big risk for Deutsche Bank, a very conservative German institution. Shortly after the announcement the deal was aborted, causing acute embarrassment for all parties, especially Breuer.

Michael Dell is also taking risks, but in his mind the issue isn't technology or markets; it's the rapid scaling-up of his business. "The real risks relate to infrastructure—how fast you can build a company," he said. "This last year, for example, we added $8 billion in revenue and fourteen thousand people and six new plants. There is risk when you are growing that fast, and it's a real challenge to do it right."

Global strategies can also be a big bet, as Roger Enrico of PepsiCo admits. We met at PepsiCo's bucolic headquarters in Purchase, New York, a large estate surrounded by beautiful gardens. Waiting for the meeting to begin, I remember staring out the window and watching someone mow the lawn ever so slowly and carefully, and wondering whether, in the middle of the global business maelstrom in which consumer products companies like Pepsi found themselves, these calm surroundings were an advantage or an impediment. Enrico's guy-next-door image is at odds with his history as the architect of a far-reaching restructuring of PepsiCo, which began in 1996 when he sold off its extensive food stores and focused the company on beverages and snacks.

"Two of the big bets we are making are on China and India," he told me, "two markets with over two billion people. In China, for example, we think there will be a huge market for our products. But it could just as easily happen the other way, and a big indigenous company could become enormously popular there and seriously challenge us." As large as the markets were, however, his company's investments were small relative to its overall operations. "It's better to invest at a relatively moderate rate for twenty years than to try to invest at a huge rate that can't be sustained," he said, "because success takes a long time to come."

James Wolfensohn of the World Bank is making some bold and controversial moves, too. He took over the world's largest development bank in 1995 in the middle of heated controversy over its role (Should it be financing government projects or the private sector in developing countries?) and its effectiveness (Did its investments really help poor people?). Since then he has forced many changes on the Bank's structure and mission. His passion about his work first became evident to me a year later when he came to Yale to speak to students. Among the many stories he told our students was one about visiting a poor town outside Rio de Janeiro where the World Bank had helped to finance the transformation of the local water utility from government to private community ownership. Before that, water had been free. Now residents received bills. A distraught peasant approached him, waving her bill in his face and speaking rapidly in Portuguese. Wolfensohn was crestfallen, thinking she was trying to tell him how poor the commercialization of water had made her. His translator corrected the impression. "This woman is showing you her name," he said. "She's saying that it's the first time she's ever seen it officially written out. She's saying that when she pays this bill, she can take the receipt to a local bank and get credit for the first time in her life." Wolfensohn described the lump in his throat as he realized what she was saying.

"The biggest single bet I'm making is that the World Bank, as one player in the whole economic development field, can have a meaningful and measurable influence on what happens on our planet," he told me in our interview. "Instead of just focusing only on individual projects, or on policy advice in particular sectors like health or environment, what I'm trying to do is move the Bank to take a comprehensive approach to economic development, not just within countries but internationally. We're attempting to do this by understanding, analyzing, and providing advice on how all the pieces of the development puzzle fit together—or don't." What Wolfensohn wants is to organize a wide array of economic development institutions that do not now coordinate their efforts. The upside is not just a much more powerful role for his institution, but also a more rational approach to helping developing nations' progress. The downside is that the World Bank is undertaking a mission that is so broad and so difficult that it will be seen as ineffective and risks losing its existing support from Washington and other governments. It has accumulated many critics for just those reasons.

CEOs have to make big bets, but how to take educated risks is the real question. A lot comes down to instinct, of course, especially since information is never complete and the terrain is unstable. The ability to take calculated gambles and still sleep at night often requires surrounding yourself with highly talented people and being able to rely on their judgment to supplement your own. Still another important attribute is to have a wide range of relationships outside of the company—a broad intelligence network—to provide a context, an early warning system and a reality check.

Some CEOs appear to relish the industry conference circuit, which has grown enormously these past few years. Some are active in business associations and government-supported commissions and task forces that draw on corporate executives. Many are on one another's corporate boards. These kinds of activities will become increasingly essential in the years ahead. Of course, the big constraint—a theme throughout a CEO's life—is having enough time to talk to people outside the company and the industry and also run a complex global operation.

✧ ✧ ✧

The cases of three CEOs who resigned under pressure since my interviews with them illustrate what happens when vision and execution don't come together.

Richard Huber was, until February 2000, the chairman, president and CEO of Aetna, a position he held for less than three tumultuous years. He previously had served as Aetna's vice chairman for finance and held top executive positions at Citibank, Chase, Continental Bank and the investment bank of Wasserstein Perella. Through a series of large-scale acquisitions, he transformed Aetna into the largest health care company in the United States, with over twenty-one million customers. Every one of these transactions was supported by Huber's board. While he was still CEO, he talked to me with great enthusiasm about a vision of linking patients and doctors through the Internet—an e-health business that was revolutionary in its scope. Not only would health costs be reduced and convenience enhanced, not only would patients benefit and Aetna profit as a company, but Huber envisioned Aetna's using its vast reservoir of medical knowledge to enable patients to ask their doctors intelligent questions, and also to educate physicians about medical breakthroughs that were taking place elsewhere in the U.S.—knowledge that Aetna would have because of the millions of claims it saw and its web of relationships with doctors and hospitals. "We have the largest health care database in the world," said Huber.

"Using it, we should be able to detect early warning signs, leading indicators, particularly of chronic diseases like asthma or diabetes. We could use information technology to scan for patterns. We could alert individual patients and individual doctors. We elevate the entire health care industry with the rich information we have mined. It's the right thing to do, and it's also a great way to retain customers."

Huber's vision, which linked health care to the Internet, had all the elements that a Stephen Case or a William Ford had in their own dreams for their companies—a business plan that was exciting for the firm and its shareholders, but also one that would transform in a positive way the interaction of the company and the broader population which depended on it. He seemed to have the ideas way before the competition—at least before anyone else had implemented them. He had the corporate apparatus, including the links to health care recipients and providers.

So what happened? The problem was in the execution. It wasn't as if Huber didn't know what in theory had to be done or the difficulties in making it happen. "The technology is there already," he told me, "but making the conversion from our current systems—that's a big deal. There is only one way to do it—fast, because whoever does it will have first-mover advantage, and in this world that counts for an awful lot. We are very well positioned to be that company."

But it turned out that Aetna was also preoccupied with digesting the large acquisitions it had made when it acquired U.S. Healthcare and Prudential Healthcare to reach its critical scale. The obstacles of post-merger consolidation, combined with pressures to run the business in the face of all the ongoing changes in the health care arena, proved too much for Huber to orchestrate all at once. The price of the company stock plummeted, and Huber was forced to resign.

Richard Thoman was president and CEO of Xerox, and on the road to being chairman, when he resigned under board pressure in May 2000. It would be hard to identify someone better trained to run a global company. With degrees in economics from the finest Swiss universities, plus a Ph.D. from the Fletcher School of Law and Diplomacy at Tufts University, Thoman had held senior positions at American Express and RJR Nabisco and had been chief financial officer at IBM. In June 1999, he presented a compelling picture to me of the need to thrust an old-line company that made copying machines into the new economy. He talked about the critical importance not just of generating information, but also of sorting it, transferring it, preserving it. "I believe that knowledge is the most critical business asset," he said. "And the striking thing is that over half of it is in people's heads, so when they walk out the door, the knowledge goes with them. Companies spend billions of dollars on technology and have given little organized thought to where the knowledge resides, how to share it, how to keep it when people leave. We intend to be in the middle of the revolution to enhance the use and the retention of knowledge." To hear him talk, Xerox would become an icon of the new economy, with a new generation of high-powered digital copying and printing machines, and take its place alongside Intel and Microsoft and Dell Computer as a company that would help define today's information revolution.

But, Thoman also ran into execution difficulties. It wasn't that he didn't move fast or aggressively; indeed, he reduced costs quickly, slimming the payrolls by fourteen thousand people in two years. He radically reorganized the sales force to focus on providing upgraded services. He re-aligned the organization from one based on geography to one based on large customers. He concluded alliances with Sharp, Fuji Photo Film and Microsoft. Commenting on Thoman's departure, Paul Allaire, Xerox's chairman, said that he had fully endorsed Thoman's strategy, which he and the senior management were all partners in developing. The reason for the ouster? "We haven't implemented strategies as well as we should have," said Allaire.

In late August 2000, Rebecca Mark resigned from Azurix Corporation, a company that was set up to win large concessions to manage and operate water and wastewater assets as the industry was privatized, particularly in developing countries. Azurix was formed in June 1998 and went public a year later. Enron Corporation, the principal shareholder, controlled the board. Mark had come from Enron, where she had risen to vice chairman and become one of the most visible female executives in the global arena. The story is also one of a vision that couldn't be executed.

Just a year before she resigned, I interviewed Mark in the coffee shop of the Four Seasons Hotel in Washington, D.C., where she was attending a conference. She described a super-ambitious game plan. Azurix would take on the world-wide water industry—a market estimated in the media to be on the order of $400 billion—in the same way Enron achieved such success in the global energy sphere, she said. Many of the same elements were present: pressures for governments to attract private capital to develop a natural resource; increasing consumer and industrial demand because of population pressures and urbanization; need for expert management; and so on. In addition, Mark was intent on using the Internet to quickly create a market for water equipment and technical training and information for managers, to create new billing systems and to organize procurement on an international basis. "I think we can create a new way of thinking about water and running a water industry," she told me. "The greatest problem right now in the industry is that it has a very low level of sophistication and a high degree of fragmentation. So I think we can modernize it within a very short period of time."

It was a big idea, but it built on Mark's substantial knowledge and experience in overseas markets. Nevertheless, political problems with deregulation in developing countries delayed projects, some key executives left and the stock dropped almost 45 percent in the first eight months of 2000. "Analysts said Azurix's chief problem from the outset was overpromising future results," wrote Hillary Durgin and David Owen of the *Financial Times*. "Azurix may have overestimated its ability to compete in a business that has been dominated by old competitors, is rife with political sensitivities, and requires not only huge amounts of capital but a long-term [horizon] to turn a profit." Compared to other projects in which Enron had invested, the financial return on Azurix was unacceptable to Kenneth Lay, Enron's chairman, and the person who wielded the most influence over Azurix's fate. "A lot of capital has been chewed up," he told the *Wall Street Journal* on the day Mark resigned. "I think it's best for Rebecca to start afresh."

❖ ❖ ❖

What are the lessons of the Huber, Thoman and Mark situations? In all cases, the vision was a far-reaching one but only half the equation. In Huber's case, his major talent may have been in reorienting a company and expanding it, primarily by acquisition, as opposed to "roll-up-the-sleeves" management. One of Huber's mistakes was to allow himself to be chairman, president and CEO, rather than to build a broader top-management team to implement his vision. Huber was also the victim of circumstances beyond his control —political and social forces which were changing the way health care itself needed to be delivered.

Thoman's situation illustrates something else: The dilemma of speed versus impact. For all the talk about having to make changes quickly, it is wise to remember that change ultimately entails human behavior. Thoman went for the hundred-percent solution: Do it now, do it quickly and thoroughly, and get it behind you. Was there an eighty-percent solution—take it a little slower, allow a little more slack, don't strip the gears? Maybe, but Thoman was facing huge expectations on the part of investors. He was facing stepped-up competition from Canon and Hewlett-Packard. Wall Street had expectations of a swift turnaround. Until the last minute, Thoman was supported by his board. It may have been, as in Huber's case, that given the information available at the time, together with the broader forces at play, stumbling was inevitable, and a better strategy was recognizable only in hindsight. Shortly after Thoman's departure, he admitted that although he had pushed through a massive reorganization a year earlier than planned, the morale of the organization was destroyed. "I clearly did not get enough Xerox people to understand it was going to work the way they wanted," he told Pamela

Moore of *Business Week*. "You could argue that I was tone deaf to a degree around people's concerns simply because I was worried that if we slowed down we would never get there. I felt that we did not have the luxury of changing over a five-year period."

For Rebecca Mark, the vision may have been too grandiose and too reliant on many business and political factors coming together. On the other hand, she came from a culture—Enron—where she and others had been highly successful in mounting difficult mega-projects, and she had every reason to believe she could change the world again. I recall her words to Yale students when she came to New Haven in October 1997: "We at Enron have a mentality of taking a good idea and putting some money behind it. You can't create that kind of environment without an extraordinary sense of vision. We like to dream very big," she said. "We have a saying around Enron that we don't just like to create our own rules; we like to create our own game. We like to change the environment so radically that we force the rest of the industry to move toward what we are doing and to have to see the world in an entirely new way."

Huber, Thoman, and Mark all show that while vision is a prerequisite for being a great CEO, it is the failure to execute well that gets chief executives into trouble. Sometimes it's not enough speed, and sometimes it's too much of it; sometimes it's failure to follow through; sometimes it's not having the right people in the right places; sometimes the trends go against you; sometimes the vision may simply be too grand. As the record shows, even highly experienced and skilled CEOs can crash.

In fact, we may well be entering the "era of execution," as opposed to the "era of vision." Brent Schendler of *Fortune* put it well when he wrote,

> As exciting as the past five years have been, the next decade will mainly be one of painting by numbers—realizing the potential of broadband and wireless, beefing up the infrastructure, implementing new, networked-based entertainment, information and commerce services and otherwise fulfilling what [Bill] Gates and [Andy] Grove and other technovisionaries have already sketched out for us.

> Schendler then quotes Peter Drucker.

> This is the third or fourth time in American history when we had all this emphasis on the 'genius CEO.' The last time was in the 1920s, and before that in the 1880s. That always is the sign of a big economic transition. But it isn't going to last, because the transition to the information economy has already happened.

Perhaps so. But eras don't end so suddenly. For years to come we will demand CEOs with bold visions and CEOs who can execute with great skill. Few will be able to fulfill our expectations for both at the same time.

6

Shareholders and Stakeholders

"I look at shareholder value as the result of several things," said Unisys chairman Lawrence Weinbach. "To me, if you take care of your people and your people then take care of your customers, your shareholders win. The vision of the company is to increase shareholder value and what I tell everyone here is, shareholder value is the result of what we call our three-legged stool. If we get it right with customers, employees, reputation—then shareholders win. If we get it wrong, they lose. I'm very mindful of shareholder value, but I don't look at it as the single reason I'm in business. I think of it as the result of what we've been able to accomplish."

Since the rise of national firms in the United States at the end of the nineteenth century, there have been two conflicting philosophies concerning the purpose of the corporation. One says that the sole role of a business organization is to enrich its shareholders. This idea has often been embraced by Anglo-Saxon countries, but rarely elsewhere. In the United States in particular, the shareholder emphasis reached a feverish pitch in the 1980s, when swashbuckling leveraged-buyout firms dismantled one company after another in an effort to unlock immediate shareholder value while giving scant attention to the fate of a company's employees or of surrounding communities. The contending theory about the purpose of a company takes a broader view, asserting that a corporation needs to concern itself not only with its shareholders, but also with other "stakeholders," who include customers, employees, suppliers and even communities. This more holistic view has been especially prevalent in Europe and Japan for over a century. In the 1980s, for instance, Europe and Japan prided themselves on fostering a different kind of capitalism from that in the United States—one which was more inclusive, more stable and more caring.

Given the last few years of extraordinary activity by an ever wider range of investors in the stock market, it would seem that "shareholder capitalism" ought to be more intense than ever, not just in the United States but in the many countries where market philosophies have taken hold. You would think that CEOs would be totally obsessed with how the stock market rates them day to day, and that they would gear all their policies to this end. However, the actual picture is more complex. Of course, increasing profitability and shareholder value constitute the major responsibility of any CEO, and they all realize that ultimately this is the standard against which they will be measured. What's important, however, is not whether creating value for shareholders is the ultimate goal but how and over what period of time that objective is achieved.

While the shareholder–stakeholder controversy is an old one, it is worth reexamining, because in the new economy the boundaries of commercial organizations are beginning to disappear. In the industrial age, a firm could be defined by its physical and human assets—the factories it owned and the people on its payroll, for example. A large number of old-line companies were vertically integrated; that is, automobile companies, steel firms and the like owned their own sources of raw materials because they found it more efficient than to buy supplies from third parties. Today, however, companies are no longer relatively self-contained organizations. They specialize in what they do best, and either outsource the rest, or create alliances and partnerships with other companies to handle all the noncritical activities they once did in-house. Horizontal links are replacing vertical ones. As Jack Welch says, your back office should be someone else's front office— meaning that if another company specializes in something that you are doing only as a support activity, it is probably better at it than you are because that is its primary business. You should therefore subcontract to that company and devote your own resources to what you do best and where you add the most value.

In this environment, the new business model looks more and more like an open network; it is a model based on the idea that a huge amount of interaction between a company and *all* of its constituencies will create the maximum value possible. For a CEO, moreover, keeping the company competitive entails not only close association with various constituencies but also managing their interaction in such a way that the company is more than the sum of its individual parts. For example, it is not enough just to get a precise reading on what a customer wants; you must also trigger a chain reaction down to the supply subcontractors so that the product is automatically assembled to the customer's requirements whenever that customer places an order. All along the way, employees should be learning how to get even closer to customers and further perfect the system of flawless custom-tailoring and quick delivery. In this way, more value—more speed, lower cost, and enhanced sales and service—is extracted at every stage of the process. A similar case can be made for integration with suppliers, who need to work closely with producers to create the necessary innovations and efficiencies. The critical role of employees needs no elaboration, but the importance of links to the community may at first appear remote from the company's objectives, yet these ties are essential not only to retention of customers and employees but also to the company's general reputation.

The dilemma for a CEO is stark and possibly irresolvable. Creating value today rests on establishing strong links with a wide range of constituencies, which requires taking a long-term view. Meanwhile, financial markets are more riveted on short-term results than ever, and investors have become merciless in their quarterly referendums on a CEO's performance.

❖ ❖ ❖

Let's take a look at how CEOs think about some of their constituencies, starting with customers. Yes, business has always been about customers—What's the point of creating a product or service if no one wants to buy it?—but it is becoming harder than ever for companies to keep them. As regulatory and trade barriers have fallen around the world, many more companies have entered the game. For many industries, such as automobiles, aircraft and electronics, industry estimates show that there is massive production overcapacity, sometimes by 30 percent; this leads to too much supply searching for too little demand. Competition has also been aggravated by the Internet, which has greatly empowered customers by giving them access to more information about what they are purchasing, including the ability to easily compare prices. Consumers have also come to expect more customized and efficient service, and on-line consumers can switch brand loyalty with a click of the mouse. All this is true whether the customer is a retail consumer or another business.

The most successful executives see customers not just as people or organizations to sell to, but as sources of knowledge that are essential to a company's business. They can and should be partners in anticipating the products and services that will be required in the future. Companies need their frank and continuous feedback in order to create, distribute and service top-of-the-line customized products; in this sense, customers are the key to remaining competitive. The more intimate a company's relationship with a customer, the better the sharing of knowledge.

One CEO who has achieved phenomenal success by showering attention on his customers is Michael Dell. I met him in his company headquarters, a nondescript box building in Round Rock, Texas, just north of Austin. For most of my other interviews, I had been met in the reception area by someone from the CEO's office who escorted me to the executive suite. As I sat in Dell's vast lobby, marveling at the sense of space and the number of people, most of them very young, coming and going at a rapid pace, I was suddenly conscious of someone standing beside me. I looked up to see Dell himself, who had come out to get me, and we walked together to a small conference room on the periphery of the floor.

Dell began his career when, as a teenager, he learned to take apart an Apple computer and discovered that he could order the components and assemble a machine for much less than Apple's sale price. In his first year of college at the University of Texas—which turned out to be his last year of formal education—he figured out that he could make computers to order by adding customized features, and eliminate the middlemen by selling directly to purchasers, many of whom were his friends. It was to become a business model that thrived even more when e-commerce came along. As the business grew from a room in his dormitory to one selling a million dollars' worth of computers each day—in 1999 Dell was the top personal computer retailer on the Web— Dell's "mass customization" became the new standard both for manufacturing and the provision of services to computer buyers.

Michael Dell's starting point is finding out precisely what his customer wants. He makes it exceedingly easy for someone to specify the type and specific features of the computer he desires. Armed with this information, the company can deliver a custom-made product in record time. Dell's system allows the company to keep minimal inventories, and all human resources can be devoted to increasing the efficiency of the assembly and delivery of the made-to-order product. This kind of extreme customer orientation extends to after-sales service. The same kinds of linkages extend from Dell to equipment suppliers, with joint teams working to make production and delivery of supplies cheaper and faster. Dell refers to the entire system as "virtual integration." "We try to get so close to the customer that the only thing closer would be a kind of mental telepathy," he told me with a smile. "You think you want a computer and it just shows up."

Dell keeps refining his customercentric approach. "You have a series of interactions with the customer—some on-line, some on the phone, some face to face—and they are all intertwined to create the optimal mix of mutual understanding between us and the customer," he said. "Even as Internet communications become more widespread, the human element becomes more important—maybe less frequent, but more important because you can resolve the routine problems on-line and save the human communication for the tougher, more unique challenges." The company now creates Web pages, specific to each customer, to provide extensive information about that customer's order. It has also developed software that integrates Dell Computer systems into a corporate client's software systems so that when a company orders from Dell, not only is a chain reaction begun between Dell and its suppliers, but the customer's own systems—approvals, budgets, inventories—swing into action, too. Dell's people also stay close to their customers, some even working on the customers' premises. To illustrate the point, Dell described to me how the company services GE. Dell personnel are in the plants to ensure that the computers run smoothly. They aren't just making house calls; they work there. And while they are at it, they work with GE engineers to design the modifications to the systems that GE will want in the future.

This obsession with getting closer to customers is becoming more common. Frederick Smith of FedEx has made it easier for retail and corporate customers to transport everything from letters to equipment—FedEx handles over 3.2 million daily shipments, utilizing some six hundred aircraft and forty thousand trucks—faster, more reliably and cheaper. Federal Express was the first transportation company to provide software to its corporate customers so that they could fill out their own shipping forms and then later track shipments automatically with a single number. Today two-thirds of FedEx's customers use the Internet or their own private computer networks to arrange their shipping and to track packages.

"One of our primary objectives has been to help our business customers take advantage of the global economy by exploiting all its efficiencies in finding supplies and customers," said Smith. "Our job is to take a tremendous amount of time out of the production process by streamlining the entire inventory process. This entails moving supplies in smaller amounts, increasing the speed at which inventory can be turned over—and all this relies on the customer's being able to know where the inventory is at all times. This means his being able to see it, to track it. This way he feels secure that it will be delivered just in time and he knows he'll have it just when he needs it, just as if it were in his plant. Inventory at rest is an outdated concept. We're in an era where fast-cycle distribution is critical."

The end result is more than a revolution in logistics or a way for companies to reduce inventory costs, important as all that is. The shortening of inventory cycles means that manufacturers can better serve customers' rapidly changing needs and preferences. It reverses the trend, prevalent just a decade or so ago, whereby manufacturers got progressively farther away from customers because of all the intermediaries between them, and because of the time lag involved in updating the portfolio of products the customers required.

As with Dell Computer Corporation, the line between FedEx and its customers often isn't easy to identify, so great is the interaction and intimacy. For companies like Apple Computer, Hewlett-Packard, National Semiconductor and Cisco Systems, FedEx coordinates the global supply chain— helping customers find components anywhere in the world, facilitating the assembly of finished products and delivering the product to the ultimate consumer. Fujitsu, the Japanese computer maker, is a good example. In the mid-1990s it was losing out to competitors because customers had to wait ten days between the time they ordered a laptop and the time it arrived at their door. Fujitsu then decided to turn over much of its computerized distribution system to FedEx. Today FedEx flies in parts from Asia to its own warehouses in Memphis, where they are configured into laptops and shipped out the next day. Customer waiting time from beginning to end is five days or less. FedEx orchestrates the entire process.

FedEx helped companies like National Semiconductor Corporation to reduce overall logistics costs, as a percent of revenues, by some 30 percent in the 1990s. It realizes that many companies who want to reduce inventory costs need to radically redesign their entire manufacturing processes, too—all the more so in a global economy. The company has therefore been training salespeople to be able to help clients do just that.

Michael Armstrong is also preoccupied with building a customercentric organization. "We are in the early stages of a communications revolution," he said. "But this revolution isn't about AT&T or any of the other companies trying to make it happen. This revolution is about consumers. These days you have to ask, What is the real value that you bring to the customer? You have to eliminate the processes that have no value—the costs that add nothing to what is most useful to the customer. The paperwork, or the distribution, or the service system, or many of the other things you spend money on—you think they are of value to the customer but they are not, and someone else who can supply the pure value without the added costs will take your business away."

He gave me an example. "Today when you get a phone bill, you get call detail. It tells you where you called, how long you were on the phone, what the originating number is, what the completion number is. Call detail costs us $250 million dollars a year. We think of that as a service. It costs us $50 million dollars to produce it, the cost of switches. It costs us $200 million to answer the phone on questions about it. If we put that all up on the Web, which we have done, we will give customers themselves the ability to sort all the information the way they want it. How many times last month did I call Jeff Garten? All you have to do is hit the mouse and it sorts it. Or say, instead of seeing it in chronological order, I'd rather see it sorted by states, or in the order of the dollar amounts. So let's give people the ability themselves, rather than paying two hundred million to staff for what I used to call a wonderful service, when in fact it's really a cost."

✧ ✧ ✧

Many CEOs, particularly in the technology business, believe that customer service is synonymous with providing a "total solution" to a customer's needs. As the complexity of various technologies has increased, customers need simple ways to use them and seamless ways to link them. As technology companies differentiate themselves by becoming ever more specialized, however, no firm can deliver from in-house resources everything a customer needs. Many corporations are therefore taking on the role of "solutions provider"— that is, coordinating the work of several firms in order to deliver one product.

Motorola is a good example. "What our customers want are solutions to complex problems," Christopher Galvin explained to me. "They want the pieces of the communications puzzles and the software puzzles and the architectural puzzles to fit together to meet their needs. They don't really care about the uniqueness of the technology they use. They just want plain answers. So we restructured the company these past few years around this concept—a radical change from the old culture in which we prided ourselves on having the most unique technology. It's all about listening to what the customer wants, not selling just what you have. And what people are saying is, 'I don't want to buy just the box from you. I want you to put the software in it. I want you to install it.' They might even say, 'Run the system for me, get the backup electricity organized, manage the technical people.' And what we're saying is, 'We'll get it all set up for you. We'll bring you the solution."

"Suppose the customer wanted the Internet on a wireless system. Someone has to build the handset that has a screen on it, and the screen has to contain a microbrowser. You then have to have someone organize a server, and so forth. In the old days we'd walk in and say, 'Let me show you my handset, it's the niftiest one you can find.' And the customer would buy it. And then he'd have to go somewhere else to get the software code written. And somewhere else to get the phone connection hooked up. And to someone else to integrate it into the rest of his communications system, and then test it. Now we do all that—often with partners or subcontractors like Cisco Systems, for example. We get the end-to-end solution done."

Michael Bonsignore is also enthusiastic about providing solutions. "Honeywell is uniquely positioned to be of long-term value to customers because we have become much more than a vendor," he told me. "We are really a solutions partner. We don't go to these customers anymore and talk to them about selling our products. What we try to understand is the nature of their total problem in all its details. And then we come back to them with a solution—which may or may not involve a preponderance of our products."

He described how and why Chevron recently awarded Honeywell total responsibility for process automation at its huge facility in Richmond, California. "When we started, we didn't try to sell them anything," he said. "We went out and did an audit of that refinery against world-class business practices that we had seen around the world. And we gave them a report in which we said, 'This is how your refinery stacks up against the best in class.' Then we made a proposal to close any gaps. We had to think in terms of assuming responsibility for the total automation needs of a refinery. We didn't go gathering up a truckload of Honeywell equipment. We had to think much broader, because the refinery was asking a big question: 'How are we going to save a dollar a barrel over the next few years and what hardware and software do we need to get the job done?' We were in effect a systems integrator— a manager for the whole project, which may involve many subcontractors, each with much different expertise. This is the first time in history that a major oil company has ever out-sourced its entire automation responsibility for a refinery. That would have been heresy five years ago."

Victor Fung, chairman of Li & Fung, transformed his trading company from one that simply matched buyers and sellers to a "solutions" company as well. Founded in 1906 by his grandfather in Guangzhou to bring goods in and out of China, the company was floundering in the mid-1970s when Victor and his brother William were called back from their respective teaching careers at MIT and Harvard to reinvigorate the firm. Instead of being just matchmakers, they decided to help corporations like The Limited and Reebok integrate their entire manufacturing strategies in Asia. They saw a problem that clients had—how to coordinate all the necessary manufacturing activities throughout a huge region—and they solved it by utilizing their talents and networks. The client company would give them sketches and ideas of the fashions it was thinking about for the next season. Li & Fung would take the sketches and produce a variety of samples of what the product might look like, using textiles, weaving and dyes not just from sources all over Asia but from some thirty countries around the world. Once the client agreed on what he wanted, then the trading firm would orchestrate

the production process, overseeing everything from production schedules to quality control—indeed, the entire
supply chain. "We hand hold them through the process,"
said Fung. "We are the ultimate outsourcer, almost a virtual
factory." Now Fung is providing solutions not only to western companies looking to find supplies in Asia but also to
companies in Asia wishing to import materials and components from around the world.

For companies like Dell, FedEx, Honeywell, Motorola and
Li & Fung, attention to customers goes beyond customer service as it used to be practiced. What emerges is a kind of sym-
biosis in which information flows both ways and buyers and
sellers merge. In the old industrial model, there was a one-
way flow from producer to consumer. This is what mass production was about—"Produce it, and they will buy it." Now
consumers want and expect more. In fact, the more innovative companies are giving customers tools to design their own
products. Procter & Gamble's Web site, for instance, enables
customers to create their own cosmetics—and even their own
packaging. Nancy Peretsman of Allen & Company predicts
that consumers could eventually put out bids for telephone
contracts that meet their specific needs instead of settling for
any of the packages that AT&T or Sprint or MCI might offer.
"Ultimately, I might look at my profile and say, I need a cellular package for x hours, I want x number of lines connected
to the Internet, I don't use long distance, I'm never home
during the day so don't charge me for day usage, and so on,"
she said. "Consumers are going to want choices that make
sense for them, and on an individual basis they will want to
trade off price, convenience, quality in a way that meets their

precise requirements." These new possibilities to meet consumer needs require a new mind-set for CEOs and the companies they run, an endless quest to determine precisely what each individual customer wants and how it can be efficiently delivered and serviced. The mind of the CEO needs to get into the mind of his customers.

❖ ❖ ❖

A second set of stakeholders is the people in the company itself. Finding, retaining, and motivating top talent elicits considerable passion from the CEOs as a group. Time and again I heard that there was "a war on" for talent. Compared with the emphasis on people, the word "technology" hardly arose.

The effort to hire and retain talent has reached almost indescribable proportions. In a world where so much value has been placed on the softer assets and skills—creative ideas, ability to put together and manage teams, and so on—talent is relatively scarce. In addition, the high-technology industries and the new Internet start-ups have used either cash or generous stock-option plans to offer unprecedented opportunities for employees to amass wealth in a short time frame. Money hasn't been the only factor; the New Economy has held out a vision of a more rewarding way of working—free of bureaucracy, and more conducive to liberating personal entrepreneurial talents. Companies with successful track records for finding and keeping the best people rely on a variety of devices: fostering a sense of community; investing heavily in training and mentoring; providing a wide range of interesting jobs within a company so that employees won't have to look outside; giving exceptional attention to welcoming new employees from acquired firms; being a market leader and instilling great pride in the workforce; providing services like child care.

Kenneth Chenault of American Express discusses something that all big companies face, and he is realistic about the problem and the solution. "There is a brain drain from large companies to small and medium-sized entrepreneurial entities," he told me. "The battle is going to be for ideas and non-traditional thinking. If you expect to get all those ideas and non-traditional thinking in a large company, you are kidding yourself. And my personal view is that the large company that understands how to form partnerships and alliances with those types of people. . . is going to have a major advantage because many of those types of individuals want to work on a very large stage. They just don't want to deal with all the stuff that goes with it."

Chenault did not specify what form these partnerships and alliances could take. But such arrangements are easier said than done. It's hard enough to link two large organizations where the balance of power might be more-or-less equal. But the cultural and psychological questions inherent in asymmetrical relationships between big organizations and small entrepreneurial teams will require deft handling to succeed.

Michael Dell deals with a personnel situation that has become increasingly relevant these days: How to motivate employees who have become fabulously rich. "The good news is that our business has pretty lucrative rewards, and we have a history of sharing rewards with our teams. But there is a related challenge where you get to a point where a certain percentage of the people have made so much money that it's not even other jobs in the company that excite them," he said. "At the core you've got to think about what really motivates people, what gets them excited, and you need compelling and exciting projects that keep those folks engaged. You've got to be kind of loving them and paying a lot of attention to them. Being part of something interesting and something that has impact is much more important to them." One of Dell's mechanisms for opening new opportunities for his best people is his strategy of segmentation. As soon as a part of his business shows real promise, he splits it off into a new line and puts someone in charge. That provides a chance for a talented person not just to lead but also to expand the segment into a big enough business so that it is once again segmented into others.

"I believe that the key is the quality of our people, and always will be," Henry Paulson told me. "If we are able to hire the best people, which is increasingly a big challenge, pay them well, motivate them, help manage their careers to make this an attractive spot, put the people where the opportunities are—if we can do all that, we are going to stay on top, and if we can't, we won't. No matter what happens with technology or globalization or anything else, this won't change. But I can tell you this: there is going to be a huge fight for talent. Just a huge fight. And I am increasingly thinking about our competitors as anyone, no matter what industry, who is competing with me to hire the best people."

✧ ✧ ✧

CEOs are uniformly committed to making sure that their companies are active and constructively involved in their communities—yet another constituency. Virtually all CEOs would endorse a comment from Lawrence Weinbach of Unisys. "I believe business has a social responsibility," he said. "That commitment isn't to full employment, but . . . in the communities that your people work you ought to help create an environment where you can develop and attract the kind of people you need. You have a responsibility to customers, suppliers, local educational institutions." Michael Bonsignore underscored a similar idea with respect to his overseas operations when he said, "The idea of taking from a foreign investment and giving nothing back to the community is history."

Some chief executives make a direct link between social responsibility and the morale and loyalty of their employees. Jorma Ollila ruminates about the culture of Nokia. "People want their company to be a good citizen," he told me. "They want it to show true concern for the world, for the environment. They want it to have a social conscience. There is now a very clear expectation, which is coming from political life as well as from our own employees, that companies will have to have a soul—a state of mind which represents a social conscience. That's very different from the early 1990s, when we were applauded just for employing more people. There is a very high expectation, something I did not see when I started as CEO in 1992."

Consumers are increasingly swayed in their purchase patterns by the overall image of a company, and Martin Sorrell, too, sees social responsibility as an important part of a company's brand. "Part of the brand will relate to trust," he said when we met in his New York offices. "Companies that we trust will have a huge competitive advantage. It has become in a company's commercial interest to be seen as a good citizen. It's another differentiator. There are positive benefits to being a good citizen; it's not avoiding a negative, and it's not a neutral position." Royal Dutch/Shell's Mark Moody-Stuart told me, "We've done surveys of our customers which indicate that people like to buy from companies they feel comfortable with. Frankly, they like to deal with companies they wouldn't mind their friends seeing them buy from. I see it our role to deliver what the customer wants and deliver it in a way they find acceptable. But this is not some woolly philanthropic thing. This is real, because we in our company are part of the same society. We worry about the same things our customers do. We may not have the solutions, but we're working on them and want to be seen working on them."

❖ ❖ ❖

Jürgen Schrempp tries to come to grips with the balance between a focus on short-term shareholder value and other needs. "There is a tendency in Germany to put social responsibility before shareholder responsibility. Is the tendency right? I think it can go too far. But then flying over the Atlantic there can be a tendency which is also not right. It's the same tendency that you see in South America or Asia. . . . We [CEOs] shouldn't be short-term thinkers. We should be medium and long-term thinkers. We have to deliver results in the short-term, but we must not eat our seed, as many do at the moment. We have a major battle with our American friends [at Chrysler]. The year 2000 will be a challenge. I want them to get me the profits. But I'm saying at the same time, 'I want to continue expanding the range of products, I want you to be in the lead as far as environment and safety issues are concerned.' Then they say, 'Hang on, you cannot ask for both at the same time.' And I say, 'Yes I can.' It is the [prerogative] of top management to balance short-term and medium- and long-term goals. That's our job. The job of a leader is to bring them into balance."

Said BP's John Browne, "I know some people assume our interest lies solely in the maximization of short-term profit. I'm a great believer in having to deliver a highly competitive return to our shareholders every quarter. But I see no trade-off between the short term and the long. Companies can only flourish when they serve their customers and their communities and when their employees feel valuable and productive," he said. "These are the conditions in which we can best pursue our business."

Of course, there is often a big gulf between knowing what to do and having the intentions to do them, on one hand, and being able to achieve your goals on the other. Again, the Ford Motor Company is perhaps the most poignant example. Before the tire recall, William Ford put his finger on the problem when it came to his passionate environmental goals. "The big issue, of course, is practicality," he said. "How fast can we achieve our social goals while still creating value shareholders expect? And at what cost?" After the tire recall became a major crisis for the company, leading a company in a holistic way became even more difficult. On September 11, 2000, the company, worried about its sagging share price, announced that it was buying back $5 billion of its stock. Consumer groups could have been excused for wondering whether, at such a time, Ford should have been devoting more of its resources to them. The ability of William Ford to continue to position his corporation as a leader in social responsibility was being severely tested. At a September 14 news conference he said, "The . . . path we're on and the path that I am personally on is not going to waiver for the next twenty, thirty years, however long I am here. . . . Early on people asked me is this flavor of the month and I said no, it's flavor of a career and flavor of a lifetime."

PART THREE

LEADERSHIP IN SOCIETY

7

The Biggest Blindspot

B y now it should be clear that CEOs have their hands full in responding to the rise of the Internet, the intensification of globalization, and the excruciating dilemmas and trade-offs of running big companies. I could stop here and conclude that their task is prohibitively difficult and becoming more so. That is certainly true. However, in this and the next two chapters I will identify even more tough issues for CEOs—those that they do not recognize clearly or urgently enough.

✧ ✧ ✧

CEOs want to be seen as good citizens, and they make substantial efforts in that direction. They point to their heightened commitments to protect the environment and lift labor standards in developing countries. They talk about the range of their efforts to advise government officials and to participate in trade groups that make recommendations about social and economic policy. Still, they seem uncomfortable with the growing pressures for global corporations to go where governments now tread. They argue that they have enough concerns in running their companies; they do not want to be held accountable for policies they may not be able to implement and goals they may not be able to achieve. Nor do they want to be caught in the crosshairs of political controversy.

All this is understandable. Yet these leaders are badly underestimating the rise of global problems that will affect their firms and the environment in which they operate. They are failing to see the gap between society's expectations of what they should do and what they seem prepared to do. They face three kinds of risk.

First, the trend toward freer trade and investment around the world could falter unless many social and economic problems and inequalities are addressed, and unless a sound regulatory structure is put in place to deal with such matters as trade, finance, economic development, cyberspace, the environment and labor. Capitalism requires a strong foundation of rules and institutions, and in the international global arena these are sorely lacking. Unless CEOs play a leading role in fashioning sensible pro-market arrangements, there will either be increasing chaos in world markets or ill-conceived governmental regulations—or, most likely, some combination of both.

Second, as noted in the previous chapter, companies that are not seen as progressive leaders on social problems will be far less attractive to talented employees, who are interested not only in financial remuneration but in doing work they can be proud of—nor are such companies likely to attract high-quality customers and consumers. Third, unless CEOs construe their mandate in a broader societal context, they and their companies risk becoming targets of resentment for public-interest groups and ordinary citizens who see globalization as a negative trend.

All these pressures are sure to increase. The phenomenal business expansion in the United States, which has had a powerful spillover effect abroad and has lifted the entire world economy, cannot continue indefinitely. When the downturn comes, CEOs and their companies could find themselves in more tenuous political positions. In the United States, at least, this is all the more true given the number of citizens—half of all households by many estimates—who are depending on the stock market for their future economic security. And we've seen only the beginning. The combination of the Internet and globalization will continue to shift the location of production toward developing countries. This will lead to more political and social anxieties among workers and social activists in the richer countries and also in emerging markets, where billions of people will see their traditional cultures disrupted.

It's not just a recession that could be the cause of increased public frustration with big business. Amid the greatest economic expansion in American history, anxiety is already building about the overwhelming role of markets in society. "Prosperity isn't enough to protect economic openness," wrote columnist Virginia Postrel in the *New York Times*.

> . . . It's easy to take good times for granted. . . During good times it's a lot easier to sell contempt for materialism and consumerism and for open economic policies that make them possible. The New Left, after all, defined itself in the Port Huron Statement not as the voice of the poor but as a movement of the disillusioned and discontented middle

class, 'people of this generation, bred in at least modest comfort.' More recently, the young activists campaigning against global trade are not complaining about economic sluggishness. To the contrary they see growth as the problem.

A third problem is the sheer number of new and pressing issues that confront both governments and business executives, ranging from the possible effects of global warming to the implications of genetic engineering to the rise of international crime syndicates. All of these will complicate the functioning of markets and raise near-intractable questions about the rules of the game: What are they? Who makes them? How well do they work?

Here we shall take a look at some of the pressures chief executives face in dealing with society at large. The next chapter explores some of the activities CEOs ought to contemplate above and beyond what they are already doing. Following that, we'll look at what American CEOs, in particular, should be thinking about and doing.

✧ ✧ ✧

Since the late nineteenth century in the United States, when the railroads and telegraph helped firms like Coca-Cola and Procter & Gamble to expand from coast to coast, the large corporation has been one of the defining institutions in society. In Germany, Japan and elsewhere, companies like Deutsche Bank and Mitsubishi Corporation have played pivotal roles in their countries for over a century. In the three decades after World War II, large companies around the globe took on ever-increasing social obligations. Using their size, scale and resources, they provided secure jobs, good wages and guaranteed pensions, not to mention generous support for economic development in their communities, including contributions for culture and charities. Leaders of these companies had almost unlimited discretion to set the goals and priorities of their organizations, as well as to allocate resources to objectives not directly relating to shareholder value. In the United States especially, where relatively limited government has always been the prevailing philosophy, large companies played a partnership role in the public sector. In fact, companies provided so many services and such a high level of security that a private welfare state was possible without the expansion of government power and expenditure.

A lot has changed in this country and others. Under the pressure of international competition, companies have increased their preoccupation with the bottom line. The implicit contract between management and labor—the two-way loyalty—has disappeared in the United States and is in the process of substantially loosening up in Europe and Japan. The world has moved from managerial capitalism, where CEOs and their top management had the ability to allocate their companies' profits with relative freedom, to what might be called "investor capitalism," where shareholders exercise substantial control over how corporations distribute their profits.

In today's New Economy, governments are being pared down, market-oriented policies are gaining ground, and the norms for CEOs and their companies are changing. Where is the balance between private and public interests settling, and is that the right place? What do CEOs think their responsibilities should be when it comes to labor, education and the environment? What do CEOs want their roles to be in developing global rules and institutions to guide society in this new century?

✧ ✧ ✧

These are potentially explosive questions. Although any society wants some agreed sharing of roles among business, government and citizens, the balance of power and influence among these groups is in great flux in all countries today. The uncertainties are compounded in the global arena, where there are not only few rules but vast disparities in wealth and expectations between people of different histories, cultures, and economic and political systems. "There is a worldwide effort to find the right balance between business and government," said Franklin Raines, formerly the director of the Office of Management and Budget in the Clinton administration and now chairman and CEO of Fannie Mae, the world's largest financial institution devoted to housing finance. "And through much of the century, we haven't gotten the balance right around the world. While spending an enormous amount of time trying to figure out how to divide up the pie, we didn't grow the pie as much as it could have been grown, and therefore we're having these intense battles." Raines also put his finger on an endemic problem everywhere. "Deep down in a lot of people in government there is sort of a confiscatory urge. [They] will convince private capital to come in and then [they'll] grab it and go back to command and control. There's a tough issue here: How does government encourage markets, encourage private capital, but not get into micromanagement in a way that ultimately drives away the private capital?"

CEOs face a number of constraints in dealing with their part of this balance. For understandable competitive reasons, they are reluctant to engage in activities that do not contribute to their companies' profitability. They have little time to spare for anything else. Whatever broader role they are called on to play, they fear that they can never do enough, for the more expansive their efforts, the higher the expectations are raised; in other words, they worry about being held accountable for commitments they cannot deliver.

Even so, virtually all CEOs recognize the obligation to be leaders in civil society. Most CEOs believe that they are socially responsible. They emphasize the importance of helping wherever they can, of shaping the environment, of knowing what works in practice and of the need to contribute their expertise to global problems. John Browne of BP, Mark Moody-Stuart of Royal Dutch/Shell, William Ford and others talk about the strides they are making on environmental issues, setting internal targets for emissions, publicizing these goals, submitting to outside audits—all of these being measures that are revolutionary compared to corporate behavior just a few years ago. American CEOs, in particular, point to China as an example of progress they are bringing to emerging markets.

Honeywell's Michael Bonsignore is proud of what his company has done in China. Elected chairman of the U.S.–China Business Council in 1999, Bonsignore leads a company that entered China in 1986 and has since provided a range of on-site services ranging from the installation of safety controls in Chinese mines to providing technology to improve air-traffic control. Some of Honeywell's activities have involved strategic partnerships with companies like the

National Petroleum Corporation. In August 2000, Honeywell set up its first dot-com outside the United States in conjunction with the Chinese Ministry of Construction, Tsinghua University and the Hong Kong Productivity Council. The objective was to offer information on the Web on procurement in the construction industry, project leads and on-line training for customers like the China State Construction (Shenzhen) Design Company, and the China Construction Third Engineering Bureau.

"I think that companies like ours have been and continue to be great role models as social reform is going on around the world," Bonsignore told me. "They can help create the conditions which make economic prosperity easier rather than harder. They can show the way with regard to the best practices and the highest standards for respecting the individual in the workplace. When I sit down with our Chinese employees, the one thing that comes through to me over and over is how proud they are to work for our firm, because of our standards, our integrity, the way we treat them, and the way we deal with customers. And I believe we will have an influence on future generations of leaders. That's why I have been a proponent of engagement with China—not because I'm less unhappy with them about nuclear proliferation or human rights or other things, but I just say to myself, 'It's absolutely essential that we share some of our social values so that we begin to change how people think and behave. If you want to call that cultural imperialism, so be it.' "

PepsiCo's Roger Enrico feels the same way. Pepsi was one of the first American companies to invest in China in the 1970s. It sells both soft drinks and snack foods, such as potato chips. It has competed with Coca-Cola and, more recently, with local soft drink manufacturers for Chinese consumers. Its visibility in the Middle Kingdom was enhanced in 1999 when the company signed a five-year contract to sponsor China's national soccer league. Enrico has also been a vocal proponent of normalized trade with China. In fact, I first met him in 1998 at a meeting of the World Economic Forum in Singapore. He was chairing a panel of which I was a member, on why China should be allowed into the World Trade Organization. I asked him if I could argue against Beijing's entry, just to get a debate going. Enrico said he would be delighted to mediate the controversy that would ensue. In our interview, he said, "A lot of people would argue—and I tend to agree—that running a successful company is the most important thing I could do not just for the company but for the broader world. Take China, for example. The things we and other American companies do there are so far superior to what China has had in the past. There's more democracy in our company and among our employees there. There is open competition among our Chinese employees and PepsiCo employees around the world, which opens the horizons for Chinese workers and makes them see that they can be world class. We're bringing not just capital to China but a modern operating mentality, which is invaluable to China's workforce."

✦ ✦ ✦

CEOs also understand some of the anxieties that are building up in developing countries as the global society threatens to overwhelm deeply rooted cultural values. Susan Berresford of the Ford Foundation articulated what is happening. "This is a period in which the pace and the depth and the extent of change in the world that we work in, in communities around the world, has been deeper than any that I remember. The economies have changed. The political structures have changed. The ideologies have shifted. . . . In periods of great uncertainty people search for anchors and some find the most comfortable anchors in things from the past. . . In many of the countries that we work in, including the United States, where we used to be able to work with an assumed set of values, there now has to be a discussion and a search for the adaptation of traditional values to modern needs."

She used as an example programs that try to connect human rights values—which seem to many to have emerged from the United States and Europe—to traditional religious beliefs in developing nations. "There is a need for people to find their own language and their own interpretation of what human rights may have meant in the evolution of their own cultures," she said. "Of course there are always going to be people who think their interpretations of the old values are the values, period. But they are not acknowledging that at every time there was probably a variety of interpretations of every tradition, and it has tended to be one set of views that prevailed. But if you go back to the historical records and early writings, you often find there were debates about these things, and people want to give contemporary voice to them."

She talked also about the Ford Foundation's efforts to promote folklore in India, "Not because folklore is some quaint thing that ought not be washed away by McDonald's, but because people in that country are saying that the globalized culture—the kind of homogenized international culture that creeps in or sweeps across country after country—does not feel authentic to them. All of these things connect to what I see as an enormous search for meaning and value and distinctiveness."

Richard Thoman, then president and CEO of Xerox, saw similar pressures arising. "I think there is an interesting thing happening in Europe and that's what I call the conflict between the economic and cultural agenda, on the one hand, and the political agenda on the other," he told me. "Businesses are gaining increasing global scale but at the same time there is growth in most parts of Europe of a fairly localized phenomenon around language, culture—look at the Basques, the Scots, the Welsh. You see the differences that have been submerged within the nation–state for hundreds of years increasingly emerging. The problem is that you have an economic agenda which calls for bigger and bigger scale and a political agenda which places value on catering to local drives. It's a potentially combustible issue." Deutsche Bank's Rolf Breuer expressed the same concerns. "To be frank, I see a renaissance of nationalism," he said. "Look at the Balkans. Look at the Middle East. And look even at the European countries on the continent and how they are all defending their finance industries. In fact, in my view it is nationalism and not globalization that is growing fastest." Jürgen Schrempp agrees. "You will see a tremendous backlash in the twenty-first century," he told me.

Some CEOs are particularly sensitive to the inequality of wealth and income around the world, and to the implications of these disparities. "When you are thinking about free markets, the trend is our friend," said Roger Enrico. "But if that also means that government is not working so hard to balance the distribution of wealth, we have to care about that, because the fact of the matter is that we have a consumer-driven market. If there is a shrinking middle class, that's not a good thing. I worry that if current trends continue here and abroad, down the road socialism—or worse—will again be an attractive alternative."

At the World Bank, James Wolfensohn raised a host of related concerns. "The biggest challenge that the global community faces, by far, is population growth," he said. "We have just passed six billion people on the planet and we will move to eight billion in the next twenty-five to thirty years. The gap between rich and poor is increasing. These issues are not local anymore, because the world is now linked by financial systems, trade, environment, health and immigration." Technology could cut one of two ways, he said. "There is an opportunity for the developing world to fall behind another generation, or catch up a generation. The challenge is enormous, because technology itself won't be enough. There must be organization, there must be coordination among development institutions. . . . Today, for example, there is no real coordination on almost any subject. And if you get into a plethora of initiatives being taken with new technologies and it's not all brought together, you could have bedlam. On the other hand, if you can utilize technology to deliver information and knowledge to build capacity at all levels of government in developing countries—judges, customs officials, and so on—you're talking tens of thousands of people who can benefit. The potential is just monumental."

I asked every interviewee the question, "What most keeps you awake at night?" By far the largest number of responses reflected a fear of a major disruption—rarely precisely defined—in the process of globalization. Henry Paulson, Jorma Ollila, Rolf Breuer, Hiroshi Okuda, Rebecca Mark and others all said that their entire business strategies were based on the assumption of continued momentum in global economic liberalization. John Browne worried about adverse developments in the Middle East. U.S. executives Frederick Smith, Roger Enrico, and Michael Bonsignore and Asian CEOs Stan Shih, Hiroshi Okuda and Victor Fung were deeply concerned with the future of China generally, and U.S.–China relations in particular.

❖ ❖ ❖

While business leaders understand the issues, if you listen to what they say—and if you think about what they *don't* say—you can see that most of them are very careful to set limits on their political and social responsibilities. They are trying to balance a wide range of opportunities and risks, and in the end there is little enthusiasm to undertake anything that goes beyond what they are currently doing. Their views are thoughtful and subtle, but most of them approach their obligations very gingerly and with more sense of constraint than of possibility.

Richard Thoman, for one, has been a proponent of CEO leadership on some of the bigger social questions, but he believed that chief executives will have to link their activities to their specific firms, rather than play a more general role in the making of national policy. "The smart CEO will recognize that part of his own success is in creating an environment where his company and others get better results," he told me. "But it has to be done more thoughtfully and deliberately than in the old days. The old model is one in which the CEO spent a lot of time outside the company, but today's model, in which the CEO must deliver corporate performance, requires more direct linkage to your own business."

Thoman may have been reacting to the experience of working for James D. Robinson III, then chairman and CEO of American Express, in the late 1980s. Robinson became a global business statesman to such an extent that he neglected the running of Amex, which fell on hard times. He became a leading figure in promoting trade negotiations, in opening Japanese markets, in restructuring Third World debt after the Latin American financial crisis earlier in the decade. At the time, I worked for Lehman Brothers, which was then owned by Amex. The enormous time and energy Robinson poured into global affairs seemed excessive—even to someone like me who applauded the intent—especially at a time when the company was losing ground to competitors. The clear lesson is one that we have heard before in this book: first you have to be competitive and profitable. Without that, nothing else will work.

Lawrence Weinbach of Unisys advocates staying close to home in another way. I proposed a hypothetical situation to him. Suppose, I said, a U.S. president asked you to bring Unisys into a program to help students in the inner cities, to contribute money and people. What would your response be? "My notion of social responsibility would really go to the communities in which we work and therefore I believe that business has a responsibility to do what you are suggesting," he replied. "I would choose those communities where we have people. I wouldn't pick Pittsburgh because we're not there, but I'd pick Philadelphia because we're there, we have people there."

Mark Moody-Stuart of Royal Dutch/Shell is also careful when it comes to his specific social responsibilities, even though his company has gone to great lengths to be an environmental leader. Big companies ought to be willing to give their advice to governments, he says, but the overall picture of who calls the shots is not as simple as it used to be. "In trying to achieve the balance between economic and social objectives," he explained, "it is really the whole of society, including consumers, community activists, government, and our own employees that will judge us and keep us in bounds." In other words, don't get too far out in front.

Some CEOs support the proposition that they have obligations beyond managing their own companies, but they express these in personal and even somewhat casual terms, rather than as official corporate duties. "I think that it is difficult for any business leader of a major company to ignore the governmental and social issues that confront not only the market but the world at large," said Kenneth Chenault. "And what will need to happen is that leaders will increasingly take a role in some form of change. Some will be focused on education, some on the environment, some on international affairs. I would say, ten years ago that was more of a hobby. Now it's become a necessity, and will increasingly."

"I can look at having created value in the company so my shareholders are happy," Jürgen Schrempp mused. "And I've come to the conclusion that it is important but it's by far not all. I can also contribute to charity, ten thousand dollars here, ten thousand there. That's simple. Taking my own time to help [governments] in southern Africa, and make a real contribution as Jürgen Schrempp—not on official Daimler-Chrysler business—that's important to me. I take this part of the world. Others may take other parts."

Some CEOs choose their words cautiously when it comes to anything approaching a too active role for business in areas once dominated by government. In my interviews I put one question this way: "Do you think that in this market-oriented world, business leaders will play a more prominent and active role in proposing and designing regulations, or in helping to strengthen existing institutions like the World Bank or even in establishing new ones?" Rolf Breuer of Deutsche Bank answered: "I couldn't agree more that there is an obligation of business leaders to care for the wider issues," he said. "It is not enough, as maybe it was the case in the [post–World War II] years to concentrate on business only." He paused, and I felt that he had became uncomfortable. "But in these days when business is really pushing policy and politicians . . . the discussion turns to, who is driving who? That is the discussion which is on in Europe. Is it that business is driving politics or is politics still in the driver's seat? And that is a very dangerous discussion because it goes toward the fundamentals of democracy. And there are limits, and I believe you have to observe them. Business is not the decision-maker. [Business leaders] should make suggestions. They should give ideas. They should contribute everything they can. But the final decision has to be taken by someone else—namely those who are accountable to the democratic process."

Speaking to an audience at St. Anthony's College in Oxford in 1998, John Browne talked about BP's work in emerging markets, including Colombia, Russia and China. "We'll work with local authorities and others to encourage innovation and investment in new business. We'll provide training... Our responsibility is to give the communities in which we are operating the chance and the time to make the transition in ways which do not destroy those communities.... But I do want to stress the limits of the corporate role. Companies have no democratic legitimacy. It is not our role to make choices. Our role is to expand the range of choices available, in ways which may be beyond the capacity of the public authorities."

When the CEOs talked about their activities in the policymaking arena, I frequently detected a less-than-enthusiastic note. For example, Honeywell's Michael Bonsignore talked of the importance of trade associations as vehicles for CEO policy activity, but when pressed about their true effectiveness, he responded, "I don't know if 'effective' is the right word. But I keep thinking, Where would we be if we didn't have them at all?"

Andrew Grove, the chairman of Intel, hesitated when I asked him what he thought about his company's social responsibility and involvement in public policy. "Actually I'm ambivalent on the question," he said. "But ambivalence aside, we are getting more involved. We have spent over $100 million on science education—K through 12 science and technology education — and that would have been unheard of ten years ago. We have become much more involved in politics nationally and locally. There are two reasons. One is that we have become more enlightened, whatever the reason for that. And second, we have become bigger. Ten years ago we were a $2 billion company. Today we are a $30 billion company. Our impact on the communities we are in is proportionately much larger. Our potential impact on public policy should be bigger. [On issues like taxation and immigration] we'd better talk to the subject and participate. We may not have the answers but we have a perspective."

I asked Rupert Murdoch, chairman and CEO of The News Corporation, how he thought of the interaction of business and society. Having studied at Oxford, he started his career at twenty-three after inheriting 50 percent of a small newspaper in Adelaide, Australia. From there he went on to buy a failing media group in Sydney, then onto England, where he fought his way into the cozy Fleet Street Club—the move that launched him on the path to becoming the world's best-known media mogul, owning as he now does the 20th Century Fox studio, the Fox news channel and twenty-three television stations, newspapers including *The Times* of London and the *New York Post,* satellite groups including British Sky Broadcasting and Star TV in Asia, and publishing operations including HarperCollins. We met in his New York office around a coffee table. In a soft voice that was difficult to hear, he spoke extremely slowly. Oftentimes I thought he was finished speaking, and then, after a long pause, he continued, as if he were weighing every word. He said that the "market rules" and that he felt virtually all CEOs, himself included, think about expanding their businesses with little or no consideration for anything else. He cited his own experience in entering India. "We did it to build a business," he said. "There was no sense of mission or idealism to save India." He pointed to the DaimlerChrysler merger as another example. "There was a lot of talk about rationalizing the industry," he said, "but the motivation on both sides was clearly shareholder wealth and nothing more. It's dishonest to pretend otherwise."

Murdoch's view of a company's responsibility rests on what happens after it enters a country. He believes that the act of opening markets and bringing investment is in itself an incalculable benefit. With regard to the media business itself, he gave Yale students a flavor for his thinking in early 1999 when he reflected on his long career. "I think one thing I learned from my father is that in the media you [must] always be prepared to challenge the status quo and to particularly challenge the elites." He talked about his experience of being a newspaper owner in England. "It's not that we haven't made mistakes," he said. "But one has to face it that when you are a catalyst for change, you are going to make enemies. The real point is that we are giving people choice. We are providing an alternative, and I hope we enrich society by doing that," he said.

I asked Murdoch whether he and the leaders of other major media concerns—Time Warner, Disney—had an overall vision of where this influential industry was going. I threw out an assumption that they were operating in an environment with virtually no global rules or standards, an idea he did not dispute. He replied that there was no choice but to let the market take its course—to let the interplay of consumer demand and new technologies unfold in a competitive way, creating the landscape and the new rules in the process. Government regulation, he felt, was one of the biggest potential problems on the horizon that could undermine economic progress. There were many issues that I wanted to pursue, including his view on standards for media content, but we ran out of time. I was left with what he told Yale students in a lecture a few months before our interview: "We follow public taste more than we lead it, which is nothing to boast about."

George Soros, Chairman of Soros Fund Management, and perhaps the world's best-known global investor, has a skeptical view about an enhanced leadership role for CEOs. A Hungarian-born Jew, he survived Nazi invasion during his teenage years by posing as a godson of a Hungarian official. After the war he moved to London, where he graduated from the London School of Economics. He came to the United States in the late 1950s and beginning in 1969 ran one of the earliest and most successful investment funds to take advantage of developments in global markets.

In 1992 Soros was alleged to have forced the devaluation of the British pound through shrewd speculation. Since then financiers around the globe have watched his activities for clues about how markets would behave. Drawing conclusions from his behavior has not been easy, however, because he has played three roles simultaneously: private investor, public commentator and global philanthropist. In the first, he moved markets with lightning strikes against weak currencies. In his policy pronouncements, he has bemoaned the lack of regulations for global markets. As a generous contributor to charities, he has supported causes from New York to Moscow. In a 1998 interview with Timothy O'Brien of the *New York Times,* he talked about his multiple roles. "We have to distinguish between playing by the rules and making the rules," Soros said. "Playing by the rules, one does the best one can, irrespective of the social consequences. Whereas in making the rules, people ought to be concerned with the social consequences and not with their personal interests—in other words, not to bend the rules to their benefit or their advantage. This is a principle which I certainly have observed."

I once saw firsthand how gingerly bankers could react to Soros's overlapping personas. The scene was the World Economic Conference in Davos, Switzerland, in late February 1998, and Soros was a participant in a private meeting of about thirty of the world's top financial figures. On and off during the session he gave his views about global regulation—or lack of it. At one point he asked a technical question about how a particularly complicated transaction worked. The room went silent. Bankers' eyes shifted back and forth. You could sense what they were wondering: Why does he want to know this? What move is he planning next?

On the subject of who bears the responsibility for leadership, Soros doubts that business executives can be counted on. "I don't think that businessmen—or civil society of any kind— will be able to solve problems we are currently confronting," he told me in his New York office. "So we need government, and particularly we will need to strengthen international institutions to deal with that. How is it going to happen? I have no answer. But I think it has to be political leadership because it's a political problem. So unless there is a politician–statesman who can articulate [the right policies] and then get support, I don't think it's going to happen."

Franklin Raines of Fannie Mae, reflecting on his experiences in government and private finance, drew a similar conclusion. He believes business ought to devote its attention

almost solely on its mission of serving shareholders and customers, but that it must support a strong public framework
which markets require to function. He worries that governments will levy too many requirements on business to perform social tasks, making those businesses uncompetitive or
driving them to other countries. "The only solution I see," he
said, "is you have to develop confidence in government to run
the social safety net, and the people in business [will have to]
pay for that. And then business can go and do business, and
government [would] not try to force upon them [social mis-
sions]—because if it does, ultimately the capital will flee."

The picture that emerges is a mixture of many views:
good intentions, concerns about pressures and the risks,
carefully hedged willingness to expand the scope of leadership, and opinions that CEOs are not in a good position to
lead outside the relatively narrow orbit of their companies.
Still, chief executives will have to do a better job of coming
to grips with their roles in society, for serious problems
threaten to engulf them.

❖ ❖ ❖

Business leaders are potential targets for a variety of frus-
trations relating to globalization and technological change.
At a time when unprecedented prosperity masks growing income inequalities, and when stock prices and CEO pay packages are sky-high while workers worry about job security,
there is growing public angst concerning the lopsided distribution of income. As local communities and national governments appear increasingly impotent in the face of vast
mega-mergers and sudden movements of capital, all of

which alter the location of production and jobs, more people are feeling that they have no one to whom they can voice their complaints. Who, after all, is in charge of the world economy? And how do you lodge a protest or register support in an effective way?

Even today, with so much prosperity in the air, change and uncertainty have become disorienting, public anxieties are at high levels. A *BusinessWeek*/Harris poll in the spring of 2000 found that most Americans believe that globalization drags down wages. A poll on "Americans and Globalization" conducted at the same time by the University of Maryland concluded that "a strong majority of [the U.S. public] feels that trade policies haven't adequately addressed the concerns of American workers, international labor standards, or the environment." In early May 2000, a *Wall Street Journal*/ NBC poll showed that 48 percent of Americans thought trade harmed the economy, compared to 34 percent who thought it helped. In August 2000, a *Business Week*/Harris Poll indicated that 72 percent of Americans feel that business has too much influence. Two-thirds of the population believed that big companies place profits over safe, reliable, quality products for consumers. All of these worries are aggravated by a sense that the phenomenal technological development we are seeing is beyond our control—not just in communications but also in genetic engineering and robotics. Even an establishment figure like Bill Joy, chief scientist for Sun Microsystems, says that we are being propelled into this new century "with no plan, no control, no brakes." Says Gene Sperling, head of President Clinton's National Economic Council, "Despite the growth in our economy, despite the record unemployment, you see nothing but increased anxiety about globalization, technology and trade. It's everywhere."

A number of public policy problems are piling up, too—all involving high-stakes corporate interests. They include the debate over taxation of the Internet, the "digital divide" at home and abroad, international rules to prevent global monopolies, protection of intellectual property rights around the world, a framework to balance science and morality in the biotech revolution, the delivery of affordable health care, and the security of pensions for aging populations—not to mention such threats as the growth of global crime syndicates, and the spread of infectious diseases in areas where people are too poor to buy medicine. "[We haven't] been in such a state since the early part of the last century, when a set of decisions shaped the relationship between the industrialized economy and the government for decades to come," wrote Bob Davis and Gerald Seib in the *Wall Street Journal*.

Finally, whatever the situation today, many trends point to much more pressure on the workforce in industrial societies. Jobs will shift to developing countries in magnitudes never before contemplated. One reason is that the Internet will not only help companies find partners but it will help train and integrate foreign workers into their central operations. Years ago, American and European firms began to move parts of their back offices to the Caribbean or India, for example, but we've seen just the beginning of the transfer. All this will be happening at a time when more efficient use of the Internet will allow big companies in the United States, Europe and Japan to do more work with fewer people anyway.

In developing countries, the new jobs will of course be welcome. However, the digital divide that separates those who can take advantage of modern information technology and those who cannot is likely to get wider before it narrows. The reason is that those who can afford computers or cell phones will be able to exploit the new opportunities that are continuously offered, whereas people who live on a dollar or less per day, and who have never made a phone call in their lives, have priorities that come before logging on. So the poor and less skilled people will fall farther behind—all the more so, given the pace of progress.

Unfortunately, political leaders are increasingly leaving the resolution of social and governance problems to markets and the private sector. The rhetoric from government officials may not indicate a reliance on business—because it wouldn't be good politics—but we should watch what public officials do rather than what they say. Most analysts agree that there is no longer any meaningful debate between the right and the left. Nearly everyone is trying to reduce the size and scope of government, nearly everyone is "pro market" and looking for ways to attract more private capital, technology and management. While no one can predict how long this trend will last, the momentum is strong. Global markets are forcing governments to rein in spending or face debilitating interest rates on their borrowing. They are pressing governments to eliminate regulatory red tape or face loss of foreign investment. At the same time, political leaders see in the private sector the resources they need to do their job, whether it's building infrastructure or shoring up the social safety net. The expectations that companies will deliver such services are bound to be dashed. Then CEOs may well become the scapegoats for the failure of the public sector to handle its increasingly complex political and economic problems.

❖ ❖ ❖

Alongside the unrealistic expectation that companies will fill the vacuum left by the inadequacies of government is a growing campaign by activist groups to highlight what is being done badly by the private sector, or not being done at all. The activist non-governmental organizations known as NGOs have discovered that they can band together and direct public attention to a variety of problems that they say are caused by corporate irresponsibility or globalization, or both. Most of these NGOs are defining globalization as a bonanza for global companies and a disaster for everyone else.

It would be a mistake to think of the new protest movement as ephemeral. In recent years NGOs have mustered the clout to change the policies of companies like Nike (on its treatment of workers abroad), Monsanto (on genetically engineered food), Royal Dutch/Shell (on environmental problems) and Starbucks (on prices it pays to third-world farmers). Because they are often on the politically correct side of these questions—who is against a cleaner environment or less exploitation of poor workers?—NGOs have achieved legitimacy in the eyes of a good deal of the public. They have skillfully exploited the void between shrinking governments unable to cushion the impact of change on ordinary citizens and the multinational companies that are seen as the agents of that change. NGOs have gained influence by joining forces across borders, aggregating power under umbrella groups such as Consumers International, and building alliances with unions such as the AFL–CIO. They have harnessed the Internet to form global coalitions and coordinate lobbying in multiple national capitals. While governments and CEOs bore the public and the media with sterile abstractions about free markets, NGOs tap into the anxieties of local communities around the world. Their effectiveness is enhanced by their unconventional organizational structure, which has no central leadership and only shifting coalitions, making it a difficult movement to counteract. In short, the NGOs have now become a powerful new force on the world scene.

In late November 1999, NGOs mounted a large-scale demonstration in Seattle before the ministerial meeting of the World Trade Organization, which was therefore unable to hold the negotiations it had intended to launch at that meeting. How much of this failure was due to the NGO protests and how much to genuine policy differences among the governments can be disputed. But in April 2000, similar protests took place in Washington at the semiannual meeting of the IMF and the World Bank. In September 2000 the same groups gathered at another set of IMF and World Bank meetings in Prague. As the pressure mounted, each of these international institutions emphasized the changes it was making to respond to charges that their activities were deepening poverty and worsening the environment. Some of them were quite significant. For example, the IMF, long accused of operating in secrecy, began to offer seminars to NGOs on how its programs worked. The World Bank accelerated efforts already underway to promote a new and broader concept of what it would take to help poor countries. Both institutions agreed to speed up debt relief to poor relations. Equally significant was the change in tone of top financial officials. No longer were they exalting free trade without also pointing to the need to tame capitalism's excesses. U.S. Treasury Secretary Lawrence Summers set the tone at Prague. Speaking about the extremes between unfettered global capitalism, on one hand, and protectionism and anarchy on the other, he said, "If we want a more vibrant, more truly inclusive global economy then there is no alternative to finding some way in between these extremes."

The Nike case is illustrative of how the pressures of NGOs have also changed the attitudes of CEOs. Once branded as an exploiter of poor workers around the world, this consumer icon is in the process of an abrupt about-face. How else to explain the article by Philip Knight, Nike's chairman and CEO, in a recent issue of the *Financial Times*? "We believe in a global system that measures every multinational against a set of core, universal standards, using an independent process of social performance monitoring akin to financial auditing," he wrote. This trend cannot remain limited to the garment industry. As the production of everything becomes even more globalized, multinational companies will be increasingly involved with the labor pool of emerging markets. Even if there is a rise in standards—environmental, labor, human rights—these companies will now be operating in a fishbowl. They will be held accountable for every social aspect of their business. It will be a new world for them.

NGOs' attack on the international institutions has significance beyond these organizations themselves and the relatively few companies they have as yet targeted. The serious and responsible NGOs are trying to convey a message: that globalization is more than trade and finance, that it has repercussions for personal security, individual welfare, quality of work and life, national culture. NGOs are convinced that they have no way to attract public attention without attacking existing institutions. Globalization is creating problems faster than they can be handled. Says Moisés Naim, editor of *Foreign Policy* magazine, the backlash isn't just about trade. "The WTO has ended up being a dumping ground for important global issues that have no home," he told *Time*.

Although NGOs represent a variety of causes, they are united by the belief that corporate and financial interests are being placed ahead of the concerns of ordinary people. Their clout is bound to increase as they become more sophisticated in their on-line activism—from wider dissemination of more and better information to disruption of Web sites and other methods of electronic civil disobedience. The physical violence which took place in Seattle and Prague could also get much worse, especially if the radical elements in the NGO coalition win in the internal power struggle which is emerging. Alternatively, and just as significantly, if the NGOs get organized, and if they create a more positive and coherent message about globalization with reasonably practical proposals for reforms, they could have the field to themselves because neither governments nor global companies have done much to be proactive with a competing vision and a strategy that have broad resonance.

In any event, the next stage of global activism is likely to spread from international institutions to companies which are much more vulnerable to such pressure. Ironically, the

biggest threat to corporations comes not from the developing countries—which crave the investment, technology and
management that multinational firms bring—but from the
countries where corporations are headquartered and where
the biggest and most painful labor dislocations will be occurring. This is a more serious danger to multinational companies because the protests are closer to the financial and
media centers of the world. What CEOs need to worry about,
therefore, is whether their corporations will be the next targets of organized protests, and whether these will translate
into tarnished public images, disruption of business operations and government pressure to regulate business behavior. They would be wise to assume that all of these possibilities are real. Jürgen Schrempp is one who believes the
tendencies of governments are moving in this direction anyway. "Politicians—mostly in Europe, but you'll see it in America, too—are eyeing what they see as the overwhelming influence of big companies," he told me. "They ask, what kind
of influence do these companies have? Are they playing one
country off against another? Are they using their investments
to gain undue leverage over policies? You hear all these
noises, and soon the politicians will be asking for a set of new
organizations to control global companies like ours. I'm worried that politicians around the world are getting together
and saying 'Look, we have to stop these companies.' "

8

A Broader Agenda

"People often overstate how much power [global companies have]. But we cannot pretend we have none at all," John Browne told an audience in Davos, Switzerland, in 1998. "Obviously, we cannot substitute for governments. But we can help deliver concrete results. We can cooperate with a wide range of partners—governments, other companies, non-governmental organizations. We can provide a level of practicality."

Yet how far can these thoughtful sentiments be carried? What constitutes a robust but responsible and achievable role for CEOs in the new global economy?

The times call for a much higher order of leadership from business leaders than most of them now envision. Great CEOs ought to go beyond the philanthropic activities they engage in as individuals, and they need to do more than cast their corporations as "socially responsible." They should strive for a level of leadership which transcends the usual involvement in commissions, trade associations, public-policy study groups and high-powered lobbying for policies relating to narrow self-interest. The imperative for them is to acknowledge the importance of strengthening a market-oriented economy and the central role they must play alongside government to do it. They are not a substitute for government, of course, but with the resources and intellect at their command they can provide a level of leadership beyond what most of them are now contemplating.

I present these ideas not as a criticism of chief executives but as a missed opportunity for society. These top business leaders are the people who best understand the effects of change, technology, globalization. They are the ones who know what it means to set concrete goals and meet them. We need a new way of thinking about business and society that recognizes the multinational corporation as a key player in our social and political evolution and asks much more of its corporate leaders.

❖ ❖ ❖

There are a range of economic and social policies that CEOs could collectively pursue. These go beyond the self-interest of any company or industry to the creation of a version of globalization that is sustainable because it is deemed fair by the growing number of people who are presently left behind or who fear they could be vulnerable in the future.

My suggestions go in two parallel directions. First, CEOs need to be more forward-looking, and more proactive in articulating what they themselves need to do to build a stronger world economy. Second, they need to support the public sector's efforts to do the same.

For example, in their lobbying, in their trade associations, and in their pronouncements on national policies, CEOs ought to be vigorously promoting ways to improve education at all levels. A closer, clearer and more powerful identity between business leaders and schooling and training should emerge. Imagine the gains if the top three hundred global corporations decided that in the jurisdictions in which they operate, illiteracy would be eliminated within a decade and an extensive web of vocational training facilities would be established in a range of industries. Global companies wouldn't have to do it alone. They could form partnerships with local governments and businesses, with institutions like the World Bank, or with any number of non-governmental organizations.

CEOs ought to be out front in proposing ways to shore up social safety nets around the globe. A particular opportunity is presented to those chief executives in the United States, where projections show huge budget surpluses for years to come. Fiscal policy should cause more than a political fight in Washington: a genuine national soul-searching, with prominent CEOs speaking out about how to use this bounty to invest in the people and infrastructure that would promote full and confident U.S. leadership for a more open world economy. U.S. business leaders ought to be thinking big about what their country ought to look like a decade from now. What kind of social safety net should there be? What kind of school system? What kind of communications and transportation infrastructure? These issues are not strictly in the private sector arena, by any means, but the vision of our corporate leaders could be a powerful aid to the U.S. government and its citizens.

CEOs should be far more influential in the public debate about globalization, not just reluctant defendants. In the

United States at least, they become visible mainly when there is a very close vote in Congress on important trade legislation, such as NAFTA or China's entry into the World Trade Organization, but rarely at other times. During the Seattle and Washington demonstrations, for example, there were few corporate voices providing any context or contrary arguments; in fact CEOs, even those whose companies had an enormous stake in new trade agreements, were nowhere to be seen.

The job of educating the public about globalization won't be easy, but CEOs can start with the hundreds of thousands of their employees, who in turn will have an impact on others in their communities. They could fund major research projects in think tanks and universities on various problems of globalization.

CEOs should give attention to the rules and institutions necessary for regulating the world economy because these are essential to the public perception that globalization is for everyone, not just big corporate interests. Surely capitalism could not be politically sustained in the national context without an effective framework of governance, so why shouldn't the same be true on an international scale? "We need a framework within which to invest; a framework that provides the right incentives for development of skills, for the right environmental policies, and for the efficient use of resources," John Browne told the Council on Foreign Relations in November 1997. "Investment and anarchy don't mix. Many of the problems faced by companies—in ethics and in environmental policy and in dealing with people—occur in areas where government lacks legitimacy. The need for effective government is true at the local and national level. The need for effective public institutions also exists at the international level."

New institutions are required for financial stability. Financier George Soros is among the most thoughtful in debunking the optimists who say that regulation is sufficient. "The disappearance of obstacles to the free flow of capital has been nothing short of revolutionary," he told me. "You now have a free flow of capital with countries and companies competing to attract [it] and therefore capital is in the driver's seat. That is a big turnaround in the balance of power between states and governments on the one hand, and markets on the other." His view is that economic theory does not explain what is really going on. "The danger is that there [is] a fundamental misunderstanding of [how the market operates] because there is an underlying belief, left over from a bygone era, that markets reach an equilibrium on their own," he said. "This market fundamentalism is a false perception." He explained the thought by a twist of an old metaphor: Think of the market as a pendulum, he suggested. It has been an article of faith among traditional economists that eventually the pendulum stops swinging and comes to a resting point. This conviction is used to avoid more regulation, on the theory that all's well that ends well. However, Soros likens the pendulum instead to a wrecking ball, knocking over one economy after another, and coming to rest only temporarily.

Soros attributes the fragility of the financial system to the lack of any institution capable of effective oversight of global markets. "There is a central incongruity or tension associated with an economic and financial system which is truly global now and the political system, which is based on sovereign states. . . . So the market has effectively escaped regulators."

Soros's concerns have not been heeded. During the Asian financial crisis and even as it subsided, there were many calls for reforms of the financial system. Numerous high-level studies were done, many specific proposals were made, but the efforts to create a "new financial architecture"—a term which was in vogue around the world in the 1997 to 1999 period—withered. Governments are to blame for failing to persevere in their efforts, but so are the leaders of the world's major financial institutions. From Goldman Sachs' Henry Paulson to Deutsche Bank's Rolf Breuer, there is acknowledgement that the international financial infrastructure needs shoring up. "I don't think we have the kind of protections we need," Paulson told me. "These aren't global markets. They are regional markets with different degrees of transparency, different degrees of regulatory enlightenment, different degrees of technology. They're all linked, and they all impact one another. There is going to have to be a group of people who figure this out. They'll be governmental people and regulators, but companies too will have to do it out of self-preservation. The system is not working globally as it should." Said Rolf Breuer, "We were obviously not successful in preventing the crisis in the developing countries. The private sector, including the banks, can and should help. We have vital information to share." Left unsaid is why the big financial institutions, with their enormous influence, haven't done more to lead the way.

It will be difficult to get consensus on how to create stronger foundations for the world economy, but that speaks only to the magnitude of the effort and the time required, not to the need. At a minimum more attention should be paid to reinforcing the strength of the World Trade Organization, the International Monetary Fund and the World Bank. This would include CEOs working more effectively and visibly to build public support and lobby for adequate public financing for these organizations. It would also involve putting pressure on those institutions to win public support by being more open and transparent in their deliberations, rather than making decisions in the equivalent of smoke-filled rooms, as is now the general perception. The IMF and commercial financial institutions need to work more closely together when crises hit, rather than fight with one another at precisely the time when cooperation is urgent—as happened during the Asian crisis in 1997 to 1998 when banks and governments argued about their relative roles in helping the floundering Asian economies. CEOs need to support a new round of trade negotiations in the WTO. They also must press their governments to adhere to WTO decisions designed to settle disputes, or else the credibility of the organization will be severely undermined. With regard to the World Bank, the opportunities for partnership between it and global companies on development projects are enormous.

Creating new institutions for issues like the environment or antitrust is a more complicated matter. I suspect most CEOs would prefer fewer and more effective organizations. They would agree with Jürgen Schrempp who said, "Obviously, a free market without rules would be a disaster. But I would urge against every time you have an issue, you create an institution. Let's make what we already have work."

My interview with Schrempp underscored the intractability of some of these issues. I asked him to reconcile a few of the ideas he expressed to me in our two-hour session. He had told me he believed in a world of nation states and had no interest in world government. He said he did not want to see more international institutions, but preferred to rely instead on what already existed and on the cooperative interaction of business and government leaders. I asked him to explore this line of thought with regard to environmental protection. In particular, in the absence of specified and well-enforced global regulations for environmental protection, would he as a global CEO ask his company to uphold the same environmental standards in China as he did in Germany? I wanted to know who, under his laissez-faire framework, would set the rules and how they would be carried out.

He talked about his experience in southern Africa and how the leaders he met complained that the West, which took "a hundred years" to get its environmental policies on track, was now asking developing countries to achieve the same thing in an impossibly short time—and in the face of very high unemployment. "I agree with them," he said. "and then I say, 'Let's agree on a step-by-step plan—another 10 or 15 years or whatever . . . to bring standards to a uniform level.' This is practical. I talk to them on this basis. And then I say, 'Look, that is a fair way to do it.' . . . I see myself always balancing three issues. One is the social one, the second is environmental, and the third is the economics one."

I was left with a range of unanswered questions about the role of top business executives. The biggest were these: Since negotiating a deal between a company and a government is only a small part of what needs to happen to set standards, are the standards the sum of the private deals? What if the CEO in question doesn't care about the environment as much as Schrempp does? What if a chief executive negotiated a deal and either he or the government reneged on it; who would enforce the agreement? This part of our interview reinforced my conviction that there needs to be more rules and clearer enforcement authority—but also that CEOs must be involved, deeply and constructively, in the process.

On all these questions CEOs should not be slaves to their own organization. I recall what happened on the U.S. trade mission to China in 1995. As part of this trip, Secretary Ron Brown led some twenty chief executives to meet various ministers in Beijing to try to close a variety of pending deals in which U.S. companies were involved. During a few hours' break, Brown asked the CEOs to join him for coffee in a small hotel conference room. Jackets were removed, ties loosened. Brown asked the leaders whether there couldn't be some breakthrough on business attitudes toward human rights. Why, he wondered aloud, was it so difficult to get major U.S. companies to agree to a general code of conduct that would cover their worldwide operations? Surely, no one there was against improving human rights, he said, and if all of the companies here signed up, no one would be competitively disadvantaged. After some back and forth as to what would be in the code, one CEO said, "Well, I don't see any big problems here." Others nodded their agreement. After some more discussion, Brown asked if this group of business leaders could sign on to a code as soon as they returned to Washington. Everyone agreed.

Unfortunately, it never happened. Although Brown sent around a draft code within a week, it found its way to the various legal departments and trade associations. In short order, virtually all the CEOs had backed away "on advice of staff and counsel." We ended up with nothing.

Business executives could do more to forge better understandings with labor leaders. Union membership in the United States is a pale shadow of what it was in the 1950s and 1960s, and the role of labor unions in Europe and Japan has weakened considerably, but it would be a mistake to assume that workers do not have legitimate problems that globalization intensifies. Lacking alternatives, they will find ways to form organized resistance to change—especially when the current period of prosperity ends. An analysis by Aaron Bernstein in *Business Week* in August 2000 underscored the point.

> The best economy in 30 years has brought a bounty of jobs and exuberant spending. But . . . last year 43% of workers at large corporations "find it very difficult to balance my work and personal responsibilities" according to Chicago's International Survey Research . . . 44% said they are "very much underpaid for the work I do" . . . an astonishing 40 million employees say they would vote in a union today if given the chance.

The issue isn't just a defensive one, however. The New Economy is foremost about people, and about creating an environment in which they can be productive and able to take advantage of changing opportunities. How much time do CEOs spend trying to forge alliances with labor organizations rather than opposing them? How much do they think about innovative ways to jointly lower health care costs while improving care, or to create joint training programs, or programs which help dual wage earners with day care, parental support, stress reduction, and the like? How many high-level discussions have occurred concerning the forging of a New Economy agenda, including provision of lifetime learning opportunities and the portable benefits that a highly mobile workforce needs?

❖ ❖ ❖

John Browne, Mark Moody-Stuart, William Ford and others have made progress in the environmental arena, articulating specific goals, discussing them with NGOs and governments, allowing third-party audits of the results. But businesses, governments, international institutions and NGOs are just learning how to communicate with one another. For the most part, cooperation is at best tentative on the environment, labor, human rights, genetically modified products and economic development in the poorer countries. Nevertheless, certain companies are exploring new approaches which others should emulate. For a good deal of 2000—and before the Firestone tire recall—William Ford and his team met on several occasions with some of their harshest environmental critics. Similar efforts have been made by BP and Royal Dutch/Shell. In addition to trying to understand one another's goals and constraints, the benefit of these meetings is the establishment of an air of openness. This kind of atmosphere becomes invaluable when a crisis hits. William Ford told the *Wall Street Journal* that the activists he's been meeting "don't expect us to be perfect. They expect us to be open and honest and responsive." Under these circumstances, companies have a much better chance to get the benefit of the doubt as they work through various problems.

One example of a promising effort is the Fair Labor Association (F.L.A.), a group formed by eleven leading apparel companies, including Nike, Patagonia and Liz Claiborne; by NGOs like the Lawyers Committee for Human Rights and the National Consumers League; and by 141 universities. With encouragement from the U.S. government, the F.L.A. is working to eliminate sweatshops around the world. Members have developed a code that prohibits forced labor and child labor, and supports freedom of association, minimum wages, maximum working hours, clean bathrooms, and similar rights and amenities. The group has begun to monitor one another's facilities abroad and to conduct surprise inspections. To inform consumers, companies in compliance with the code can put F.L.A. labels on their products. Though more such inspections are needed and more public transparency regarding the results, the F.L.A. does reflect the understanding that consumers care about the conditions under which a product is made. Other industries should emulate these practices, using the F.L.A. model for how business, enlightened social activists and governments can work together.

Another example is the simply named "Global Compact" organized by U.N. Secretary General Kofi Annan and signed in July 2000 by Nike, DaimlerChrysler, Royal Dutch/Shell and dozens of other global companies, together with twelve labor associations and public-interest groups, and aimed at improving human rights, eliminating child labor, and protecting the environment. In one way it is a rhetorical document, since there are no sanctions for violation. However, the companies have committed themselves to important first steps, such as posting on their Web sites progress made in implementing the principles, and agreeing to a series of meetings to explore ways to promote the Compact's goals. The Compact came after an accord signed a few months before in Paris by the twenty governments of the Organization for Economic Cooperation and Development regarding how corporations should act to safeguard basic environmental and labor standards. The accord recognizes that many of the big, contentious economic and social issues can be handled only with global companies in the lead.

The upshot is that CEOs need to get in front of movements they see coming, rather than always fighting a rearguard action. It has taken a while but a number of companies have moved in this direction when it comes to environmental protection. BP, Ford, DiamlerChrysler, IBM, Royal Dutch/Shell, and Johnson&Johnson have pledged to make big cuts in greenhouse emissions in advance of any law or treaty obligations. Several of them are joining with the Environmental Defense Fund, an NGO, to develop specific plans for implementation and measurement of performance. But there are counter examples, too. Consider the pharmaceutical industry, which has recently succumbed to pressure to contribute subsidized medicines to combat AIDS throughout Africa. It is inconceivable that these companies, with their international reach, were not aware that these diseases were spinning out of control in poor countries. Yet they waited until governments and the U.N. highlighted the crisis and pointed to both the availability and the high cost of certain drugs. Admittedly, from the corporate standpoint there is some logic in holding back until public problems are adequately defined and a

course of action is clear and supported by governments involved. But the inevitable result is that companies are seen as
doing too little too late, and then as merely waging a public relations campaign. An alternative would have been for a group
of CEOs representing the leading pharmaceutical companies
to have worked together and taken the early lead in defining
a solution that would have entailed private–public partnerships. This might have included specified roles not just for the
companies but for national governments and international institutions. It would have been a real demonstration of business
leadership of the kind it's hard to discern today.

Economic development is one area where business can
do much more alone and in partnership with other sectors.
James Wolfensohn advanced specific ideas for what corporations can do to tackle some of the problems that the world—
and by implication what they themselves—face. "I think
there is no doubt that big business has to think more in terms
of social and economic policy than they have," he told me.
"One reason is that there are fewer of them, because of so
many mergers, and they are becoming greater concentra-
tions of power in the private sector. Their relative importance is becoming significantly greater as a creator of jobs,
conveyor of knowledge, and source of innovation. But too
few industrial leaders think out of the box in terms of their
perception of their broader responsibilities to society."

Here are some of the things Wolfensohn would like to see
business do: "First and foremost is the issue of contribution
to the social context, the social structure, workers' rights, human rights, conditions of employment," he said. "Secondly,
health, education, and welfare of their employees. Third,
community involvement—sharing leadership in the commu-

nity. A lot of these business establishments are closed at night, but they have computers, they have bright young people, and they could help the community with training, they could work in helping young entrepreneurs, and generally they could interface with government in an effective way to create an environment in which private investment flows."

Among the most innovative corporate attempts to make a contribution to global advancement is a recent partnership between Cisco Systems and the United Nations Development Program (UNDP) focused on using the Internet to alleviate poverty in the Third World. Cisco is taking responsibility for creating and maintaining a Web site that allows people and organizations everywhere to better understand the nature of poverty, to get personally involved in specific programs, and to match up their own capabilities with specific needs in poor countries. On the Web site a donor will be able to identify a problem in the Third World, make a contribution to its resolution, and then track the impact of the commitment. UNDP is the on-the-ground agent in over a hundred countries. The partnership, which is called Netaid.org, plans to involve other corporations. This is an experiment, to be sure, but the combination of corporations, public entities, and the use of new information technology hold great promise.

❖ ❖ ❖

Then there is the need for rules for cyberspace. The newness of the technology and the number of emerging public policy questions make this area both difficult and important for CEOs to address. Stephen Case is the only CEO I interviewed who underscored the unresolved regulatory problems which the Internet has revealed. In so doing, he expressed the concern that business leaders will take too narrow a view of what they should do. "I think the biggest risk is that we are at a unique point in time when the Internet is big enough to matter, but still young enough and small enough to be shaped," he said. "So it's important that business leaders take a step back and don't just focus on building their own services and their own companies but also focus on building a medium we can be proud of. Otherwise, there is a real possibility it could go wrong. It's going to require a sustained commitment and a genuine dialogue between business and government and consumer groups to make sure this is done right. . . . There's a growing need for the Silicon Valley culture to recognize that it is winning. It is having the kind of impact on people's lives it always wanted to have. But with success comes responsibility."

Case has been relentless in pushing the communications industry to involve itself in a host of public policies which affect it. In an extensive series of public pronouncements—and also in his interview with me—he not only enumerated many of the issues but suggested an Internet model of addressing them, one based on extensive partnerships between industry, government and consumers. "The goal of building a framework for Internet self-governance is no doubt ambitious—particularly in an industry of such diversity and dynamism," he told me. "Certainly the Internet is like no other medium. It has no center and no edges. Its stakeholders include not only a wide variety of businesses, but also advocacy and public interest groups, and, of course, consumers. And so self-governance of the Internet will be something different, something that reflects the unique nature of the medium—as well as the unique characteristics of our Internet community."

AOL's chief executive prescribes what many of the partners in this endeavor should do. Government must preserve an open playing field, revamp its outdated telecommunications regulatory process, and help see to it that everyone has access to the Internet. Industry has an obligation to ensure that consumers can trust the information they get through cyberspace and that privacy is protected, and it must enlist the help of nonprofit organizations to address educational needs. Industry needs at least to help bridge the technical gap that divides people. Consumers, for their part, need to get more involved in understanding the medium, making their views known as parents and citizens.

Case talks about the need for extensive partnerships and alliances among groups that have rarely talked to each other, in order to get a handle on changes in the world that the Internet will force—from taxation to censorship. "This new paradigm of communications will enable people— already has enabled people—to talk to those they otherwise wouldn't talk to and engage them on issues they might otherwise not engage," he said. "The Internet is largely the force that is blowing up traditional walls that separate industries and countries."

Just how far can Internet self-regulation go, and how much government involvement will be required? An enlightened position for CEOs would be to accept a significant dose of both. In a period of enormous change, the government would be foolish to overprescribe and stifle innovation—yet companies cannot be the sole arbiters of the public interest. Collective decisions must be made, not just by industry but by a wide range of other constituencies, and that can only happen through the formal institutions of democratic governments. CEOs should be working closely with governments to anticipate where new laws and regulations will be required. For example, I do not believe commerce on the Internet should escape taxation, since fees are levied on all other types of commerce. Aside from the sheer unfairness of this lopsided arrangement, too much tax revenue essential to the functioning of economies would be lost. The questions ought to be "What kind of tax system can work?" and "How would cybertaxes relate to the various systems in place now?" Privacy is another matter that cannot be left just to industry. In all cases, future solutions will have to be global in scope, matching the reach of the Internet. Now is the time for global CEOs to join forces to help sketch out what these international regimes will look like.

❖ ❖ ❖

Global CEOs also ought to play a more effective role in influencing top government leaders at the annual heads-of-state summits and at the various ministerial meetings of the IMF and WTO. Today they appear on the fringes of these events, as hangers-on. There is no clear, concerted business voice. A major business summit in advance, in which CEOs project their collective views of the world and their agenda, would get considerable attention. Provided that it wasn't just a business agenda but a broader picture of how to promote globalization, it could have even more impact than the governmental meetings, with their stale communiqués and vacuous soundbites. Top corporate executives ought to be presenting their views about the agenda in a way that gives governments and the public something to react to. We would benefit by knowing what CEOs think about where the IMF, the World Trade Organization and the World Bank should be headed. The last time there was fresh thinking about the landscape of global economic institutions in its entirety was a half century ago in the aftermath of World War II. With the end of the Cold War, the advent of the Internet, the rise of big emerging markets in the world economy, the intensifying globalization of trade, finance and foreign investment, and the explosion of critical issues relating to the environment, why don't CEOs call for another round of thinking similar to the 1944 Bretton Woods Conference? It would be less effective if they conducted a conference on their own, for government leaders are essential. So are CEOs, though, and nothing is stopping them from trying to get such an event launched.

✧ ✧ ✧

The range of business challenges faced by CEOs makes a broader leadership role in society problematic, to be sure. But if we conclude that more business involvement at the top is essential, then the model of what today's CEO is and does needs to be modified. At least two changes could be made.

First, it is difficult to envision global companies being effectively run by one person who is chairman, CEO and sometimes president, too. Together the burden of all these responsibilities is too great not to be shared. No one formula will fit all companies, but someone at the top—probably the chairman—needs to have as a major responsibility the kinds of broader societal issues discussed here.

There are in principle many options, each of which needs to fit into the particular situation and culture of any specific firm. Frederick Smith points to his own model at FedEx, which consists of an "office of the chairman," a team that includes himself and several others. "We have a small group of very capable and sophisticated officers in the chief executive unit," he said. "It is a five-person executive committee which oversees the operations of our companies—including the complexities of the global environment, a demanding Wall Street, and the press. [In addition to me] it includes the chief financial officer, the chief information officer, the head of marketing and communications, and the general counsel. We didn't invent this system but I believe it is catching on in many big companies."

In late 2000 the pressures on Ford Motor Company showed that running a big multinational company may be too much for one person. Because of the crisis surrounding faulty Firestone tires, Ford faced a serious setback to its vision and reputation as a consumer products company and good global citizen. Its U.S. business was losing profitability (and might have even more difficulties because of fallout from the Ford–Firestone ordeal.) Its European operations were hemorrhaging cash (for reasons as yet unrelated to the recall). Its intention to purchase Daewoo Motors in South Korea had to be put aside because of the entire array of pressures on top management in Detroit, thereby undercutting its Asian strategy. Surely these challenges would require all of the efforts of both the chairman, who might have been best positioned to deal with the political and social issues, and the CEO, who was needed to attend to the company's core operations. Admittedly Ford faced an extreme situation, but every global company has to be prepared for a big crisis. After all, that's when its leadership is tested and its reputation hangs in the balance.

Nancy Peretsman of Allen & Company muses that particularly for high-technology companies the jobs of chairman and CEO may need to be separated. "What we've seen is that certain founders or those with a large financial stake in the company are turning over day-to-day management of the growth to partners so that they can focus on strategic positioning. Particularly at a time when so many of the rules are changing, someone's got to be paying attention to where the business [needs] to be, and then someone has to be running the hyper-growth of the business." In this model, the chairman's vision could include the company's relationship to and involvement in broader social issues. Peretsman may be identifying a strong trend, for in recent years even the most powerful and successful chief executives have opted for a strong partner. In late 1999, for example, Bill Gates made Steve Ballmer CEO with all responsibility for Microsoft's day-to-day operations. In mid-2000 Louis Gerstner promoted Samuel Palmisano to the vacant position of president and chief operating officer of IBM to be in charge of daily operations, and designated John Thompson to become vice chairman for new growth areas. Over the last several months Michael Dell has turned over most day-to-day oversight to two vice chairmen, Kevin Rollins and James Vanderslice.

A second way for business leaders to be better able to shoulder the job of running their companies and broadening responsibilities for the global economy is for their associations to evolve beyond the narrow lobbying groups they now are, or

for new ones to be devised. A good example of a business organization that has fallen significantly short of its potential is
the Business Roundtable, which was established in 1972 as an
association of U.S. chief executives committed to advocating
public policies for the U.S. economy. According to its charter,
the Roundtable was designed to enable CEOs representing
different sectors of the economy—manufacturing, finance, retailing, mining, transportation, communication—to work together to present government and the public with "knowledgeable, timely information and with practical, positive
suggestions for action." Only CEOs of major U.S. companies
are members, and they head up and constitute many specialized committees. In the first half of 2000, the Roundtable's
major public announcements centered on applauding Congress's passage of normal trade relations with China, opposing the patients' bill of rights in Congress, complying with
the SEC's request for views on international accounting standards, and opposing class-action lawsuits. These are important issues, to be sure, but they also reflect a relatively narrow
and technical perspective of the organization's mission.
More effort is devoted to government lobbying than to thinking about a serious business role in shaping a national
agenda. It's almost as if the Business Roundtable doesn't
want visibility beyond the narrow confines of immediate legislation. Certainly the organization doesn't envision a leadership model that departs from the existing pattern—government leads, government is responsible, and business
executives are confined to making their views known and trying to influence Washington's decisions. There is no effort
among chief executives themselves to take the lead in iden-

tifying what the government ought to be addressing but isn't. There is no effort to identify what CEOs themselves ought to be doing independent of the government. None of the other business associations—the National Association of Manufacturers or the U.S. Chamber of Commerce, for example—has risen to the occasion either.

✧ ✧ ✧

At the beginning of *One World, Ready or Not,* his thoughtful book on the global economy, William Grieder asks his readers to close their eyes.

> Imagine a wondrous new machine, strong and supple, a machine that reaps as it destroys. Think of the awesome machine running over open terrain and ignoring familiar boundaries. It plows across fields and fence rows with a fierce momentum that is exhilarating to behold and also frightening. As it goes the machine throws off enormous mounds of wealth and bounty while it leaves behind great furrows of wreckage.
>
> Now imagine that there are skillful hands on board, but no one is at the wheel. In fact, this machine has no wheel nor any internal governor to control the speed and direction. It is sustained by its own forward motion, guided mainly by its own appetites. And it is accelerating.

No analogy is perfect, of course. Nonetheless, as this new century unfolds, Greider's rudderless world economy will serve the interests of neither citizens nor business leaders. Herein lie some of the most crucial questions that CEOs face. To what extent are they aware that for capitalism and democracy to survive, society—including them—must find a way to ease the social costs of a free-market economy? To what extent do they understand that despite the current prosperity, huge problems loom, from a crisis-prone financial system to rapidly widening income gaps? To what extent are they prepared to step up their contribution to economic—and, by implication—political and social stability?

The answer to all these questions is the same. As individuals, CEOs are aware and concerned, and they are trying to contribute in the way they think they should. Yet as a group they are too much on the margins of the big problems of the day.

9

Pax Americana?

In May 2000, Novartis AG, the gigantic Swiss pharmaceutical firm, went public on the New York Stock Exchange. Until then, Swiss firms had been reluctant to list themselves on a U.S. stock market, because it meant adopting U.S. accounting standards and complying with the Securities & Exchange Commission's stringent information disclosure requirements. Novartis's chief financial officer explained to a *Wall Street Journal* reporter why the company had changed its long-standing policy: "To become a truly global player, able to attract the best talent in our industry, sooner or later we'd have to play by U.S. rules," he said.

Novartis is one of the many foreign firms that have restructured their financial reporting systems in order to appeal to U.S. investors. This is a major change for such companies, because it means making their internal operations transparent to the public, in contrast to the long tradition in continental Europe, Japan and other non-Anglo-Saxon areas of disclosing as little as possible. The reason for this about-face is that America has the largest and most liquid pool of capital in the world, and almost everyone wants access to it.

In 2000, for instance, foreign funds were flowing into the United States at a rate of $1 billion per day. Foreign companies want to use their U.S. shares as a currency to make acquisitions in the United States. Going public is good publicity, too, and can contribute to American consumers' awareness of a foreign firm and its products. The last half of the 1990s has been a particularly good time to tap into the market, given the high valuations, though the desire of foreign companies to list their shares in America has been increasing for over a decade. But financial prowess is just the beginning of U.S. power.

Most CEOs believe that the influence of the United States—its political, economic and technological clout, even its culture—is one of the most powerful forces acting on markets. It would be impossible to understand the climate in which business leaders will be operating in the early twenty-first century without dealing with the implications of the Americanization of the world. But what exactly is this phenomenon? Is it as real and deep as it looks? To what degree should top U.S. executives be thinking about deliberate strategies to prolong America's substantial influence over the world economy? And if they conclude that they need to become more proactive, what role can they play?

My view is that as formidable as Americanization seems to have become as a force, its depth and longevity should not be exaggerated or considered inevitable. The popularity of American capitalism rests in large part on the unprecedented business expansion of the last decade, a trend that obviously can be reversed. It wasn't so long ago, after all, that Japan was widely admired for devising a system that promoted growth, innovation, respect for workers and social equity. Then its economic bubble burst, and with it virtually all foreign confidence in the country's ability to handle its own problems evaporated. We are making an assumption that the Internet, invented in the United States and dominated (for now) by U.S. companies like Intel, Cisco, Microsoft and Oracle, will accelerate Americanization. Another scenario is that this new communications technology will give a greater voice to more groups who want to go their own way, and more clout to minorities who want to preserve their own cultures and will be able to do so by linking up their disparate communities around the world into powerful ethic networks that supersede all nationalities.

In addition, many societies have grafted American capitalism onto deep-seated cultures with markedly different histories and priorities. While seeming to embrace Americanization now, these countries may in time reject the U.S. system, or major parts of it. History shows that empires breed a degree of hostility in other nations, both friends and foes. Some of this resistance is becoming all too evident in Europe, Russia, China and Japan.

If U.S. CEOs thought about these trends, many would probably say, "The time frame is too long to affect me. Anyway, it's all too big and fuzzy for me to influence, maybe even too much for Washington." However, challenges to Pax Americana pose a threat to U.S. firms that is more imminent than it appears—especially in the context of the general backlash against globalization, not to mention the inevitability of an economic downturn at some point. Besides, U.S. foreign policy can count: Washington does influence how the world views the United States, whether it finds Uncle Sam a congenial superpower, whether it is more or less willing to accept our notion of democracy and capitalism. If American CEOs recognize that, then they ought to wield more influence on U.S. foreign policy than they now do. They ought to seek more involvement not only in international economic matters but also U.S. statecraft. In the mind of the CEOs in the United States, there appears to be little room for such thinking now.

✦ ✦ ✦

There is ample evidence of the enormous influence that the United States has had on the world economy. The predominance of U.S. financial markets is indisputable. Although the United States accounts for about 25 percent of global production, in the last few years its stock market capitalization has hovered around 50 percent of the world total. And this is not the whole story. Markets everywhere are heavily influenced by what happens in Wall Street and Silicon Valley. They base their behavior on U.S. interest rates, on the pattern of securities trading, and on the trends in venture capital. The views and actions of the Federal Reserve chairman or the Treasury secretary can influence markets from São Paulo to Shanghai. In the financial services industry, too, U.S. firms dominate the most dynamic businesses around the world, such as mergers and acquisitions, securities underwriting and trading, and financial restructuring. At the end of 1998, the Bank of Japan, equivalent to the U.S. Federal Reserve, called in McKinsey & Company to help it reorganize its management and systems. A year later, Merrill

Lynch was called on to help with the consolidation of Fuji Bank, Dai Ichi Kangyo and the Industrial Bank of Japan, three of Tokyo's largest and most important financial institutions. In May 2000, when the London and Frankfurt stock exchanges were contemplating merging—a major milestone in European financial history—Goldman Sachs was the principal advisor to the German exchange, while Merrill Lynch performed the same function for the British.

Finance is only one arena where the United States casts a long shadow on the global economy. In the high-technology arena, firms like Cisco, Intel, Microsoft and Oracle predominate. In media and entertainment, few foreign companies compete with Disney or Time Warner, and those that can, such as Sony, are able to do so only because they bought U.S. studios and operate from a U.S. base. More than companies of any other nationality, U.S. firms have brought their distinct management styles, their technology and their cultures to foreign countries. In addition, U.S. universities have been importing some of the world's best talent and creating new generations of engineers, scientists and MBAs, who have in turn spread their knowledge and skills well beyond U.S. shores.

In developed countries like France, Germany and Japan, radical economic changes are occurring along the lines of the U.S. model: less regulation, more financial transparency, more accountability to shareholders, more mergers and acquisitions, more entrepreneurship, more flexible labor markets. For the first time, many foreign companies are focusing on modern corporate governance, which makes companies more accountable to private citizens who own the company's stock. In Germany and Japan, the cozy system of companies holding one another's shares is breaking down, creating more agile corporate structures. In Germany, workers' participation in management boards, a major feature of the country's postwar economic structure, is declining. In Japan, the system of lifetime employment is ending. In France, the state is shedding its ownership stakes in such industries as air transport, banking, insurance and telecommunications. It would have been unthinkable just a few years ago for Europe to have been the scene of gigantic takeover battles, such as occurred in 1998 to 1999 when Olivetti acquired Telecom Italia and Britain's Vodafone Airtouch bought Germany's Mannesman.

One powerful force opening these economies is the Internet, invented, inspired and driven by Americans—and the ultimate creator of new and more democratic markets. In Japan, known for its cultural rigidities, the Internet has allowed housewives to come together to start businesses. It has opened up opportunities for employees in big companies to bid on other jobs within those companies, outflanking the rigid hierarchies. In Germany, entrepreneurs have become the new corporate heroes, replacing the CEOs of big established companies. Many countries have many similar stories.

In emerging markets the U.S.-style changes are equally dramatic. Lowering trade barriers, encouraging foreign investment, privatizing state-owned companies, stepping up banking and securities regulation, devoting more attention to sound corporate governance, establishing modern bankruptcy laws—these are just some of the measures most of the countries in Asia, Latin America and Central Europe are taking. Here, too, the tightly woven ties between government and business, and the links among big businesses themselves, are breaking apart with increasing speed.

The U.S. system does in fact have features that suit it to deal with the kind of changes sweeping over the world today. In the early twenty-first century, corporate competition will be based more than ever on such factors as the effectiveness of a country's regulatory systems, including the balance between markets and governmental intervention; the environment for scientific research and technological development; the system for educating, training and management of the workforce; and the openness of a society to change. On every count, the U.S. has a commanding lead. The integrity of the regulatory structure, based as it is on transparency and legal protections, gives people confidence in financial markets. The fluid labor markets ensure that workers can move to where they can be most productive. The antitrust laws help create a level playing field. The education–research complex fuels new technologies. The willingness to accept immigrants in large numbers creates a steady supply of labor and skilled talent. All this fosters widespread entrepreneurism, a trait that is critical to succeeding in an era of rapid change. "It's a post-industrial world," wrote *New York Times* columnist Thomas Friedman, "and America is good at everything that is post-industrial."

✧ ✧ ✧

Evidence of Americanization can also be seen in the minds of business leaders. CEOs from many different countries share a lot of ideas. They buy into similar models of leadership and strategy. They are equally obsessed with the Internet and with global strategy, and they are struggling to deal with the same daily management problems, and to find the right level of involvement in the social and political arena. They are generally optimistic about the future, and while some worry about the backlash against globalization, either in the form of rising political and cultural nationalism or trade protectionism, they are proceeding at full speed, as if these trends will not seriously disrupt the momentum for a more open world economy.

These similarities among business leaders may not seem surprising, but they represent a marked change from the 1980s and early 1990s, when perceptions were more divergent. Back then, many observers were critical of the U.S. model because it seemed to have lost its competitiveness, and they were touting Japan as the next superpower. In 1992, in a book entitled *A Cold Peace: America, Japan, Germany and the Struggle for Supremacy,* I identified three quite different forms of capitalism. At that time, for example, German executives were promoting "Rhineland capitalism" and pointing to the cooperative ties among their companies, their banks and their labor unions as a key to their success. They claimed that their system was more stable than ours and allowed more long-term thinking and investment. Half a world away, Japanese CEOs were proud of their corporate links within families of firms called *keiretsu,* and were more interested in gaining market share than in earning profits. They also touted the importance of being able to plan ahead and to take advantage of "patient capital." Some prominent commentators asserted that the U.S. system was seriously flawed and would be outdone by others. M.I.T.'s Lester Thurow's best-selling *Head to Head* (1992) predicted that European-style capitalism would dominate the world. In *Changing Fortunes* (1992) former Federal Reserve chairman Paul Volcker explained why Japan was assuming global financial leadership. We all vastly underestimated several aspects of the U.S. economy and society: The incentive that competition would provide to change; the extreme flexibility of U.S. capital and labor markets to effect change; the willingness and ability to take the best from abroad—such as Japanese-style quality control or just-in-time delivery methods—and adopt it as our own; and the decentralized technological base that allowed for widespread experimentation and implementation—to name just a few of America's positive qualities. Nevertheless, it would have been difficult even in the early 1990s to see how completely world capitalism would converge by the end of the century.

❖ ❖ ❖

But converge on what? Has there been some mixing of the three systems, or is everyone adopting the U.S. model? "What I think is going on in the world is not globalization—it's Americanization," WPP's Martin Sorrell told me. "And I don't mean that in the nasty French sense. America dominates everything we do, whether it be education, industry, services. That's a fact of life. And if anyone wants to build a global business, I would say it's potentially fatal not to have the strongest franchise in the United States. The importance of the American market in terms of influencing what goes on in the rest of the world is quite extraordinary."

Sorrell's ideas are privately shared by other global CEOs, although sometimes with important nuances. European executives like Jorma Ollila, Jürgen Schrempp and Richard Branson see the pendulum swinging toward America, especially when it comes to issues such as paying more attention to shareholders, disclosing more information, strengthening corporate governance, engaging in the rough-and-tumble world of mergers and takeovers—and even tolerating sizable layoffs of employees to reduce costs. Their thoughts have little to do with ideology but entail instead a pragmatic recognition of what it will take to compete. "The new European corporate stars are convinced that time is running out for the old order—the unholy trinity of meddling politicians, hidebound trade unions and business dynasties for whom national interests always come first," wrote Richard Tomlinson in *Fortune*. "With a global outlook comes a healthy respect for American capitalism. Business leaders like John Browne and Jürgen Schrempp are such masterly global operators that it is doubtful whether their corporate style is any longer distinctively European."

Some European leaders also draw distinctions between their own belief about how capitalism should function and what they believe to be the U.S. model. According to Rolf Breuer of Deutsche Bank, his institution, while shareholder oriented, accords more loyalty to customers and other relationships than do his U.S. counterparts. He sees U.S. banks as more likely to abandon a client if a better deal comes along. "I think one of the many [different] points of emphasis we put on is trust. We don't believe in a commodity trading [philosophy] of business," he said. "We are loyal. We are not for the quick buck. We are not fly-by-night bankers. . . . Also, we don't believe in prima donnas—the stars. What's necessary is that the team is rewarded—not the leader, the star, the prima donna."

In Japan, Toyota's Hiroshi Okuda is quick to acknowledge that U.S. principles of economics and business are having a strong influence, which he says is a good thing. However, he feels that at least one aspect of the U.S. system will not be accepted by his countrymen: the wide disparities of income between top management and the general workforce which characterize the American scene. Nor does he believe that the Japanese system would tolerate widespread layoffs of the kind that were common in the United States through the 1980s and 1990s.

Finland's Jorma Ollila of Nokia and Japan's Yoshihiko Miyauchi of ORIX no doubt represent many other foreign CEOs when they say that they would like to soften the harsher edges of U.S. capitalism. They appreciate the virtues of the American model and are proponents of most of what it represents, but they would prefer a more humanistic approach, particularly when it comes to providing more job security for workers. This entails not only a reluctance to lay off thousands of employees at a time but also a sense that companies and the government have a responsibility to maintain an effective social safety net. To be sure, this "capitalism with a human face" philosophy is easier to talk about than to implement. British Prime Minister Tony Blair and several of his European counterparts have called for a "Third Way"—something between American and old-style European capitalism. But the concept has floundered because it is so difficult to translate into practice. In the global economy, either you are competitive or you are not. What's in between?

Most of the U.S. CEOs I interviewed seemed subdued on the subject of the triumph of the American model. A typical response was to praise U.S. capitalism, but also to acknowledge that while it may be sweeping through the world, it was not a foregone conclusion that this would always be so, and certainly not inevitable that U.S. firms would be able to maintain their current competitive dominance. The memories of U.S. deficiencies in the 1980s are still vivid. Michael Bonsignore and Michael Armstrong, both of whom have lived in Europe and run substantial businesses there, have a healthy respect for the likelihood of growing competitive pressures from abroad. So does Rebecca Mark. "There are cycles to these things," she said. "It's inevitable that we'll once again see European and Japanese firms challenge us in the way they did a decade or so ago." Based on my own experience in four administrations in Washington, both Republican and Democratic, it is clear that the rhetoric of the U.S. economic agencies—the Treasury, the Trade Representative, the Commerce Department—is far more boastful about the superiority of U.S.-style capitalism than what American CEOs have to say.

❖ ❖ ❖

How sustainable is the U.S. influence over the global economic and business environment? From the standpoint of those who find advantages in the continued spread of U.S.-style capitalism—presumably most global CEOs—there are several causes for concern. One is whether the strength of the U.S. economy can continue. Looking ahead, it is certainly possible that we could see big setbacks.

U.S. consumers and businesses are soaking up foreign goods, services and capital at an unprecedented rate. In 1992 the U.S. trade gap totaled $36 billion, whereas in the first half of 2000, it was running at $30 billion per *month*. This is leading to current-account deficits (the broadest definition of gaps between our imports and exports) of a projected $400 billion in 2000, over 4 percent of the GDP and 24 percent higher than 1999, which itself was a record year. If history is any guide, whenever a country's trade gap widens so dramatically, foreign holders of its currency get worried and begin to sell it. Thus the United States could be vulnerable to a weakening dollar and a reversal of the inflow of foreign capital that has helped fuel the stock market. At that point, the Federal Reserve would have to raise interest rates to prop up the greenback, but in so doing it could choke off the business expansion.

Another crisis could arise if politicians in Washington actually implemented a broad and deep tax cut while the U.S. economy remained strong. The stimulative effect, on top of economic growth already in the 4 percent range, would be like pouring gasoline on a fire. As in the previous scenario, the Fed would have to tighten credit, this time to ward off inflation. As in the first case, that would spell the end of strong economic growth in the United States, at least for a while.

These economic shocks could bring with them a shift of psychology, as the American economic machine is no longer seen as invincible. Foreign economies, which have become so dependent on selling to a booming U.S. market, would incur huge problems. Opponents of U.S. economic influence would come out of the closet, much as they did in the 1980s when big budget deficits and uncompetitive U.S. firms were a major feature of the U.S. scene, and Washington became the whipping boy for profligacy and bad policies in capitals from London to Tokyo.

Perhaps none of this will occur. Still, there are other trends which could undermine the continuation of Americanization as we know it. Consider the Internet. It is possible that the U.S. will not dominate the information that flows through cyberspace—the "content." Rupert Murdoch, Michael Bloomberg and Stephen Case all emphasize the growing importance of sensitivity to local cultures. They are preoccupied with finding local programming to use in other countries—local news, local talk shows, local sitcoms, local gossip. In fact, rather than reinforcing U.S. culture, the Internet may be the device to promote the cultures of other nations and subnational regions. It could be the means for Spanish-speaking people or people of Chinese origin to communicate no matter where they are. It could give local cultures a way to forge relationships and alliances around the world in ways and with an intensity that has never been seen in modern times. The previous chapter explored the power that the Internet gives to NGOs opposed to globalization or its current direction, and similar patterns could emerge for any cultural or ethnic groups wishing to develop tighter bonds—and not ones which mirror U.S. culture.

❖ ❖ ❖

A more deep-seated problem for Americanization lies in the frequent incompatibility between U.S.-style markets and the underlying U.S. culture. Ultimately you can't have one without the other, and therein lies the potential for serious tension. This distinction between markets on one hand and politics and culture on the other is crucial to understanding what globalization is all about, and why CEOs may ultimately encounter stronger political headwinds in their quest for an open world economy than most now anticipate. Today's version of capitalism is less regulated and more ruthless than that of the 1950s and 1960s, says author–commentator Will Hutton in his book *On the Edge.* "Its overriding objective is to serve the interests of property owners and shareholders. Its ideology is that shareholder value must be maximized, that labor markets should be 'flexible' and capital should be free to invest and disinvest in industries and countries at will. It is the capitalism of both Wall Street and financial markets and of street trading and street markets. It's a very febrile capitalism. . . ."

There are many aspects of our system that have no historical counterpart in non-Anglo-Saxon cultures. Who else tolerates such rapid turnover of products, companies and organizational models? Who else has so lenient a bankruptcy law, which allows businesses and individuals to fail and come back relatively unscathed? It is easy enough to see how this kind of capitalism can succeed in America, because the infrastructure and experience are here—the institutions, the laws, the history. But this system is at great odds with the European and Japanese traditions, to say nothing of those of China or India. In those societies, stability takes precedence over dynamic change. Individual freedom—political and economic—takes a backseat to public order. Everything about the American way is a challenge to the traditional values of these cultures.

If all this is true, why haven't we already seen the revolt over American intrusion? Answer: It's true, there has not yet been a concerted backlash, but it's too early to rule it out. In many countries, the reforms—the legal changes, the enforcement, the implications of transparency and accountability—are either very recent or still lie ahead. The fact is, markets move much faster than the foundations on which they rest. A decade of political and economic change abroad, most of it occurring against the backdrop of rising prosperity, is not long enough for Americans to declare victory. It remains to be seen how a European Union with over a dozen new members will ultimately try to shape its political and social compromises. U.S.-style capitalism is just now beginning to penetrate Japan, and has a long way to go there. Moreover, it's not at all clear that in the developing world the U.S. system will be the preferred approach to dealing with the crushing burdens of poverty, population growth and environmental pressures.

In many emerging markets, there is a great difference between form and substance. There may be lots of new regulations, but they cannot be implemented, because of a lack of human and technical resources. I remember sitting next to a minister from the Chinese government at a banquet in Washington in 1994. We were talking about the need to protect intellectual property rights, a highly sensitive topic at the time, since the Clinton administration was about to threaten the imposition of large sanctions for Chinese violations of agreements. The minister didn't deny the importance of intellectual property rights, but he explained the difficulty China had in dealing with the issue. "We accept the need for new laws," he said. "We've even written them and put them on the books. But we don't have a court system to enforce them." Without a system of adjudication and enforcement, I realized, all the assumptions that my colleagues and I were making about China's ability to undertake new obligations for protection of copyrights, trademarks and patents were flawed.

There is a similar question when it comes to other aspects of the transition that China is trying to make to a market economy. In the summer of 2000 Chinese workers held six foreign managers hostage for forty hours in a factory outside the industrial city of Tianjin. The angry workers had been laid off, just as many other Chinese workers have been and will continue to be as inefficient state-owned enterprises are closed or sold to private investors. Elizabeth Rosenthal of the *New York Times* identified the horrific picture that will be emerging when she wrote, ". . . It has been painful and confusing for China's tens of millions of workers, echoing similar privatization efforts in the former Soviet bloc. The workers are unfamiliar with the intricacies of buyouts and severance packages, generally lack effective labor unions and have little outlet for their complaints. . . ."

Finally, while no one doubts America's overall technological supremacy, here, too, it's possible to become too complacent. A good deal of the U.S. lead derives from enormous defense-related investments during the Cold War, the Internet being a prime example. It may well be impossible to keep up the pace without a foreign threat, and it is unlikely that private companies, obsessed as they are with the bottom line, will entirely fill the role the Defense Department once played in encouraging and funding innovation. In addition, the diffusion of U.S. technological genius to other countries is sure to accelerate, undercutting its advantages. As multinational companies like IBM establish state-of-the-art research labs all over the world, employing highly skilled foreign nationals in all of them; as foreign companies like the former Daimler-Benz increase their acquisitions of U.S. companies; as an ever larger percentage of engineers trained in the United States comes from abroad; as the Internet weakens protection of intellectual property—as all this happens it will become increasingly difficult for the United States to maintain the overwhelming technological edge it now has.

❖ ❖ ❖

Will the United States be up to the task of creating the right political environment for its economic goals to be achieved? Market forces, entrepreneurship and the desire for free choice are all embodied in globalization, and these forces have strong momentum. However, economics has never existed in a political vacuum. An economy, national or international, needs someone to set the rules and someone to enforce them. In the last golden age of capitalism, 1860 to 1914, that role fell to Great Britain. After World War I, the mantle was transferred to the United States. In the 1930s, Washington ignored its leadership responsibilities and thereby contributed to the economic breakdown, itself one cause for World War II. For four decades afterward the United States played the role Great Britain once did with regard to the non-Communist world. Since the collapse of the former Soviet Union, the United States has been the sole global leader. Is it inevitable that this will continue?

There can be no definitive answer, of course, but it is instructive to look at some of the anti-American measures which are building. Even as consumers everywhere embrace Hollywood, McDonald's and the National Basketball Association, there is growing displeasure with the way Washington has thrown its weight around in NATO, the WTO and the IMF. There is particular suspicion almost everywhere in the world about our tendency to act unilaterally—such as in our public pronouncements about what other countries should do regarding human rights, birth control, narcotics, weapons sales, or relationships with Cuba and our threats to apply economic sanctions if they don't change their ways.

America's trade and foreign policy in the early-to-late 1990s is a textbook case of throwing one's weight around in a counterproductive way. Some of this activity was understandable; some went too far. Admittedly, I played a part in it.

When Bill Clinton was elected president in 1992, there was still a widespread perception in the United States that U.S. competitiveness was lagging, particularly vis-à-vis Japan. There was a consensus among the president and his top economic officials that companies in Japan and Europe were deriving significant benefits in international competition because they were being supported by their governments. The new administration was keen to show that it, too, could play that game. Secretary Ron Brown had a common refrain. "We don't want just to level the playing field," he would say, "we want to tilt it toward American firms." The administration proceeded to move aggressively on behalf of U.S. companies. There were high-profile government-led trade missions in which the country's top CEOs enthusiastically participated.

There was presidential arm-twisting of foreign governments to persuade them to award contracts to U.S. firms that were competing abroad with companies Washington alleged were backed by their governments. A "war room" was established in the Department of Commerce to organize U.S. government help, including financing, to hundreds of U.S. companies, big and small, to win foreign contracts.

None of this was really critical to an economy that was gathering steam from the early 1990s recession, moving from a GDP of $6 trillion to $8 trillion and about to launch a third industrial revolution fueled by a level of innovation not seen in at least a century. Economics wasn't the point, though; power politics was. The nation that had just won the Cold War and had emerged with unprecedented military power was signaling that it would not take a backseat to anyone economically, either. Commercial diplomacy would be a major part of U.S. foreign policy. For Washington in the 1993 to 1995 period, this was the new world order.

Most of the top officials in the administration supported this effort for two reasons. First, governments in Europe and Japan had much closer and longer-term ties to their companies than Washington did with the U.S. private sector. The administration and a good deal of corporate America felt disadvantaged—especially when it came to winning big international project bids in developing countries like Saudi Arabia, China, Indonesia and Brazil, where governments themselves were involved in selecting the winners and were susceptible to the kind of foreign pressure that Europe and Japan typically exerted on behalf of their firms. Second, wielding a big club was good domestic politics, because to the extent that Uncle Sam was seen at home as doing all it could for its companies abroad, Congress and the public were more relaxed about the administration's efforts to negotiate new trade-liberalizing agreements.

Still, the approach had its flaws. I was constantly asked by Americans and by foreign officials if the United States, as the only power capable of shepherding the world toward an open economy, could pursue this type of gunboat economic diplomacy and still be a credible leader. There were no easy answers to that one.

Washington's actions grew from a gray area to something less ambiguous when it started to pressure emerging markets to follow U.S. economic-policy blueprints. Here U.S. assertiveness morphed into arrogance. The Clinton administration—and I was definitely one of the culprits—used its leverage, which was growing with the strong U.S. economic recovery and the sudden reemergence of supercompetitive U.S. firms, to press countries in Asia, Central Europe and Latin America to open their markets to foreign capital to an extent unseen in over fifty years. The administration pushed hard, as did U.S. firms, for the dismantling of trade and investment barriers around the world. We were asking other countries to make painful transitions well before they had adequate underlying regulatory systems. Kenneth Courtis, then a strategist for Deutsche Bank, described what this meant for a small country like Thailand. "Asking it to link itself into the global financial system in this way was the equivalent of hooking up a lightbulb to a nuclear reactor, whose power keeps ebbing and flowing," he told me in February 1997. Washington's overzealous policy contributed heavily to the beginning of the Asian financial crisis. As the Asian countries went into deep recession, moreover, the administration pushed the IMF toward demanding too much austerity, a mistake reminiscent of that made in the early days of the 1930s depression, when President Herbert Hoover tried to balance the budget in the middle of a deteriorating economy.

Today the Asian financial debacle is over. It is inconceivable that it has not created latent resentment about U.S. pressure. The crisis, though, should not be seen in isolation from other sources of foreign anxiety about U.S. dominance. A good deal of foreign opinion worries about the world's only superpower becoming too powerful for its own good and that of other countries. It's no wonder that the European Union is visibly striving to be a counterweight to the United States, or that Russia and Germany are talking about a new strategic partnership, or that French officials are calling the United States a "hyperpower," or that China rails against U.S. hegemony. "It is impossible to pinpoint the moment when America's successes in the 1990s moved from a topic of grudging admiration around the world to a constant source of annoyance at Washington's triumphalism to a rationale for mistrust and resistance," wrote David Sanger of the *New York Times.*

> Perhaps the clincher was the envy over the Dow's dramatic ascent from a little over 2,000 at the start of the decade to a little over 11,000. Maybe it was the dawning realization that people around the globe are all flicking on the same Windows operating system in the morning on their way to navigating an Internet dominated by American innovations and businesses and driven by Intel inside everything. Maybe it

was when the United States, in the wake of the Asian economic crisis, began offering tutorials on American-style capitalism, and insisting that the world's financial architecture be rebuilt to American building codes.

But surely, Sanger says, a capstone was the high-tech intervention in Kosovo and "the image of those B-2 bombers lazily lifting into the air over Missouri at midday, flying an 11,000-mile, 32-hour mission to drop laser-guided weapons over Belgrade—and getting back for dinner the next evening."

Perhaps these are straws in the wind, temporary manifestations of frustration that will eventually blow over. But just as likely they are the initial stirrings of a countermovement to U.S. power. After all, no empire has been able to avoid the coalescing of a new one arising in opposition to it. Of course, Pax Americana is young and could continue for a long time—but CEOs in the United States will have to work toward that end, for it is not preordained.

✧ ✧ ✧

What then should U.S. CEOs do? Because an open world economy works well for the United States, they can begin with the measures cited in the previous chapter regarding more concerted policies to make globalization sustainable: a clearer and bolder economic and social agenda, more support for a strong regulatory framework for cyberspace, and more active involvement in the establishment of other international rules and institutions for the global economy. Beyond this, they need to think through an agenda for U.S.

foreign policy and then, as a group, press U.S. officials to move effectively to keep Americanization a powerful force for a long time.

An example of the role that U.S. CEOs could have played but did not was in helping to devise policies and strategies after the Berlin Wall came down and the former Soviet Union collapsed. I had a ringside seat from the Commerce Department, being one link between high-level business leaders and the first Clinton administration. In retrospect, the changes that Washington expected to occur in countries that had either been behind the Iron Curtain or had yet to embrace free markets as Americans understood the term seem highly unrealistic. It was surprising how little capability the U.S. government had for understanding the political and economic dynamics of the "newly liberated" nations. U.S. embassies were disproportionately staffed with people who understood Cold War military politics, but not economic affairs—even fewer who knew the business world. The U.S. business community, with its global reach, its extensive involvement in emerging markets, its powerful research capabilities, its vast intelligence network—actual or potential— should have known better, but didn't help much at all. There were almost no conversations that I recall in Washington between the government and business on the best way to help emerging markets make the transition to capitalism, other than to agree to push ahead as fast as we could, press for market opening on all fronts, and lobby for U.S.-style regulatory institutions. Had U.S. companies construed their role differently, they might have counseled us to go a bit slower and make sure that there was broad local political support for economic reforms. Advice from U.S. financial institutions would have been particularly useful in warning against the excesses that were building and about to cause the Asian financial crisis, which spread to Russia and South America. The point is not to apportion blame—there is more than enough to go around in business and government—but rather to suggest that CEOs construed their role in a global economy narrowly, despite the fact that they were major players and had a lot of important things to say and do to help build a foundation for stable global capitalism.

Turning to the future, CEOs of U.S. companies have already pressed the U.S. government to reduce one of the great irritants—the tendency of successive Congresses and administrations to levy unilateral economic sanctions—and they should not let up on these efforts. Aside from sanctions being relatively ineffective, nothing is more irritating to foreign leaders. CEOs understand, as well, the importance of allowing emerging markets like China into the WTO. They did a good job in pressing the case, but a test still lies ahead, as China will inevitably have trouble conforming to the elaborate rules of the trade organization. Business leaders will now need to help Washington steer a fine line between blustery threats and steady pressure for Beijing to make the necessary changes in its behavior. This will surely be a difficult task for at least the next decade.

U.S. CEOs also need to work much harder to create a national consensus for trade liberalization generally. They should have worked much harder than they did to help President Clinton win "fast track" authority from Congress to negotiate new trade agreements, rather than watch as he lost the battle—with enormous damage to the credibility of the United States as a free trader. As noted, polls show substantial skepticism in the U.S. public about the benefits of trade to the U.S. economy, and President Clinton was unsuccessful in getting authority to negotiate major new trade agreements. These problems worry foreign leaders. Says Mitsubishi Corporation's Minoru Makihara, "Of great concern to Japan and all other countries is the possibility of protectionism emanating from the U.S. Today U.S. capitalism is often characterized by a self-righteousness and a sense that you can't do anything wrong. Of course, there has always been some of this, but it becomes more serious when the U.S. is so predominantly the leading economy in the world. Any kind of leader has to lead by example—not just by sheer power." Jürgen Schrempp of DaimlerChrysler is also concerned about U.S. protectionism. "There are going to be many concerns about moving ahead with trade liberalization in the U.S.," he said. "And remember this is a situation where unemployment is very low and the U.S. economy has been booming for years. Just put yourself in the situation in which there would be a major downturn."

A prime requirement for U.S. foreign policy is to support and expand the New Economy on a global basis. The combination of deregulation and entrepreneurship, and the enhanced productivity which innovative technology has brought to the United States during the late 1990s and into the new century has fostered the economic freedoms and the social mobility which has always constituted the American dream. To the extent that these conditions can be spread and sustained abroad, the United States would win in many ways.

There would be more economic growth around the world, and more open markets for U.S. competitive industries. Countries enveloped by the New Economy are more likely to value individual liberty and be vibrant democracies. It has always been a tenet of U.S. foreign policy that democracies are less likely to start wars, and so the right economic conditions could also lead to a long peace dividend.

There are a number of ways that American business leaders could help Washington to export the New Economy. First, U.S. companies could accelerate their efforts to help establish more U.S.-style business schools abroad, in alliance with local universities and U.S. MBA programs. Second, U.S. CEOs could work with their government and with international organizations to further narrow the digital divide between the haves and have-nots. Third, as James Wolfensohn mentioned to me, multinational corporations could do a lot with their own employees, helping with their formal education and their vocational training, including in all aspects of computer competence. U.S. firms could also devise programs, perhaps in conjunction with the U.S. government, to finance teams of economists, accountants, financial experts and lawyers to help foreign entities think through the laws and institutions that support new economic activities, including tax and regulatory regimes. To be sure, some elements of these programs are already in train. But it's hard to discern a concerted business strategy to extend America's New Economy to other countries. And these efforts must be made in ways that other nations are comfortable supporting, and—in contrast to the policies of the mid-1990s—within a time frame that recognizes political and social constraints, as well as the need for certain policy foundations to be in place.

Another place where business can help is the promotion of American culture. There was a time, particularly during the first two decades of the Cold War, when the U.S. government went to great lengths to finance the promotion of U.S. libraries, permanent cultural exhibits and traveling theater and dance groups abroad. In a world of CNN, MTV and the Internet, the role of Washington is diminished, of course. Federal support for cultural programs abroad is a pale reflection of what it used to be. But, the market alone is not enough. Adam Smith's invisible hand will not explain to citizens of other countries what the rule of law is in the United States and why it's so important. It won't promote U.S. history or the kind of culture seen on the Public Broadcasting System. It won't honestly expose the serious difficulties we have with race or crime in a thoughtful, historical way and therefore build up U.S. credibility as a society worth respecting for its earnest attempts to deal with its problems in an open way. It certainly won't carry the American message—beyond its pop incarnation—to the poorer regions of the world.

The fact is, new generations are rising to power abroad with no memory or experience with the United States as the ultimate defender of democracy in the mid–twentieth century, and as the most generous victor that history has ever seen. If the United States does not find ways to keep alive the history of its extraordinary magnanimity, no one else will. It is a story that can be told through many lenses—but it must be told repeatedly. Otherwise the power that emanates today from the United States will have no context—or the wrong context—and all of the tendencies for other nations to react negatively will be heightened that much more. Bottom line: If CEOs care about the prolonging of the American century, it will take continued work. The U.S. government cannot be expected to bear all the expenses, or even most of them, and great U.S. companies ought to be more heavily involved by getting together and helping Washington mount cultural efforts suitable to the post–Cold War era.

An example of innovation from the U.S. private sector is the effort being made by Ira Millstein, senior partner of the law firm of Weil, Gotshal & Manges, who has organized groups of U.S. executives to meet with their counterparts in other countries, mostly emerging markets, like Brazil—and to explain in nondogmatic ways how the U.S. economic system works to provide a legal and commercial infrastructure in which companies can flourish. Millstein teaches part time at Yale on such issues as strategy, leadership and corporate governance. In addition to his law practice and teaching, he is also involved in the World Bank and the Paris-based Organization of Economic Cooperation and Development, helping companies and governments around the world to create the right policies to prosper in the global market. We talked in his corner office, which towers over New York's Central Park, a fitting location for a former chairman of the board of the Central Park Conservancy. "There are legitimate arguments about who should take the lead in building the right platform for global markets," he said. "But before you assign roles to the public or private sector, you need to know what the right platform is. I happen to think it's sensible regulation of securities, antitrust, and so on; lack of corruption in general and in particular in judicial systems;

transparency and appropriate corporate governance—all to the end of countries and companies being able to attract global capital to build competitive enterprises which in turn create jobs and economic welfare. CEOs and their successful enterprises can be the 'voice' which understands and insists on what is needed. They must not be passive bystanders. If they are, it won't happen."

In our discussion, Millstein mentioned that he was about to take a trip to Brazil with a group of U.S. executives who represent major investing institutions. "We're going [down there]—we'll have seminars, discussions, different kinds of get-togethers—and hopefully we'll leave on the ground in Brazil a group of local business people who are becoming convinced that if Brazil is to develop [it will] need to end corruption, to have a better judicial system, and so on. I think the message comes better from an investor group consisting of their peers than it does from the OECD or the World Bank or anyone else that looks like a group of bureaucrats who are coming to give them a lecture. And ultimately, only if local businesses exert pressure on their government will things change enough."

Millstein feels that this kind of message, which he was planning to deliver to several other countries including Russia, will be effective if done with humility. "We need to admit all the mistakes we [Americans] have made. And we did. Foreign corrupt practices, fraud, and so on—we did it all. Monopoly, raping minority shareholders. There isn't a mistake we haven't made in the United States as we developed this great system we have." He wants to share the experiences and the lessons.

✧ ✧ ✧

Beyond the economic and business arena, U.S. business leaders could play a more effective role in more traditional foreign policy. No doubt most U.S. CEOs, political leaders and even many citizens will recoil at the notion of crossing the line between economics and politics. If ever there was a bogus distinction, though, this is it. Putting "business and economics" in one box and "politics and security" in another amounts to misreading the nature of global interaction today. Virtually all countries are concerned with all dimensions of their existence. They want growth and prosperity, of course, but they want freedom of action and dignity, too. In this regard, foreign attitudes toward Americanization of the markets cannot be divorced from foreign views about broader U.S. behavior. If CEOs want the EU and Japan to let up on nationalist drives in the commercial sphere, then other governments will have to be given some "face" in other areas, so that they do not feel totally cornered by Uncle Sam. There is a seamless connection between economics and politics when it comes to anti-Americanism, in particular.

For example, the European Union wants a stronger defense capability with some independence from the United States. A confident U.S., reflecting its unequaled strength, would not fight the proposition, as seems to be the case so often now. It would see political merit in encouraging a strong and confident Europe which could, on its own, handle crises in its backyard such as the civil wars in Bosnia, Serbia and Kosovo. It would work with Europe to build transatlantic defense companies in which both sides received their share of procurement. This is the best way to relieve pressure on nationalist tendencies, and U.S. CEOs should be helping U.S.

officials to understand the eventual liability of "winner-take-all" strategies.

A final area of U.S. foreign policy which ought to concern CEOs is adequate funding for the full range of U.S. diplomacy. As the number of complex problems increases—from trade and finance to illicit drugs and terrorism, from protection for our diplomats to protection of the environment—the nonmilitary international affairs budget continues to shrink. The United States doesn't pay its full dues for U.N. peacekeeping. It doesn't lead the way in adequately funding the WTO and other global institutions. Many of its embassy facilities are in a state of crisis. U.S. CEOs ought to weigh in forcefully on the side of Washington having the tools to conduct a modern foreign policy.

REFLECTIONS

Historians cannot agree on what happened in the past, so it is little more than speculation to suggest how, looking back years from now, they might view our times. During my interview with Emma Rothschild, who runs the Center for History and Economics at Kings College at Cambridge University in England, she talked about the powerful impersonal forces that created the first industrial revolution in England, ranging from the steam engine to the French Revolution. In another interview, Harvard Business School historian Richard Tedlow explained the critical role played by individual business leaders during the second industrial revolution in America. Different times, different perspectives, but it seems certain that the history of our era will also be a story of both shifting political, economic and social forces and the strenuous efforts of individual business leaders who confronted powerful trends and even tried to shape them.

If I had to guess, however, I would say that today's CEOs will be seen as captains of ships in a turbulent sea—unable to chart a steady course and to maintain control of their own fate, at least to the extent most people imagine they can. Their considerable skills and determination notwithstanding, the pressures of this era will have proved much greater than anything these individuals could handle well. The challenges that will have arisen—of the Internet, of globalization, of creating trust in the face of rapid change, of putting forward a bold vision and executing it exquisitely, of balancing shareholders and stakeholders, and of understanding the need for broader vision and leadership in society—these challenges will be assessed by historians as having been too difficult for most CEOs to successfully handle all at once.

Even in the months between my interviews and the writing of this book, the vulnerabilities of top business leaders began to emerge starkly. Aside from the fact that well-trained leaders like Richard Huber, Richard Thoman and Rebecca Mark were toppled, by the fall of 2000 the press was speculating about the vulnerability of Michael Armstrong, who was forced to break up AT&T to boost its sagging share price. The reputation of Rolf Breuer never fully recovered from the botched merger between Deutsche Bank and Dresdner, and his board took the unusual step of naming the person who would succeed him in 2002, perhaps signaling an exit for Breuer in advance of what he had originally planned. William Ford's personal agony over the recall of Firestone tires, and the ramifications for everything he wanted for the company, can hardly be imagined.

While Michael Dell's company, the single best-performing stock of the 1990s with a 97 percent average annual price increase during the decade, saw its market value drop 25 percent in the first eight months of 2000, more than a fickle stock market was to blame. "The box that made Mr. Dell a billionaire has become a commodity product no longer technologically innovative and no longer in need of replacement every 18 months," wrote the *Wall Street Journal*. "Dell needs to push into Internet servers and high end data storage. Both are largely terra incognita for Dell." In September 2000 Andrew Grove's Intel lost 22 percent of its value, the worst one-day drop in its history, because of lowered expectations for earnings but also because of anticipated changes in the market for computers. When GE and Honeywell announced that they would merge in October 2000, it seemed likely that the latter would dissolve and disappear into Jack Welch's empire and that Bonsignore would be out of a job. Amid substantial losses, George Soros slimmed down his fund management firm, saying that the business required younger blood. Motorola, Unisys and DaimlerChrysler were all experiencing serious declines in market valuation by late 2000. These price gyrations were due in part to the ups and downs of markets, but Wall Street analysts and investors were also worried about the fundamental outlook for strategies and execution.

And these were only the leaders I interviewed. Elsewhere Bill Gates was able to appeal his antitrust conviction, but by October 2000 Microsoft had lost half its value since the start of the year. Louis Gerstner felt compelled to institute a sweeping reorganization of IBM to enhance sagging revenues and better execute and plan the next stage of its Internet strategy. Jeff Bezos's Amazon.com, facing continuing financial losses, gave up not only a huge amount of its financial value but lost much of its luster as a model for the Internet age. Jay Walker, Priceline.com's founder and leader, could not have been too happy either; not only was the company's market value plummeting, but its name-your-own-price strategy had failed almost everywhere except in the travel industry. Yahoo!, dependent as it was on Internet advertising, was also worrying investors.

Of course some CEOs were still riding high—Jack Welch, John Browne, Ken Chenault, Henry Paulson, Hiroshi Okuda and Marin Sorrell among them. And many who seemed to be in trouble would no doubt rebound. But the landscape did reflect the enormity of the challenge these men and women face in simply succeeding at running their companies at this time in our history.

✧ ✧ ✧

From the vantage point of, say, 2010, we may have the answers to questions that now we can only ask. Must CEOs be in sole charge of multinational corporate Goliaths, or can responsibility be shared by separating the jobs of CEO and chairman and holding boards of directors more accountable for a company's behavior? Or is it the inevitable nature of things that, as Ralph Waldo Emerson once said, "An institution is the lengthened shadow of one man"?

A second question: In the current business revolution, with its constantly changing business models and its hypervolatile stocks, can CEOs build great enduring companies, or are they forced to respond so quickly to fickle consumers and investors that there is no time for long-term thinking?

And question three: Will we have sorted out, at least somewhat, the relative roles of the public and private sectors on both our national and international arenas, or is this destined to be a never-ending and inconclusive struggle?

If this were a novel with a plot, how would it come out? There are at least three possibilities. Global CEOs could find themselves able to remain preoccupied almost entirely with beating their competition, while some of the bigger societal issues are handled by a combination of governments, NGOs and market forces—basically, a continuation of current trends. Alternatively, hostility against global corporations could become a powerful force, throwing the companies off course and causing governments to intervene with stepped-up regulatory efforts. A third possibility is that global companies will become both business empires and social organizations, giving far more attention than they already do to deliberately shaping—and improving—the social and political environment in which they operate. Based on my interviews, I would predict that we will see a combination of all three. But based on what I believe will be required in the future for corporate success, it's the third scenario—a simultaneous focus on profits and community—that ought to become the model for big companies. Only historians will be able to assess what actually happened and with what results.

❖ ❖ ❖

CEOs—and all of us, for that matter—can be forgiven if the interaction of business and society is almost too complicated to deal with except on a superficial level. How could it be otherwise when markets, technology, consumer needs and tastes, public attitudes and the roles of governments and international organizations are all in flux? Amid such shifting foundations, the chances of finding the right answers will be related to whether we are asking the right questions. On this score, historians may conclude that our framework for analysis was itself inadequate.

Historian Emma Rothschild compared the environment for important big ideas in the first industrial revolution to that of today. "Certainly political debates and parliamentary debates were much more about ideas than they are now," she said. I asked her about the absence today of great economic and political philosophers who could shed light on changing economic and social circumstances around the world. "There is a cost to the tremendous specialization in academia," she said. "A lot of political leaders and public figures over the last ten years have been aware that we are living in a period of momentous change when ideas are very important, and they haven't found an easy way to communicate with political philosophers in universities." The problem is compounded by the need to have a discussion across borders she said. "How do you have a debate about big global changes with people who come from a completely different intellectual background where the only common language is a kind of English that nobody speaks well?"

Rothschild's lament came to mind in October 2000 when Dr. James H. Billington, Librarian of Congress, announced a $60 million grant to fund a cadre of scholars to reside in the Library, who would interact with American politicians. "These two worlds just kind of fell apart in the '60s and haven't really come back together again," he said. "We're trying to celebrate and facilitate not just the life of the mind but also the role of the life of the mind in the life of the republic." It's a start, but the experiment will eventually need to be expanded to global dimensions, and also include interaction with business leaders. Otherwise, it will be but a partial effort to come to grips with the challenges of our times.

Susan Berresford had a similar perspective. "Since we are in this rapidly, deeply, broadly changing world and everything is uncertain, one of our great challenges is to create the analytic structures to keep us reflecting on the right things. We have universities and think tanks and researchers and journalists and poets and artists who help us, but the question is whether they are up to the task, whether they are too rigid, whether they are open enough, whether they are composed of the people who are diverse enough to understand and think about what's going on together."

In light of everything else that CEOs need to do, it is not surprising that they are not often thought about as being an essential part of the dialogue on the direction of society in this new century. There are some exceptions such as John Browne, George Soros, Jürgen Schrempp and William Ford, all of whom have proactively jumped into the debates about globalization. However, many more CEOs ought to be involved, for what makes this era different from previous industrial revolutions is that the leaders of multinational companies have much more influence—by virtue of what they do or don't do—than did their forebears. This is all the more true given that we live in a global setting lacking in so many of the governing structures that we take for granted at a national level.

❖ ❖ ❖

Historians will no doubt wrestle with whether or not today's CEOs mirrored the values of our times, the best of them and the worst, and they are likely to conclude that they did. To the extent that the twilight of the twentieth century and the dawn of the twenty-first was about increasing freedom, including the unleashing of global capitalism all over the world, today's CEOs were right there, making it happen, profiting from it, and throwing off benefits for others such as consumers, employees, and shareholders. If the prevailing tendency was to concentrate on the short term, assuming either that the good times would last or that the future was too complex and uncertain to deal with, then global CEOs mirrored that, as well. If our era is judged as one of rampant materialism, greed and a callousness toward widening social inequities, then CEOs also played their part.

In *The Mask of Command,* his classic treatise on military leadership, historian John Kegan made a similar point. "Generalship is much more than command of the armies in the field," he wrote

> For an army is . . . an expression of the society from which it issues. The purpose for which it fights and the way it does so will therefore be determined in large measure by what a society wants from war and how far it expects its army to go in delivering the outcome. A general may, given strong character traits and effective behavior, carry both society and army further than they wished to travel. But he, too . . . will in the last resort act like a man of his time and place.

In sticking to their knitting, in keeping their time horizons short, in taking a modest view of their own roles in society, most CEOs are doing just what might be expected if you looked at the environment from which they come. Maybe that is inevitable. But can we not expect more? Are we not underestimating the opportunity for business leadership as we make the journey from the industrial age to the information age, with all the wonderful and painful transformations that will entail?

✧ ✧ ✧

In my five years at the Yale School of Management, I've seen hundreds of students wondering what their role as business leaders should be. Of course many of them want to lead corporations and banks, many want to be investors and start up new companies, and a good number hope to make a lot of money. But if you listen carefully to the questions they ask the many CEOs who come to campus, the theme is not stock prices but the soul of the leader and his or her company. How do chief executives see their jobs in relation to all else that is going on in the world? Where do they fit into the big forces acting on society? The students understand and respect the achievements of these CEOs in the business world narrowly defined. They want the same for themselves. But most of them seem to want more, too.

Susan Berresford raised the same issue in our interview. "One of the positive things about change and uncertainty is that it prompts a search for values that can guide people in the new period," she said. "In the 1980s we saw the rise of a sharper, more competitive dog-eat-dog kind of business leadership. In the younger generations today we may be seeing a group with a set of values and interest in the environment or poverty or health who are not going to be able to totally put those things aside as they come into leadership positions, because they are integral to their understanding of how the world should be for their own lives and for their children."

Let's hope she is right.

Appendix: CEOs and Their Companies

CEO	Company	Title	Headquarters
C. Michael Armstrong	AT&T Corporation	Chairman and CEO	32 Avenue of the Americas New York, NY 10013
G. Leonard Baker, Jr.	Sutter Hill Ventures	Managing Director	755 Page Mill Road Suite A-200 Palo Alto, CA 94304-1005
Susan V. Berresford	Ford Foundation	President	320 East 43rd Street New York, NY 10017
Michael Bloomberg	Bloomberg L.P.	CEO and Founder	499 Park Avenue New York, NY 10022
Michael R. Bonsignore	Honeywell International Inc.	Chairman and CEO	101 Columbia Road Morristown, NJ 07962
Richard Branson	Virgin Management Ltd.	Chairman	5/F The Communications Building 48 Leicester Square London WC2H 7LT UK
Dr. Rolf-E. Breuer	Deutsche Bank AG	Spokesman of the Board of Managing Directors	60262 Frankfurt Germany
John Browne	BP Amoco p.l.c.	Group Chief Executive	Britannic House 1 Finsbury Circus London EC2M 7BA United Kingdom
Stephen M. Case	America Online, Inc.	Chairman and CEO	22000 AOL Way Dulles, VA 20166-9323
Kenneth I. Chenault	American Express Company	President and Chief Operating Officer	200 Vesey Street New York, NY 10285
Michael S. Dell	Dell Computer Corporation	Chairman and CEO	One Dell Way Round Rock, TX 78682

[1]Most recent available information as of August 2000 is from *Fortune* magazine, annual reports, Web sites, and other public sources.

Nature of Business	Web site	Employees	Revenues ($Bn.)	Notes[1]
Telecommunications Services	www.att.com	148,000	62.4	Gross revenue from *Fortune*
Venture Capital	www.shv.com	18	N/A	
Charitable Foundation	www.fordfound. org	600	2.9	Gross income from annual report
Financial Information Service Provider	www.bloomberg. com	7,000	2.3	Estimated gross revenue from internal source
Diverse Technology and Manufacturing	www.honeywell. com	120,000	23.7	Gross revenue from *Fortune*
Entertainment, Travel, and Other	www.virgin.com	25,000	5.0	Gross revenue from Web site
Banking and Financial Services	www.deutsche-bank.com	93,232	58.5	Gross revenue from *Fortune*
Petroleum and Petrochemicals	www.bp.com	97,000	83.6	Gross revenue from *Fortune*
Internet service and content provider	corp.aol.com	12,100	4.8	Gross revenue from *Fortune*
Diversified Financial Services	www. americanexpress. com	88,378	21.3	Gross revenue from *Fortune*
Computers	www.dell.com	37,000	25.3	Gross revenue from *Fortune*

Appendix: CEOs and Their Companies

CEO	Company	Title	Headquarters
Roger A. Enrico	PepsiCo, Inc.	Chairman and CEO	PepsiCo, Inc. Purchase, NY 10577
William Clay Ford, Jr.	Ford Motor Company	Chairman	One The American Rd. P.O. Box 1899 Dearborn, MI 48126-2798
Victor Fung	Li & Fung Limited	Group Chairman	LiFung Tower 888 Cheung Sha Wan Road Kowloon, Hong Kong
Orit Gadiesh	Bain & Company	Chairman	2 Copley Place Boston, MA 02116
Christopher B. Galvin	Motorola, Inc.	Chairman and CEO	1303 East Algonquin Road Schaumburg, IL 60196
Andrew S. Grove	Intel Corporation	Chairman	2200 Mission College Boulevard Santa Clara, CA 95052-8819
Richard L. Huber	Aetna Inc.	Former Chairman, President and CEO	151 Farmington Ave. Hartford, CT 06156
Minoru Makihara	Mitsubishi Corporation	Chairman	6-3 Marunouchi 2-chome, Chiyoda-ku Tokyo 100-8086, Japan
Rebecca P. Mark	Azurix Corp.	Former Chairman and CEO	333 Clay St. Ste. 1000 Houston, TX 77002-7361
Ira M. Millstein, Esq.	Weil, Gotshal & Manges LLP	Senior Partner	767 Fifth Avenue New York, NY 10153
Yoshihiko Miyauchi	ORIX Corporation	Chairman and CEO	3-22-8 Shiba, Minato-ku, Tokyo 105-8683, Japan

Nature of Business	Web site	Employees	Revenues ($Bn.)	Notes[1]
Food and Beverages	www.pepisco.com	116,000	20.4	Gross revenue from *Fortune*
Automobiles	www.ford.com	400,000	162.6	Gross revenue from *Fortune*
International Trading	www.lifung.com	2,852	2.1	Net revenue from internal source
Strategic Business Consulting	www.bain.com	2,400	0.6	Estimated Revenue from Firms and Kennedy Info. Research Group
Communications and Electronics	www.motorola.com	121,000	30.9	Gross revenue from *Fortune*
Microprocessors and Computer Components	www.intel.com	70,200	29.4	Gross revenue from *Fortune*
Health and Retirement Benefits	www.aetna.com	69,811	26.5	Gross revenue from *Fortune*
Diversified Manufacturing and Trading	www.mitsubishi.co.jp/En/	11,685	117.8	Gross revenue from *Fortune*
Water and Waste Water Treatment	www.azurix.com	157	0.6	Operating revenue from annual report
International Law Firm	www.weil.com	1,700	0.4	Gross revenue from internal company source
Financial Services	www2.orix.co.jp/owf	9,503	5.8	Gross revenue from Web site

Appendix: CEOs and Their Companies

CEO	Company	Title	Headquarters
Mark Moody-Stuart	Royal Dutch/Shell Group	Chairman	30, Carel van Bylandtlaan 2596 HR The Hague, The Netherlands
Rupert Murdoch	The News Corporation Limited	Chairman and CEO	2 Holt Street Sydney, N.S.W. Australia 2010
Hiroshi Okuda	Toyota Motor Corporation	Chairman	1, Toyota-cho Toyota City, Aichi 471-8571, Japan
Jorma Ollila	Nokia Corporation	Chairman and CEO	Keilalahdentie 4, FIN 02150 Espoo P.O. Box 226 FIN-00045 NOKIA GROUP Finland
Henry M. Paulson, Jr.	The Goldman Sachs Group	Chairman and CEO	85 Broad St. New York, NY 10004
Nancy B. Peretsman	Allen & Company Incorporated	Executive V.P., and Managing Director	711 5th Avenue New York, NY 10022
Franklin D. Raines	Fannie Mae	Chairman and CEO	3900 Wisconsin Avenue, NW Washington, DC 20016-2892
Leonard Riggio	Barnes & Noble, Inc.	Chairman and CEO	122 5th Ave. New York, NY 10011
Jürgen E. Schrempp	Daimler Chrysler AG	Chairman	D-70546 Stuttgart, Germany
Stan Shih	The Acer Group	Chairman and Co-founder	21F, 88, Section 1, Hsin Tai Wu Rd. Hsichih, Taipei Hsien 221, Taipei, Taiwan
Frederick W. Smith	FedEx Corporation	Chairman, President and CEO	942 South Shady Grove Road Memphis, TN 38120
George Soros	Soros Fund Management LLC	Chairman	888 Seventh Avenue New York, NY 10106

Nature of Business	Web site	Employees	Revenues ($Bn.)	Notes[1]
Petroleum and Petrochemicals	www.shell.com	96,000	105.4	Gross revenue from *Fortune*
News and Entertainment	www.newscorp. com	30,000	13.7	Gross revenue from *Fortune*
Automobiles	www.global. toyota.com	214,631	115.7	Gross revenue from *Fortune*
Mobile Communications	www.nokia.com	60,000	21.1	Gross revenue from *Fortune*
Financial Services	www.gs.com	15,361	25.4	Gross revenue from *Fortune*
Investment Banking	N/A	200	N/A	
Mortgage Securitization	www.fanniemae. com	3,800	37	Gross revenue from *Fortune*
Book Sales	www.barnesand nobleinc.com	37,400	3.5	Gross revenue from *Fortune*
Automobiles	www.daimler-chrysler.com	466,938	160	Gross revenue from *Fortune*
Computers	global.acer.com	14,058	8.4	Gross revenue from Web site
Package Delivery	www.fedexcorp. com	156,386	16.8	Gross revenue from *Fortune*
Hedge Fund Management	N/A	200	N/A	

Appendix: CEOs and Their Companies

CEO	Company	Title	Headquarters
Martin S. Sorrell	WPP Group plc	Group Chief Executive	27 Farm St. London W1X 6RD United Kingdom
G. Richard Thoman	Xerox Corporation	Former President and CEO	800 Long Ridge Road Stamford, Connecticut 06904
Donald Valentine	Sequoia Capital	General Partner	3000 Sand Hill Road Bldg. 4, Suite 280 Menlo Park, CA 94025
Lawrence A. Weinbach	Unisys Corporation	Chairman, President and CEO	One Unisys Way Blue Bell, PA 19424
John F. Welch, Jr.	General Electric Company	Chairman and CEO	3135 Easton Tpke. Fairfield, Ct 06431-0001
James D. Wolfensohn	The World Bank Group	President	1818 H Street, N.W Washington, DC 20433

Nature of Business	Web site	Employees	Revenues ($Bn.)	Notes[1]
Advertising and Marketing Firm	www.wpp.com	39,000	15.1	Gross sales from annual report
Information Technology	www.xerox.com	94,600	19.2	Gross revenue from *Fortune*
Venture Capital	www.sequoiacap.com	28	N/A	
Information Technology	www.unisys.com	36,000	7.5	Gross revenue from *Fortune*
Diversified Services, Manufacturing, Technology, Finance	www.ge.com	340,000	111.6	Gross revenue from *Fortune*
Lending to Developing Countries	www.worldbank.org	11,300	1.5	Net income from annual report

NOTES

All quotations come from the interviews unless otherwise noted.

Chapter 1

Page 19: Examples of strategies which CEOs once employed come from Christopher Meyer, 19–22 "Ahead of the Game," *World Link,* January/February 2000, p. 81.

Page 38: Steve Case's comments about driving a racecar are from his address to the Jupiter Conference, March 5, 1998, New York City.

Chapter 2

Page 41: Paulson's quote on the Internet's being a basic business comes from Neil Weinberg, "Fear, Greed and Technology," *Forbes,* May 15, 2000, p. 170.

Page 51: Examples of potential to increase productivity and profitability come from Jennifer Reingold and Marcia Stepanek, "Why the Productivity Revolution Will Spread," *Business Week Online,* February 14, 2000; for Boeing, see Bill Gates, *Business @ The Speed of Thought: Using a Digital Nervous System,* p. 268.

Page 52: Bill Gates' quote comes from Bill Gates, *Business @ The Speed of Thought: Using a Digital Nervous System,* Warner Books, 1999, p. 412.

Page 53: Louis Gerstner's quote comes from *The Economist,* "When Companies Connect," June 26, 1999, p. 19.

Page 58: Projections about brokers come from Emile Thornton, "Take That, Cyber Boy," *Business Week,* July 10, 2000, p. 58.

Page 58–59: Information on e-commerce of DaimlerChrysler comes from Joseph B. White, Vehicle Maker Plans Upgrade For Websites," *Wall Street Journal,* July 17, 2000, p. A7.

Page 58: Toys 'R' Us–Amazon.com linkup is described in Richard
Waters, "Amazon to Merge Online Toy Stores with Toys 'R' Us,"
Financial Times, August 11, 2000, p. 1.

Page 59: *Financial Times* article is from Andrew Edgecliffe-Johnson,
"E-Revolution Shelved," *Financial Times*, August 3, 2000, p. 10.

Page 59: Size of B to B market from Steven V. Brull, "Such Busy Bees in
B2B," *Business Week*, March 27, 2000, p. 50; *The Economist*, "Internet
Economics," April 1, 2000, p. 64.

Page 59: Information on B to B markets comes from Keith Bradsher,
"Car Markets to Buy Parts on Internet," *New York Times*, February 26,
2000, p. 1; Jacqueline Moore, "U.S. Farm Sector Cultivates
E-Commerce," *Financial Times*, March 2, 2000, p. 12; Edmund L.
Andrews, "Streamlining a German Blimp," *New York Times*, February
29, 2000, p. C1; Shelly Brauch, "Over 50 Consumer-Products
Concerns to Forge Industry Web Marketplace," *Wall Street Journal*,
March 16, 2000, p. B20.

Page 61: Information on e-commerce tie-ups comes from Katherine
Campbell, "Alliances with Grand Designs," *Financial Times*, August 7,
2000, p. 6.

Page 62: Business Week quote: Jim Kerstetter, et. al., "Finding The
Right Formula," *Business Week*, October 23, 2000, p. 45.

Page 69: Peter Drucker's quote comes from Peter F. Drucker,
"Beyond the Information Revolution," *Atlantic Monthly*, October
1999, p. 50.

Chapter 3

Page 76: McKinsey & Company predictions are in Lowell Bryan et al.,
Race for the World, Harvard Business School Press, 1999, p. 3.

Page 91: Information on General Motors comes from "Latin Leap," *The
Economist*, July 29, 2000, p. 64.

Page 96: Article by Douglas Daft comes from Douglas Daft, "Personal
View," *Financial Times*, March 27, 2000, p. 20.

Page 96: Information on Procter & Gamble comes from Emily
Nelson, "Rallying the Troops at P & G," *Wall Street Journal*, August
31, 2000, p. B1.

Page 101: Merger statistics come from Louis Uchitelle, "As Mergers
Multiply, So Does the Danger," *New York Times*, February 13, 2000,
Sunday Business Section, p. 4; Nikhil Deogun and Steven Lipin,

"Cautionary Tales, When Big Deals Turn Bad," *Wall Street Journal,* December 8, 1999, p. C1.

Page 105: Robert Pittman quote comes from an interview with Catherine Yang, *Business Week,* June 14, 1999, on-line edition.

Chapter 4

Page 120: Information about Goldman Sachs' courting small investors comes from Greg Ip and Charles Gasparino, "Goldman Hopes to Court Small Investors," *Wall Street Journal,* August 30, 2000, p. C1.

Page 127: Information on CEO pay comes from See Dean Foust, "CEO Pay: Nothing Succeeds Like Failure," *Business Week,* September 11, 2000, p. 46.

Page 130: Quotes from *Built to Last* from James C. Collins and Jerry I. Porras, "Built to Last," *Harper Business,* 1994, pp. 48, 56, 57.

Chapter 5

Page 139: Ford quote from Thomas A. Stewart et al., "The Businessman of the Century," *Fortune,* November 22, 1999, p. 128.

Page 135: For background information for this entire section on AOL, I have drawn on Saul Hansell, "Now AOL Everywhere," *New York Times,* July 4, 1999, Section 3, p. C1.

Page 140: Information on Ford's approach to the environment is based on interviews and these sources: Keith Bradsher, "Ford Is Conceding S.U.V. Drawbacks," *New York Times,* May 12, 2000, p. 1; Jeffrey Ball, "Ford Contacts Environmentalists Behind Scenes," *Wall Street Journal,* May 15, 2000, p. B2; Robert H. Frank, "Feeling Cash-Resistant in an S.U.V.," *New York Times,* May 16, 2000, p. 23; *1999 Corporate Citizenship Report;* Keith Bradsher, "Ford Said to Plan Improved Mileage in Sport Utilities," *New York Times,* July 27, 2000, p. 1; "Ford's Clean Air Breakthrough," Editorial, *New York Times,* July 28, 2000, p. A20.

Page 146: Steve Balmer's quote comes from Steve Lohr, "Microsoft Starts Recruiting for Its Next War," *New York Times,* September 14, 1999, p. C10.

Page 146: Armstrong's quote comes from Thomas J. Neff and James M. Citrin, *Lessons from the Top: The Search for America's Best Business Leaders,* Doubleday, 1999, p. 37.

Page 153: Guyon article is Janet Guyon, "AT&T's Big Bet Keeps Getting Dicier," *Fortune,* January 10, 2000.

Page 153: Schiesel article is Seth Schiesel, "With AT&T at the Brink, Pressures Rise at the Top," *New York Times,* July 9, 2000, Section 3, p. 1.

Page 153: *Wall Street Journal* quote is from Deborah Solomon and Nikhil Doegun, AT&T Disconnected," *Wall Street Journal,* October 26, 2000, p. B1.

Page 161: Background on Richard Thoman comes from John Hechinger and Joann Lublin, "Xerox's Thoman Resigns Under Pressure," *Wall Street Journal,* May 12, 2000, p. 3; Claudia H. Deutsch, "After Bad Year, Xerox Ousts Top Executive," *New York Times,* May 12, 2000, p. C1; Robert C. Alexander and Douglas K. Smith, "Can Xerox Duplicate Its Original Success?" *Wall Street Journal,* May 17, 2000, p. A 26.

Page 162: Background on Rebecca Mark comes from Stephanie Anderson Frost, "Paddling as Fast as She Can," *Business Week,* May 1, 2000, p. 90; Rebecca Smith and Aaron Lucchetti, "Rebecca Mark's Exit Leaves Enron's Azurix Treading Deep Water," *Wall Street Journal,* August 28, 2000, p. 1; Hillary Durgin and David Owen, "Azurix Strategy Fails to Hold Water," *Financial Times,* September 5, 2000, p. 21.

Page 165: Pamela Moore article is Pamela L. Moore, "Xerox: Rick Thoman Speaks Up for Himself," *Business Week,* May 29, 2000, p. 50.

Page 166: Brent Schendler quote from Brent Schendler, "The Reign Is Over," *Fortune,* October 16, 2000, p. 126.

Chapter 6

Page 171: Some information on Dell comes from Geoffrey Colvin, "America's Most Admired Companies, *Fortune,* February 21, 2000, p. 110.

Page 175: Background for the discussion on FedEx comes from Jeffrey E. Garten, "Why the Global Economy Is Here to Stay," *Business Week,* March 23, 1998, p. 21; Kathy Brister, "The Human Equation," *Knoxville News Sentinel,* June 3, 1999, p. C1; Tim Smart, "Delivering Packages, Partnerships," *Washington Post,* May 2, 1999, p. H1; and Linda Grant, "Why FedEx Is Flying High," *Fortune,* November 10, 1997.

Page 179: For background on Victor Fung, I drew on Joanna Slater and Eriko Amaha, "Masters of Trade," *Far Eastern Economic Review,* August 22, 1999, p. 10.

Page 181: Background information on retaining talent comes from Nicholas Stein, "Winning the War to Keep Top Talent," *Fortune,* May 29, 2000, p. 132.

Page 187: Transcript of September 14, 2000, news conference is in Ford Motor Company news release, September 15, 2000.

Chapter 7

Page 193: Postrel article comes from Virginia Postrel, "It's Good Times, Not Bad, That Nurture the Enemies of the Free Market," *New York Times,* September 7, 2000, p. C2.

Page 197: Some information on Honeywell in China comes from *Engineering News–Record,* August 14, 2000, p. 19.

Page 207: John Browne's 1998 Elliot Lecture, St. Anthony's College, Oxford, was on June 4, 1998.

Page 210: Soros's interview with O'Brien comes from Timothy O'Brien, "George Soros Has Seen the Enemy. It Looks Like Him," *New York Times,* December 6, 1998, Business Section, p. 1.

Page 213: For poll on "Americans and Globalization," see Aaron Bernstein, "Backlash: Behind the Anxiety Over Globalization," *Business Week,* April 24, 2000, p. 38.

Page 213: For *Wall Street Journal*/NBC poll see Albert R. Hunt, "A Short Term Victory," *Wall Street Journal,* May 25, 2000, p. A 27.

Page 213: For August 20 *Business Week* survey see Aaron Bernstein, "Too Much Corporate Power?" *Business Week,* September 11, 2000, p. 145.

Page 213: For Bill Joy quote see Bill Joy, "Why the Future Doesn't Need Us," *Wired,* April 2000, p. 238.

Page 213: Gene Sperling's quote comes from David E. Sanger, "Rounding Out a Major Legacy of the Clinton Era," *New York Times,* May 24, 2000, p. 1.

Page 214: For Davis and Seib article see Bob Davis and Gerald F. Seib, "Technology Will Test a Washington Culture Born in an Industrial Age," *Wall Street Journal,* May 1, 2000, p. 1.

Page 218: Lawrence Summers quote comes form Steven Pearlstein, "A New Politics Born of Globalization," the *Washington Post,* October 1, 2000, p. H1.

Page 218: For Philip Knight article, see Philip Knight, "A Forum for Improving Globalization," *Financial Times,* August 1, 2000, p. 15.

Page 219: Moisés Naim's quote comes from Charles P. Wallace, "Davos Listens to the World," *Time* (Europe), February 14, 2000, p. 60.

Chapter 8

Page 230: Aaron Bernstein's quote comes from Aaron Bernstein, "Too Much Corporate Power?" *Business Week,* September 11, 2000, p. 154.

Page 231: Ford's quote in *Wall Street Journal* comes from Jeffrey Ball and Joseph B. White, "Ford's Chairman Speaks Out About Firestone Crisis," *Wall Street Journal,* September 15, 2000, p. B1.

Page 232: For background on F.L.A., see Thomas L. Friedman, "Knight Is Right," *New York Times,* June 20, 2000, p. A31.

Page 232: For background on Global Compact see Joseph Kahn, "Multinationals Sign U.N. Pact on Rights and Environment," *New York Times,* p. A 3; also "The Global Compact," www.unglobalcompact.org; and Edward Alden, "Multinationals in Labor Standards Pledge," *Financial Times,* July 28, 2000, p. 10.

Page 235: See Case's address to National Press Club, October 26, 1999, which is representative of many of his statements.

Page 241: For background on organizational changes see the following: On Gates, see Holly Yeager, "Gates to Step Down," *Financial Times,* January 14, 2000, p. 1; on Gerstner, see Steve Lohr, "Broad Reorganization at IBM Hints at Successor to Gerstner," *New York Times,* July 25, 2000, p. C1; on Dell see Gary McWilliams, "Dell Looks for Ways to Rekindle the Fire It Had as an Upstart," *Wall Street Journal,* August 31, 2000, p. 1.

Page 242: Background on the Business Roundtable can be found at www.brtable.org.

Page 243: William Greider's quote comes from William Greider, *One World, Ready or Not: The Manic Logic of Global Capitalism,* New York: Simon & Schuster, 1997, p. 11.

Chapter 9

Page 245: Novaris CFO's quote comes from Stephen D. Moore, "Novartis Moves to New York Stock Exchange," *Wall Street Journal,* May 11, 2000, p. B2.

Page 250: Information on Japanese use of Internet comes from Stephanie Strom, "Rising Internet Use Quietly Transforms Way Japanese Live," *New York Times,* May 14, 2000, p. 1.

Page 250: Information on German entrepreneurs comes from Roger Cohen, "German Entrepreneurs Transform, Land of Steel," *New York Times,* May 14, 2000, p. 3.

Page 251: Friedman's quote comes from Thomas L. Friedman, *The Lexus and the Olive Tree,* Farrar, Straus, Giroux, 1999, p. 3.

Page 254: Tomlinson's quote comes from Richard Tomlinson, "Europe's New Business Elite," *Fortune,* April 3, 2000, p. 177.

Page 259: Hutton's quote from Will Hutton and Anthony Giddens, *On The Edge: Living with Global Capitalism,* London: Jonathan Cape, 2000, p. 10.

Page 261: Information on factory closings in China come from Elizabeth Rosenthal, "Factory Closings in China Arouse Workers' Fury," *New York Times,* August 21, 2000, p. 1.

Page 266: Sanger article comes from David E. Sanger, "American Finds It Lonely at the Top," *New York Times,* July 18, 1999, Section 4, p. 1.

Reflections

Page 278: *Wall Street Journal* quote comes from Gary McWilliams, "Dell Looks for Ways to Rekindle the Fire . . . ," *Wall Stree Journal,* August 31, 2000, p. 1.

Page 282: James Billington's quote comes from Francis X. Clines, "$60 Million Gift Is Made to Library of Congress," *The New York Times,* October 5, 2000, p. A 20.

Page 284: Kegan's quote from John Kegan, *The Mask of Command,* New York: Penguin, 1994, p. 2.

INDEX